HISTORICAL STUDIES OF URBAN AMERICA

Edited by Lilia Fernández, Timothy J. Gilfoyle, Becky M. Nicolaides,
and Amanda I. Seligman
James R. Grossman, editor emeritus

Also in the series:

THE CYCLING CITY

THE CYCLING CITY

Bicycles and Urban America in the 1890s

EVAN FRISS

THE UNIVERSITY OF CHICAGO PRESS

CHICAGO AND LONDON

EVAN FRISS is assistant professor of history at James Madison University. He lives in Virginia with his wife and two sons.

The University of Chicago Press, Chicago 60637
The University of Chicago Press, Ltd., London
© 2015 by The University of Chicago
All rights reserved. Published 2015.
Printed in the United States of America
24 23 22 21 20 19 18 17 16 15   1 2 3 4 5

ISBN-13: 978-0-226-21091-9 (cloth)
ISBN-13: 978-0-226-21107-7 (e-book)
DOI: 10.7208/chicago/9780226211077.001.0001

Library of Congress Cataloging-in-Publication Data

Friss, Evan, author.
    The cycling city : bicycles and urban America in the 1890s / Evan Friss.
        pages ; cm
    Includes bibliographical references and index.
    ISBN 978-0-226-21091-9 (cloth : alk. paper) — ISBN 978-0-226-21107-7 (ebook)
1. Cycling—United States—History—19th century.   2. Bicycle commuting—United States—History—19th century.   3. Urban transportation—United States—History—19th century.   I. Title.
    HE5737.F75 2015
    388.3'472097309034—dc23

                                                              2015007469

Publication of this book has been supported by Furthermore: a program of the J. M. Kaplan Fund.

Furthermore:
a program of the J.M. Kaplan Fund

TO AMANDA, MILES, AND QUINCY

CONTENTS

ACKNOWLEDGMENTS

Although writing can make one feel alone, this book reflects the efforts of many people. Thomas Kessner, Gerald Markowitz, Owen Gutfreund, Setha Low, Brendan O'Malley, Mark Rose, Gwynneth Malin, and Paul Naish read and commented on earlier drafts. Their input was invaluable. I owe a special thanks to David Nasaw, who not only helped me shape the book but also convinced me to write it in the first place.

I was lucky to find a home in the history department at James Madison University, where my colleagues have been warm and welcoming. Kevin Borg, Emily Westkaemper, and Michael Douma deserve particular recognition for reading individual chapters, as do Gabrielle Lanier and Andrew Witmer (who also helped me rewrite a particularly ugly paragraph) for letting me stand in their doorways as I complained about the challenges of writing, researching, and publishing. Summer research grants from the history department and the Edna T. Shaeffer Humanist Award from the College of Arts and Letters provided the resources to finish the project. David Jeffrey, the dean of the college, kindly agreed to allocate funds to help cover the costs of image permissions.

At the University of Chicago Press, I would like to thank Robert Devens for his initial interest, Nora Devlin for assisting in some of the technical matters, Caterina MacLean for copyediting, and Timothy Mennel for expertly shepherding this book to its current form. I am especially grateful to Timothy Gilfoyle, a terrific historian and a generous man. He has now supported this project (and me) for many years, reading every word of the book and offering sage advice on how to improve it. Likewise, the anonymous reviewers read my manuscript carefully and offered helpful suggestions, as did Zachary Schrag, who read the entire book twice and provided as intelligent a critique as anyone. Foolishly, I did not follow all of their suggestions and, thus, they shoulder no blame for the many flaws that remain.

Librarians, archivists, and fellow researchers ably assisted in finding sources and making sense of them. Specifically, the staffs of the New-York Historical Society, the New York Public Library, the Brooklyn Public Library, the Historical Society of Washington, DC, the Library of Congress, the National Museum of American History Library, the Washington DC Public Library, the Minneapolis City Archives, the Chicago History Museum, the Pennsylvania State Archives, the Municipal Archives in New York, the Chicago Public Library, the Newberry Library, the Rochester Public Library, the San Francisco History Center, the San Francisco Municipal Library, the California Historical Society, the Bancroft Library, the Harvard University Archives, the Schlesinger Library, the University of Virginia Library, and the James Madison University libraries all warrant a sincere thank you. I also want to acknowledge Thomas Cameron Burr, Ross Petty, Bruce Epperson, Captain Jack, and Louis Gimelli for sharing sources and knowledge, or for helping me to remember a word that I had misplaced.

My parents, Mike and Rose, deserve special recognition. Without them, for many reasons, this would never have been possible. I was also fortunate to inherit Ellen and Les Cohen as in-laws; they have given me unbridled support ever since.

Most importantly, I need to thank Amanda. As I worked on this project, she worked just as hard as my editor, wife, friend, distractor, baker, and wonderful mother to our two boys. Miles and Quincy have made writing this book all the more difficult, but only because they have made my life so much richer. And so it is to my family—Amanda, Miles, and Quincy—that I dedicate this book.

INTRODUCTION

In the 1890s, more bicycles wove through city traffic than ever before. Spinning wheels swirled across the urban canvas, dodging carriages, rotting horse carcasses, and piles of manure. Commuters sped to work; others glided lazily around town. News, mail, and eggs all came by wheel. Merchants filled magazines with advertisements for bicycles and bicycle accessories. Folded newspapers revealed cycling-related headlines on both sides of the crease. Cycling gossip spilled out of parlors and saloons. Bicycles starred in novels, poems, and on stage. Cycling clubs proliferated, wheeled paraders regularly filled the streets, and bicycle racing attracted throngs of spectators. Politicians sought endorsements from the army of "wheelmen." Doctors, reformers, educators, engineers, and ministers preached the gospel of cycling. Restaurants and museums valeted bicycles for their patrons, while racks and garages invited riders to park on their own. It was a particular place at a particular time in which bicycles, like never before or after, shaped American cities.

Indeed, toward the end of the nineteenth century, a diverse group of men and women embraced the bicycle as a fundamental feature of urban life. They imagined, and even began building, a cycling city. For them, the bicycle appeared to solve many of the ills that had come to define American cities. Smoke spewed from factories. Office jobs furnished a regular income but a sedentary way of life. Mechanized transit brought speed but also urban thunder. In response, professional engineers sought to provide fresh water and sanitized streets, reformers launched a crusade against squalid living conditions, and city builders redesigned the urban landscape to promote efficient transportation, incorporate places of salutary refuge and recreation, and manage population growth. There was also a

growing group of advocates who began to see the bicycle as a potential solution to the problems of urban life—for good reason.

The bicycle inspired a vision of a city in which pollution was negli-
gible, transport was noiseless and rapid, leisure spaces were democratized,
and the divisions between city and country were blurred. As a private vehicle, the bicycle enabled users to redraw the urban grid. Cyclists could
pedal to work, the park, or the adjacent countryside, leaving timetables,
transit fares, and pedestrians in their wake. Bicycles moved at a clip faster
than trotting horses. They emitted no pollutants and but a faint noise, easily swallowed up by the cacophonous city. Unlike streetcars, bicycles offered the advantages of private transportation, ran twenty-four hours a day,
and required comparatively little infrastructure, including none of the
tracks that clogged roads. Used as a tool for exercise, recreation, leisure,
and transportation, the bicycle served multiple functions and promised to
solve countless problems.

Its popularity imprinted physical, social, and cultural changes onto
the city map. As cyclists pedaled across town, they complicated the way
people and vehicles moved about the city. That the population of rookie
wheelmen and wheelwomen increased at such rapid rates and that they
traveled in a way unique from all other vehicles did not go unnoticed. Carriage drivers and streetcar operators agonized over the pesky hazards and
new competition. Pedestrians, city officials, victims of bicycle accidents,
and others began to wonder if and how bicycles could fit into the urban
network. What followed was a series of ordinances in cities around the
country that, at first, codified the bicycle as a legitimate vehicle and, ultimately, led to comprehensive plans designed to improve traffic and safety
by defining how bicycles and all other vehicles could move through the
city. Cyclists occasionally wrote the laws themselves and almost always
signed off on the legislation before the actual lawmakers did. Their lobbying efforts extended into the area of road improvement, in which they
became the most vocal supporters of "good roads." The new ribbons of asphalt extended beyond just traditional roads. Bicycle paths began to flow
in and around major metropolises and stood as a clear symbol that the
bicycle had arrived. In aggregate, the paths, the improved roads, and the
new laws signaled that the bicycle had become a device with effects that
extended well beyond any individual cyclist.

While the physical changes the cyclists brought with them were
among the most significant developments, the American city of the 1890s
was a cycling city because of more than just the infrastructure on the
streets and the laws on the books. Atop a bicycle, the city looked different.

It allowed residents a new way to understand their environment, even if the nature of those perceptions varied tremendously. While the millions of bicycles looked more or less the same and while everyone may have called them bicycles, the device promised many different things to many different people. For some bicycle-commuting office clerks, middle-class professionals, and even for some working-class urbanites, the workplace no longer seemed so far from home. These same people found that beaches and quiet landscapes no longer seemed so distant. Having access to the world outside of the city made life inside it that much different. For female cyclists, the city looked alternately inviting and distrustful, depending on when, where, and how they rode. Wheelwomen remarked that the bicycle unlocked new spaces, made socializing with men easier, and was one of several factors that led to increasing independence. At the same time, it renewed suspicion that they did not belong *there*, at least not wearing *that*. For wealthy cyclists the cycling city looked even more socially rich, a place where high society could gather to promenade down oversized boulevards and inside grand clubhouses. Those less affluent saw a city, even if not quite complete, that promised mobility to nearly everyone. Reformers saw a city on the mend—a city, more imagined than real, in which hushed bicycles would spin on clean streets and riders would breathe unadulterated air. Under the new electric lights or moonlit skies, city dwellers on bicycles began to see the night as a special place for refuge, rather than a space to avoid. Doctors conceived of a new city in which the seemingly inevitable effects of urban life—the maddening mayhem, the lack of exercise, and loss of access to nature and its restorative powers—could be cured.

Americans living in the 1890s would have had difficulty imagining any future decline in cycling. After all, the cycling city was not only a place in which bicycles had an outsized presence on the landscape of the city and the people who lived there, but it was also a time in which bicycles seemed to offer great promise. Pundits heralded bicycles, and the cities they were in the midst of spawning, as decidedly revolutionary. "In its social importance the bicycle deserves to rank next to the railway and the telegraphs, among the inventions of our waning century," an admiring *Atlantic Monthly* journalist wrote in 1892.[1] Another pundit claimed, "As a revolutionary force in the social world the bicycle has had no equal in modern times."[2] Hyperbole aside, late nineteenth-century Americans looked upon the bicycle as an almost utopian instrument. The possibilities of the bicycle and the cycling city appeared limitless. "The effect upon the development of cities will be nothing less than revolutionary," a journalist hypothesized in 1892. Horses would disappear and "perfectly smooth pavements" would follow.[3] A different soothsayer predicted that cycling would soon become the "universal method of locomotion" and that it would usher in "a new order of things."[4]

In retrospect, some of the rosy prognostications about the bicycle's potential influence appear myopic at best. But the bicycle boom of the 1890s was one of those rare moments in history when a single, new piece of technology seemed to offer the chance for a complete reconceptualization of urban life. Cyclists found ways to adapt to city traffic, laws, and spaces, while the city found ways to adapt to its latest resident. And yet while many paths leading toward that future were laid, ultimately few were followed.

Despite its prominent role, few historians have examined, let alone focused on, the bicycle's relationship to the city. Perhaps bicycles' second-class status on today's roads led to this scholarly lacuna. Just as automobiles dominate our streets, so too do they dominate the library stacks. Even the bulk of the existing bicycle-related literature is, at least indirectly, related to automobiles. These histories tend to emphasize the bicycle's role as a transitional mode of transportation that laid the groundwork for the ultimate accommodation of automobiles. While bicycles were a crucial factor in the particular ways in which cities later dealt with automobiles, critical questions about the bicycle's impact on cities in its own time remain unanswered. Those who lived in the 1890s knew almost nothing of the motorcar. How they understood their urban world and how they imagined the urban ideal is often misconstrued because of our own preconceptions about the looming inevitability of the automobile. Other historians who have written about bicycles tend to be less concerned with questions related to consumption, transportation, urban space, the built environment, and cycling as a social and technological practice, but are instead interested in bicycles as a marker of innovation. Scores of scholars have, quite adeptly, explored the evolution of the bicycle as machine. Nary a nineteenth-century bicycle patent or ball bearing has escaped the meticulous eyes of bicycle historians.[5]

Quite reasonably, others have dismissed the popularity of cycling in the 1890s as just another fad, not worthy of serious study. In some ways it certainly was. It was intense, widespread, and fueled by the media. And the cycling boom did not last very long, at least by historians' standards. For strands of the cycling community, cycling was a fad. Trendsetters flaunted their elegant wheels but would inevitably move on to something else. Some middle-class professionals cycled for practical reasons, but those who joined bicycle clubs and relished cycling through the parks at the fashionable hour had other motivations. Those social uses of the bicycle disappeared quickly. Moreover, there were more than a few fads in the waning years of the nineteenth century; so much so that a writer for the *Nation* in 1893 mourned the fact that Americans had a penchant "to take nearly everything in crazes." Roller-skating was all the rage in the 1880s. In the 1890s it was the skirt dance, ragtime, commemorative (historically-oriented) spoons, and theories that promoted improved health through excessive mastication of food (thirty-two chews before swallowing, to be exact). Fads in the fields of recreation, athletics, fashion, consumption, and health again and again swept in swiftly before quietly exiting out the back door.[6] And they still do. But unlike Hula Hoops, sideburns, Beanie Babies, or Zumba, cyclists thought they were participating in something that was going to change not only their own lives but also the very nature of the cities in which they lived. So while they thought it would improve their health, make them fashionable, and open up social opportunities, they also thought it would allow them to travel outside of the city, to become more independent, and to get to work and play faster. They thought their cities of the future would be different—cleaner, easier to navigate, and designed around the bicycle. They (not just cyclists and journalists, but politicians, engineers, doctors, teamsters, and streetcar operators) thought so for a simple reason: cities had already begun to look different. In just a few short years, bicycle paths, roads, racks, and traffic laws began to alter how people moved about and experienced the city. Riders and advocates thought it was just the beginning. In some places around the world it was. Even in the United States, while the obsession with bicycles dissipated, it did not disappear as fully as most fads do. In fact, long after Americans turned off the ragtime, stopped skirt dancing, put down their history-themed spoons, and began to chew their food normally again, they kept buying bicycles, even if the meaning—the kinds of people who rode bicycles and the reasons they rode them—had changed.

No matter the era, scholars have long recognized the importance of mobility in terms of the urban environment. To be sure, some have portrayed city development too passively, focusing only on a particular agent of change (e.g., streetcars) and a particular subject of that change (e.g., suburban development), and in the process have cast the city as an inorganic blob, merely absorbing the impact of external factors.[7] But causality between transportation and city form is not a one-way street. Transportation alters the development of cities and the development of cities demands new forms of transportation. No kind of syllogistic reasoning can untangle the relationship. Like the much-studied streetcar and on a much smaller scale, bicycles altered the design of American cities. But the nature of that change was contested and filtered by the city itself. It was the city's politicians, reformers, cyclists, carriage owners; cultural tradition and predominant social mores; political infrastructure; geography and ecology; and even architectural tastes that determined the shape of urban transportation as much as urban transportation determined the shape of the city.

The fundamental relationship between transportation and the city is nothing new. Some of the very first cities in ancient Mesopotamia contained residential units, social meeting places, and trading centers all within a well-defined, dense nucleus. Mobility was limited. Thousands of years later, stone walls fortified medieval cities, confining city growth and urban mobility.[8] By contrast, wall-less American cities invited speculators and territorial expansion. But it was not until the nineteenth century, thanks to several technological advancements, that a transportation revolution occurred. Railroads and canals linked distant cities, dramatically reduced shipping costs, and unleashed an unprecedented wave of industrialism. Within America's cities, innovative transportation technology facilitated production and capital markets. By midcentury, horse-drawn omnibuses carried more cargo and people than ever before. Street railways followed, increasing speed and comfort for riders. In the early 1880s, elevated trains transported hundreds of thousands of people despite being expensive to ride, hard on the eyes, and damaging to the ears. By the end of the decade, electric-powered street railways replaced the horse-pulled variety, delivering even faster speeds. Originally devised for San Francisco's slippery hills, the cable car was ultimately adopted in Philadelphia, Chicago, and elsewhere. Finally, at the dawn of the twentieth century, Boston became the first American city with an underground train system. Urban transportation was never the same.[9] Profound innovations in the field of transportation came quickly and often in the nineteenth century. In those one hundred years, transportation technology evolved more than it had in the previous ten thousand years.

Bicycles were merely one of many modes of transportation that fueled imaginative plans for reordering the city. And its effects were, in many ways, more modest and less permanent than some of its rivals. Elevateds and streetcars could move people across great distances and over hills with little effort and, ultimately, subways would push part of the urban world to an entirely new realm, the subterranean. Nevertheless, for the men and women living in American cities in the 1890s, the bicycle had immediate consequence and almost unlimited potential. While mass transit shepherded herds of city folk to crowded train cars running on fixed tracks, the self-propelled bicycle (described as "the perfection of selfishness") was a means of private transportation that could take its rider (nearly) wherever and whenever he or she wanted.[10]

While cycling's popularity has faded, the bicycle remains, over a century later, a piece of the urban fabric. And that it does not occupy a more central role today (as it does elsewhere in the world) and that it did not bring about even more transformational change was not a foregone conclusion in the 1890s. In fact, back in 1896 one writer predicted that "when the social and economic history of the nineteenth century comes to be written, the historian cannot ignore the invention and development of the bicycle."[11] He and his contemporaries recognized the sweeping changes accompanied by the popularization of urban cycling and assumed, quite wrongly, that the bicycle's place within the American city and its place in American history were secure. For certain, bicycles, and those who rode them, affected late nineteenth-century urban America in significant ways. While the telegraph and telephone conquered distance, the cinema blurred reality, and electric lights defeated darkness, bicycles altered the look and feel of cities and their streets, enhanced mobility, fueled leisure and recreation, promoted good health, and shrank urban spaces as part of a larger transformation that altered the city and the lives of its inhabitants. Consequently, neither a history of the bicycle nor a history of the city would be complete without the other.

Any historian attempting to write about an urban phenomenon faces a methodological dilemma—whether to investigate a theme broadly across multiple sites or to instead focus microscopically. My early research confirmed that within the country's largest cities the patterns of change, the tones of debate, and the cycling landscape developed fairly consistently. Important distinctions remained, yet in more ways than not, the cycling city was truly a national phenomenon.[12] Throngs of cyclists and a plethora of cycling-related infrastructure could be found in almost any American city of note in the 1890s. Therefore, I have worked with a broad canvas. Throughout this book, I reference dozens of cities and the footnotes will lead hungry readers to newspaper articles and municipal reports from too many cities to count. Necessarily, much of my primary research was more focused. Research trips to New York, Washington, DC, Chicago, and San Francisco provided the foundation for much of my argument and, I hope, helped ensure regional balance. In many ways, these larger cities provided the model for how smaller cities would accommodate cyclists.

Municipal records, manuscript collections, diaries, visual sources, and other primary documents from these cities and others also provided a necessary supplement to the overwhelming press coverage of all things bicycle in the 1890s. As much as cyclists themselves, newspapers and magazines caught bicycle fever and sought to cash in on the nationwide phenomenon with news articles, editorials, and regular columns about anything related to cycling. For journalists, accuracy was important, but so too was entertaining readers. Young reporters, often compensated according to how much space their stories filled and how many eyes their headlines caught, frequently resorted to verbosity, exaggeration, and sensationalism. While reputations varied from paper to paper, as a whole, reports from the mainstream press need to be read soberly and in conjunction with other sources.[13]

In focusing on the physical development of cities, as well as the opportunities the bicycle offered urban residents, this study is far from exhaustive. Three of the themes most written about among the tiny cohort of bicycle scholars—bicycle technology, bicycle manufacturing, and bicycle racing—appear only peripherally. With respect to periodization, the dawn, peak, and demise of the American cycling city fall within just years of one another. By the late 1880s, enthusiasm for cycling accelerated and continued until peaking between 1896 and 1898. Press coverage of cycling, membership totals in the largest national bicycle club, and the number of bicycles manufactured domestically topped out in 1896, 1898, and 1899 respectively.[14] On average, cities on the East Coast welcomed bicycles first (likely because the earliest machines were imported from Europe) and, in turn, wished them goodbye before their sister cities on the Pacific Coast, but typically only by a year or so. Across the country, the sudden decline was evident as the century turned. Thus, although I consider some of the early origins and extended effects of the cycling city, most of this study falls within the final chapter of the nineteenth century.

The title of this book—*The Cycling City*—both borrows from and challenges the well-known classification system that emphasizes the ways in which modes of transportation affect urban development.[15] "Walking cities," "streetcar cities," and "automobile cities" are categories of analysis that can mistakenly oversimplify our understanding of the city, but they can also be useful concepts, especially insofar as they assert the significance of mobility. Nevertheless, these terms can occasionally blind us to the fluidity of urban development—the transitions, the short-lived experiments with other methods of moving about the city, and the possibilities of what might have been. In this book, I argue that there was an

exceptional moment at the end of the nineteenth century in which bicycles shaped American cities and the lives of those who lived there. Lodged
somewhere between the walking city and the age of the automobile, the
cycling city of the 1890s had a character of its own. However brief and
however aspirational, the cycling city was the culmination of a very real
faith in the promise of the bicycle.

The end of the cycling city, it is important to remember, came not because transportation technology evolved so suddenly. Bicycles were just
as useful when cyclists stopped riding them at the turn of the century as
they had been a few years earlier. Here, the label "bicycle city"—just like
its cousins the "streetcar city" and the "automobile city"—is wanting.
Yes, bicycles offered a chance to think anew about the city, but the technology did not produce change on its own. People produced the change. (In
that sense, perhaps *The Cyclists' City* would have been an even better title.) I do not mean to diminish the importance of technology, the machine
itself. Its shape, size, weight, speed, ease of use, various functions, and so
forth help us understand the attractions to, and challenges of, becoming
a cyclist. Similarly, the ways in which cities adapted to the popularization of cycling are directly related to the bicycle's physical attributes. In
that sense, bicycles did shape the city. But it was Americans in the 1890s
who fell in love with "the wheel" and Americans who soon lost interest.
The bicycle remained more or less the same. Thus, this is not a story of
a fading technology rendered obsolete but instead of the interplay among
people, bicycles, and cities.

Consequently, understanding who rode, how people rode, and why they
rode is critical. Subsets of riders imbued the bicycle with their own meaning, meaning that changed over time. For elites, cycling was initially a
way to cement their status; for the middle class the bicycle served as both
a practical means of getting around and as a social device with which to
emulate the upper classes; for the working classes, bicycles encapsulated
hopes of mobility—physically and socially. That men and women across
the socioeconomic spectrum found bicycles useful explains the enormous
popularity of cycling at the time. But it also helps explain cycling's demise. What was the bicycle? Was it a plaything, a device for recreation, or
a practical vehicle? Who was it for? In the 1890s, the answers were varied
and oftentimes contradictory. It was, though, an open question, one that
came up in cities across the country and in debates ranging from whether
or not women should ride to whether or not bicycle paths helped or hin-
dered the cyclists' cause. Part of the problem was defining the terms "cyclist" and "bicycle." They were contested terms—not in the literal sense,

but rather in what they conveyed and who was included. These varied and evolving perceptions help explain the bicycle's sudden crash. Americans did not stop cycling because the machine proved inefficient. It was not because of bad weather, ill-suited topography, or cities that were spread too thin. And it certainly was not because they started driving automobiles. Rather, in the end, distinct social groups held competing, and ultimately unsustainable, notions about the bicycle.

Cities across the United States are once again promoting bicycles and facing familiar challenges in trying to create a transportation network that encourages modes of mobility that are efficient, safe, and healthy; that can manage problems of population growth and sprawl; and that can create a cohesive system designed around a medley of transportation choices. Integrating bicycles into urban environments today is no easy task, in large part because of the choices made during the 1890s. The landscapes of American cities reflect a renewed interest in cycling but an even longer period of neglect. That bicycles are legitimate vehicles and deserve a place on the transportation network is an opinion heard more often and more loudly, but it is an argument that lost much of its traction over a century ago. Thus, although the bicycle has experienced something of a renaissance in twenty-first-century America, cycling advocates have a particularly steep hill to climb. For when the American cycling city of the 1890s came to an end, in many ways, so too did the prospect of it ever being built again.

CHAPTER ONE

The Rise of the Cycling City

"It is safe to say that few articles ever used by man have created so great a revolution in social condition as the bicycle." This bold pronouncement came not from an editorialist, philosopher, or partisan promoter but rather from the United States government. The official census of 1900 contained an exclusive "special report" on bicycles, which enumerated the economic scale of bicycle manufacturing, summarized the technological history of the machine, and waxed philosophic about the vehicle's effect on humanity. The broad scope of the report was well warranted. After all, there had to be some explanation for the seismic changes the census reported. In the early 1880s, a few thousand cyclists lived in the United States. By the end of the 1890s, millions did. According to the 1890 census—the first to acknowledge a "bicycle industry"—twenty-seven American firms produced bicycles. In 1900, 312 were in business. The newly robust cycling economy employed roughly 1,700 workers in 1890; by 1900 that number grew tenfold. By the turn of the twentieth century, American factories produced more than one million bicycles annually.[1] These statistics merely confirmed what was obvious to almost anyone living in the 1890s: bicycles had invaded America's cities. That world—the cycling city—emerged almost as quickly as it disappeared.

Even as millions of Americans bought bicycles that looked more and more like the bicycles we know today, a lack of consensus still existed about what the bicycle really was. The indeterminacy of the bicycle—whether it was a vehicle for transportation or a plaything for recreation—was a persistent theme. Manufacturers and admen marketed bicycles as everything and to everyone. They courted the wealthy and middle-class professionals; women and men; those who sought adventure, speed, fashion, or a faster way to get to work. Their success was unprecedented. While much of the demand derived from middle-class Americans, cycling in the 1890s appealed to a broad group of city dwellers who bought and rode bicycles with varying motivations. As they did, they helped construct not only the cycling city but also the meaning of the bicycle itself.

Although the bicycle era peaked near the close of the nineteenth century, earlier bicycle models enjoyed a devoted, albeit small, following. In fact, humans were captivated by the notion of man-powered propulsion for centuries. In the seventeenth century, a French physician designed a four-wheeled carriage powered by a combination of planks, ropes, pulleys, and a pair of servant's legs.[2] But not until the late eighteenth and early nineteenth centuries did the first prototypes of the bicycle emerge across Europe. Inventors initially produced "horseless carriages" that mimicked the horse-driven variety in nearly every way except for the power source. In 1816, the German forester Baron von Drais, in search of a faster way to survey his territory, designed the *laufsmaschine*, or "running machine." The device moved with force generated by the rider's feet pushing directly against the ground. Made of wood and built with iron tires, the aptly dubbed "draisine" merited a brief spurt of popularity in Europe and the United States (fig. 1.1). By the mid-1860s, velocipedes, a more modern,

Fig. 1.1. This English print, originally from 1819, features the "hobbyhorse," a slightly modified version of the draisine. Reprinted from *Munsey's Magazine*, May 1896.

pedal-powered, two-wheel vehicle, began attracting the attention of Parisian gentlemen before making their way across the Atlantic.

These machines quickly produced a mini-craze of their own in the United States. Rinks built for velocipedes dotted American cities, but the effect on urban environments was minimal. Throughout the 1870s, even as French and English riders continued to experiment with the latest bicycle incarnations, the clunky machines failed to attract a sizable following in American cities.[3] That the velocipede craze came and went so quickly rendered any future success of the bicycle doubtful.

Wandering through the Centennial Exhibition of 1876 in Philadelphia, an unsuspecting thirty-three-year-old Civil War veteran was about to eye the machine that would forever change his life and the bicycle's place in America. Albert Augustus Pope, honorifically referred to as Colonel Pope, joined nearly nine million fellow visitors in perusing the more than 250 pavilions that marked the nation's one-hundred-year anniversary with displays designed to highlight technological and cultural progress. The telephone, typewriter, and a seventy-foot-tall Corliss steam engine were among the most talked about attractions. But it was the showcase of a high-wheel bicycle that infatuated the Colonel. Despite having no idea how to ride the "Pennyfarthing," as it was dubbed in England, the Colonel was smitten. He soon set sail for England to inspect the manufacturer's factory. After just a short stay, the Colonel was convinced. The cycling industry in Europe was quickening. In Great Britain alone, 50,000 cyclists rode through the streets.[4] Pope foresaw that Americans would soon become bicycle crazy and that as a result, he would make millions of dollars. On both accounts, he was right.

The man who wore more of his salt and pepper hair on his face than atop his head did, in fact, become nineteenth-century America's foremost bicycle tycoon. Although he had already had some success in manufacturing supplies and tools for shoemakers, the Bostonian dreamed of forging a bicycle empire. Like his few early competitors, he began by importing bicycles from England to test the market, but soon he built his own manufacturing facility in Hartford, Connecticut. Pope, who split his time between the factory and his Boston home, was certainly the most aggressive domestic producer, and he came to dominate the market. He began selling his latest high-wheel bicycles under the "Columbia" brand. Featuring an oversized front wheel (at least twice the size of the back wheel, although oftentimes much bigger) and a seat that rested about five feet above the ground, the high-wheeler was capable of achieving tremendous speed (fig. 1.2). Manufacturers quickly realized that since the pedals were attached directly to the front wheel, the larger the wheel, the farther a rider could travel with just one revolution.[5]

The high-wheeler posed a series of problems. Any dress-wearing woman daring enough to mount the saddle in the sky would have adopted a rather revealing pose. Few tried and even fewer became regular riders. Universally, the lack of stability and overall safety problems added significant danger. Because the seat typically rested above the disproportionately large front wheel, crashes often resulted in "headers." Riders would fall forward, head first, to the ground. (There were no helmets.) The even bigger challenge involved mounting the bicycle. As Mark Twain, a high-wheeler disciple, explained:

> You do it in this way: you hop along behind it on your right foot, resting the other on the mounting-peg, and grasping the tiller with your hands. At the word, you rise on the peg, stiffen your left leg, hang your other one around in the air in a general and indefinite way, lean your stomach against the rear of the saddle, and then fall off, maybe on one side, maybe on the other; but you fall off. You get up and do it again; and once more; and then several times.[6]

And that was coming from a man who had spent twelve hours in riding class.

Twain's palatial, painted-brick, Victorian mansion sat just a half mile from the sprawling campus of Pope's manufacturing center. The curious author had visited the factory, paid a handsome sum for one of the new machines, and enrolled in a cycling class. Like many others, he developed a love-hate relationship with his bicycle. (He once quipped "Get a bicycle. You will not regret it, if you live.") Despite Twain's persistent instability atop the high-wheeler (a young onlooker once suggested that he "dress up in pillows") he joined a thriving class of adventurous, affluent men who adopted the wheel.[7] At a cost of $120 and oftentimes significantly more, the high-wheeler's price limited its customer base and, since cycling was not yet "fashionable" in the way that it would ultimately become, these earliest cyclists represented but a small subset of the moneyed class.[8] They tended to be young men of means, but not those who moved comfortably among the traditional elite. Mastering the high-wheeler took much skill and athleticism, virtues embraced by a sporting crowd. Still, there were enough people interested in cycling to attract a group of cunning businessmen. Together, they laid the groundwork for cycling to move into the mainstream.

THE SAFETY BICYCLE

By the close of the 1880s, the state of American cycling had come a long way since Colonel Pope first saw the high-wheeler in 1876. The packs of cyclists roaming through and between cities that once constituted only scores of riders now numbered in the thousands. The number of clubs devoted to the sport and magazines promoting it mushroomed. Nonetheless, after a decade or so of popularity, the high-wheeler began to disappear. Safety concerns, cost, and the lack of female ridership prevented any widespread adoption.[9] Not surprisingly, manufacturers and would-be riders longed for a more appealing version.

By the late 1880s and the opening years of the 1890s, the "safety" bicycle began to replace the high-wheeler. The low-mounted version had a chain drive, two equal-sized wheels, and, ultimately, pneumatic tires (fig. 1.3). The inflatable tires represented a significant advance because they allowed for greater speeds, reduced vibrations, and, in due course, a detachable tire. Ball bearings, noticeably absent from some early models, helped reduce friction, and the new, easier-to-maneuver frame featured a lowered seat that attracted many who could never have mastered the art of (or those too frightened to have even attempted) mounting the high-wheeler. The new bicycles attracted an impressive following. In 1891 alone, Americans purchased around 150,000 machines, nearly doubling the existing sales.[10] The rapid increase reflected a broader base of potential riders. After all, manufacturers derived the name "safety bicycle" in order to attract a different set of customers than the adventurous men who dominated the high-wheel market. The reduction in the average weight of a bicycle also made cycling more manageable for more people. Thanks to lighter frames, chains, and rims (wood as opposed to steel), the average weight of a bicycle dropped from about forty-two pounds in 1890 to about twenty-five pounds within a handful of years. Despite its name and the fact that it required much less athleticism and daring than what was required for the high-wheeler, safety bicycles were still popularly understood as vehicles for sport and recreation rather than utility. That the bicycle was elegant and speedy was more important than that it be durable.[11]

In contrast to other cyclists across the globe, Americans preferred their bicycles to be light and graceful above all else. To be sure, commuters, delivery boys, and other utilitarian users often emphasized the functional components of their wheels, but Americans generally stressed form over function. According to journalists at the time, the English preferred heavier, sturdier machines and the Chinese valued "strength, durability,

Figs. 1.2 and 1.3. These two machines, built less than a decade apart, illustrate the rapid innovations in bicycle technology and form. *Top* is a high-wheel bicycle produced by Columbia in 1888; *bottom* is a safety bicycle—an 1896 Model 41 Columbia, which included a drop frame for women, allowing space for a skirt to hang down. Reproduced with permission from the Smithsonian Bicycle Collection, Division of Work & Industry, National Museum of American History, Smithsonian Institution.

and cheapness, rather than lightness and comfort." The Japanese likewise selected their wheels for practical or business purposes, not leisure.[12]
Americans fancied wheels that might not have been ideal for transportation. American manufacturers, realizing the demand and helping to create
it, marketed bicycles as the lightest on the market. Indeed, the particu-
larities of bicycle design reflected more than just the ideas of an engineer;
they also reflected customer input.[13]

Some cyclists even forwent brakes. Although a variety of brakes were
available, many riders resorted to back-pedaling in order to slow their
pace. Without brakes they saved a modest amount in weight and price.
The trade-off for emphasizing light-weight was that those bicycles ideally
suited for leisure were less practical as everyday vehicles and less likely
to sustain the wear and tear of city riding. Serious buyers also carefully
considered the size and quality of the single gear that powered most bicycles—a wise precaution, as the size would determine how difficult it
was to push the pedals and the corresponding amount of power produced.
Surely, many riders—especially those who found themselves occasionally climbing steep hills—regretted their choices. While the invention
of the safety bicycle and its particular design was not inevitable, it did
represent a breakthrough. Riders demanded stronger, lighter frames. The
rough roads demanded better tires. Bicycle dealers demanded a shape that
invited women and men of all sizes into their stores. And nearly all constituents demanded that bicycles be safer. The end result was a bicycle
that is almost identical to the one we would recognize today.[14]

At the time, bicycles fascinated Americans as a modern piece of technology that could, in theory at least, usher in revolutionary changes to the
urban world and stand as a sign that the modern age had come into being.
So did its manufacturers. Nearly every year, bicycle models sported mechanical improvements and frills absent from earlier models. In fact, manufacturers in the 1890s sought patents to improve their bicycles at such an
alarming rate that the US government created a special division within
the Patent Office just to deal with bicycle-related patenting. Most of these
innovations were minor, simply an excuse to issue another model and render the older versions out of date. In that sense, bicycles were one of the
first luxury items in which both customers and manufacturers expected
that buyers would continually replace their purchase at regular intervals.
Any large-scale transformations of the bicycle, though, were a thing of the
past. In the language of social constructivist scholars, the safety bicycle
represented a state of closure. Though the machine remained much the
same, its meaning continued to evolve. Over time, and across the world,

the bicycle has served varying roles: an efficient vehicle, a child's plaything, and, once, a marker of middle-class respectability.[15]

While small changes might have been advertised as revolutionary, in reality manufacturers put more effort on advertising the quality of the many moving parts of their machines than on reinventing them. Copywriters would include inordinate detail, alerting customers to the method of construction and the value that various components offered.[16] For example, the Damascus Bicycle Catalog from 1897 explained to interested shoppers that their frames came in three sizes, two shapes, were made from "cold-drawn seamless steel tubing," and had been "brazed into forged crowns; strong, unique and reliable." It further revealed that the wheels contained either thirty-two or thirty-six high-grade swaged end spokes and were made from "carefully selected second growth, rock elm wood rims." Materials for the hubs came from "high-grade steel, hardened and tempered," the oiling device was said to be dustproof, and the ball bearings were imported from Germany. In similar detail, the catalog highlighted the size and types and manufacturing techniques used to create the crank hanger, handlebars, gearing, chain, sprockets, saddle, and pedals, as well as the company's processes for nickeling and enameling their bicycles. Should anything go wrong, buyers could dip into the saddle-matched leather tool bag that came with the bicycle.[17] Newspaper and magazine columnists equally obsessed over the specs of new models and the processes by which godlike manufacturers miraculously turned piles of steel and rubber into bicycles. Producers and users each understood and celebrated bicycles as modern technological marvels.

The rapid technological progress displayed in the birth of the safety bicycle suggested the potential of the machine; Americans speculated about the possible applications. Military men envisioned the modern battlefield lined with cycling militias. Innovators scrambled for the next great bicycle contraption: amphibious watercycles; sailing bicycles; skating bicycles; bicycles built for two, four, six, or eight. Some began to experiment with motorized bicycles. And two cyclists and bicycle mechanics from Ohio, inspired by the machines they tinkered with, rented, and built, debunked one of history's great axioms. Humans, the Wright brothers proved, can indeed fly.[18]

Despite its human power source, the bicycle was a machine that attracted those with an appetite for the latest technology and a vehicle that sparked the imagination of those who saw technology as a panacea to the problems of late-nineteenth-century American cities. Indeed, the modern safety bicycle was but one of many innovations that spurred utopian visions of the future. Even for those technologies that had already reoriented daily life, Americans dreamed up unrealistic fantasies of how their world would change even more and for the better. That electricity, for example, could light the city under the night sky was not enough for those who fancied that it might someday be used to "abolish sleep, cure disease, quicken intelligence, eliminate pollution, banish housework, and much more."[19] Earlier in the century, railroads and telegraphs reshaped the country, mass communication, culture, and commerce, but some boosters imagined even grander changes that these technologies would bring to the size, shape, and nature of cities. While Americans had long been enamored by machines, the popularity of technological utopianism soared as "the machine became not only the symbol of social change but, in the eyes of many, the primary agent of change."[20]

Nothing embodied the power of technology better than speed. While engineers and manufacturers built bicycles capable of moving faster, racers pushed themselves to set speed records. Like horse racing, baseball, and other sports, bicycle racing attracted a mass audience seeking to experience the thrill of speed and the excitement of competition. Inside arenas, jaws dropped and media outlets swarmed at the six-day races in which cyclists circled a single track as many times as they could in the 144-hour time limit.[21] But there was something different about the bicycle. Unlike trains, airplanes, or automobiles, bicycles functioned as an extension of the human body. Human power drove the chains. That is, in part, what made the machine so compelling. A human could travel twenty-plus miles per hour using just his own force. In the past, one journalist recorded in 1896, humans had depended on animals and electricity. Now, however, "he has hit upon a device which makes his own body the source of power" and "finds that it becomes really a part of himself."[22] That excitement evinced itself in special races in which bicycles raced against horses and even moving trains. It was man versus equine and man versus machine.[23]

Cyclists often defined the bicycle as part of themselves, an almost robotic tool. "The cyclist is a man made half of flesh and half of steel that only our century of science and iron could have spawned."[24] Another cyclist described the bicycle as an "echo of yourself."[25] An older, female cyclist recounted, "I had made myself master of the most remarkable, ingenious, and inspiring motor ever yet devised upon this planet."[26] The technology behind the bicycle and its every iteration was widely praised, but even more so was its ability to tap into the human body and maximize human power. Nevertheless, while speed attracted some, safety attracted many more.

MARKETING AND SELLING

The low-mounted bicycles, easier to ride and more affordable than the high-wheel variety, attracted masses of middle-class men and women. As the new bicycles increased in popularity, production boomed and prices dropped even more. Almost three hundred new firms began manufacturing bicycles in the 1890s alone. Consumers could choose from among dozens of varyingly-priced models offered by Columbia, Victor, Gladiator, Crescent, Spalding, Rambler, and scores of other brand-name manufacturers, or from lower priced machines retailed by department stores, specialty shops, and mail-order catalogs.

To attract new riders, bicycle producers marketed their products through promotional campaigns, the size and scope of which were unrivaled. In the embryonic stage of domestic bicycle manufacturing Pope and his rivals advertised relentlessly, knowing full well that no serious demand existed. Instead, the Colonel was determined to "create a demand."[27] And that he did. In 1880, Pope spent $60,000 to launch *Wheelman* magazine. His rival and one of the other few early captains of the nascent bicycle industry, Frank Weston, started the *American Bicycling Journal.* Aside from the preponderance of advertisements for Pope's Columbia bicycles in *Wheelman* and Weston's Cunningham, Heath, and Company machines in *American Bicycling Journal,* the two magazines appeared to readers as unbiased cycling periodicals chronicling the sport. Pope also had his attorney and confidant write the *American Bicycler,* essentially a book-length treatise on the history and merits of "the wheel."[28]

Pope's and Weston's bicycle magazines evolved into merely two out of the whopping fifty bicycle periodicals in circulation by 1896. In the late nineteenth century, an era of increasing literacy and cheaper printing costs, a wave of magazines and journals flooded newsstands. Many of them catered to niche audiences. The cycling magazines offered subscribers a range of articles, from pieces on how to maintain a bicycle, maps outlining favored cycling routes, and results of track races, to news from prominent cycling clubs, and even bicycle-related humor. Other magazines, like *Harper's Bazaar,* not only regularly featured the bicycle but also produced special issues or "bicycle numbers." Desperate to attract the growing population of riders, newspapers created entire news departments devoted to cycling, sponsored bicycle parades, and filled their pages with bicycle advertisements. Like most other dailies, the *New York Times* printed a regular column with tidbits from "among the wheelmen." The *New York Recorder* touted its loyalty to cyclists by boasting of its twenty-two columns of bicycle advertisements and exhaustive coverage of all things bicycle, while the *Chicago Times Herald* proudly advertised that it devoted more of its pages to cycling than any of its competitors. The *Boston Post* printed a special column in each Sunday paper devoted to issues concerning women cyclists. Even for an enthusiast, it was impossible to keep up. One such fan collected clippings from bicycle related articles printed around the country. In a six-month period from May until October of 1896, her collection spanned more than 2,500 pages in what now covers fourteen gigantic bound volumes.[29]

While Pope, Weston, and other producers rejoiced in the increasing press coverage, they maintained their own direct-to-consumer marketing efforts. "Modern technologies," advertising proponents came to realize, "needed their heralds."[30] Before the advent of full-scale advertising firms and professional admen in the 1920s, the bicycle industry was exceptional. Manufacturers took full advantage of the explosive growth of print media and impressionable consumers. Bicycle advertisements were placed in popular national magazines, including *Harper's Weekly*, the *Atlantic Monthly*, and *Scribner's Magazine*. Foreshadowing a trend in the industry, these advertisements sold the idea of bicycle riding as much as the bicycle itself.[31] Especially since cycling was still so novel an activity, manufacturers had to convince consumers to become bicycle riders first and Columbia, Victor, or some other brand's loyal customers second.

As sales grew, so did advertising budgets. By the late 1890s, the bicycle industry probably spent more on advertising than any other trade group. One historian of advertising found that the ratio of bicycle advertisements to all other advertisements combined was one-to-six. Convinced that money spent on marketing was money well spent, manufacturers and individual retail agents poured money into advertising. Illustrative of the industry, the Monarch Bicycle Co. plowed its profits back into advertising. The company began in 1893 and had a $20,000 advertising budget in 1894. Just two years later, the Chicago-based firm sold 50,000 machines and spent $125,000 on print advertisements, its racing team, balloon launches, and company catalogs. In the annual catalogs, Monarch and its competitors lavished readers with colorful images, in-depth commentary on the firms' latest models, and prominent endorsements, often totaling fifty-plus pages. The 1896 Humber Cycles catalog devoted an entire page to a list of its most famous customers (John Pierpont Morgan and the Sultan of Morocco, among others). According to the leaders of the bicycle industry, the catalogs served as the most direct form of advertisements and warranted great expense. Colonel Pope was convinced that every dollar spent on advertising returned to Columbia's coffers in multiple. Once asked about his most cherished employee, the Colonel responded: "He has been in my employ for seventeen years, yet he has never even asked for a holiday. He works both day and night, is never asleep or intoxicated, and though I pay him more than $250,000 a year, I consider that he costs me nothing. His name is Advertisement."[32]

Aside from traditional modes of advertising, Pope and his competitors found creative ways to promote their bicycles. "Columbia"-emblazoned fans cooled women on the streets, pins hung from men's lapels, and calendar pages flapped inside drafty offices. Pope sent bicycles to boys who earned top grades and prizes to scrupulous schoolteachers. A paper model of the bicycle factory in Hartford was sent to anyone who asked. As bicycle racing became a popular spectator sport that drew thousands to local velodromes (banked bicycle tracks), manufacturers signed the most famous athletes for endorsement deals. Producers sponsored racers and meets and often bragged about cycling records set atop their own brand of bicycle. Columbia widely advertised that it was the model of choice for Thomas Stevens, who became the first person to circumnavigate the world on a bicycle (boats carried him and his wheel across the oceans).[33]

With friends in the press and a keen sense of the yet-to-be-defined field of public relations, Pope's likeness regularly appeared inside newspapers. He led (and bankrolled) campaigns to improve cycling conditions and push for cyclists' rights. Pope later recalled that these public crusades, launched by himself rather than his company, "brought [them] more good, more publicity" than any other marketing efforts. As he recalled, the goal was quite simple: "to make the papers talk." In a creative marketing move that required far less capital but was widely praised, Pope installed an air pump outside his Boston office building. His customers got free air anytime they needed it. The ultimate effect of these advertising ventures was unabashed success. Probably with a grin, Pope concluded, "We created the demand for bicycles with one hand, and the supply with the other."[34]

Inside the "Vatican," as Pope's headquarters back in Boston came to be known, a salesroom welcomed visitors on the ground floor and a cycling school at the top; his offices were sandwiched in between. Pope's was the largest, but far from the only, riding school in town. Throughout the 1890s, schools opened in nearly every major city. Since virtually no one had ever ridden a bicycle, adults had not gone through what later became a childhood ritual of learning how to ride. Standing on their two wheels, bicycles naturally fall over. Balancing on a bicycle was a new skill that needed to be mastered. So was steering. Some Americans may have ridden on streetcars and carriages, but few had ever driven them. Even for those that had, they experienced nothing like the feel of handlebars that with just a slight push on one side could turn so sharply and easily. The millions of cyclists in the 1890s had to either teach themselves or patronize one of the many schools emerging in urban centers. The schools offered more than just an elementary education in cycling; they provided a private setting where would-be riders could avoid public embarrassment. New York City had more than a dozen such academies alone. Retailers owned some of the schools, like Macy's Cycling Academy; manufacturers operated others, including Spalding's fifty-instructor academy at Madison Square Garden; and private individuals managed some as well. Schools boasted about the size of their open floor space ("no posts" here) and their amenities, which often included private changing rooms and places to store or rent bicycles. The method of instruction varied depending on the "professor's" preference, but the technique used at Washington, DC's Columbia Bicycle Academy was not uncommon. There, instructors tied leather belts around their pupil's waists and, with one hand on the belt strap and the other on the handlebars, guided the novice across the polished floors. In subsequent lessons, the instructor held the student's saddle, walking alongside the bicycle. For the final lesson, the teacher rode side by side with his now semi-confident student, keeping one hand on each bicycle.[35]

To sell machines, bicycle distribution, just as advertising, developed through national (and sometimes even global) channels. In the earliest years of the 1880s, bicycle salesmen visited cities, performed public demonstrations, and sold directly to consumers. But this was a temporary measure. Pope and Weston both envisioned their companies as national entities and established retail channels throughout the country. At the height of the bicycle boom, Pope opened "branch houses" in New York, Chicago, San Francisco, Pittsburgh, Providence, Rochester, Buffalo, Detroit, St. Louis, Portland, New Orleans, Milwaukee, Louisville, and Washington, DC. Yet, most machines were sold through retail outlets ranging from large sporting goods stores to specialty bicycle shops. By the last year of the century, there were about 40,000 bicycle dealers.[36] In several cities, "Bicycle Rows," districts with a concentration of bicycle shops, where riders could purchase, rent, or repair their wheels (or simply socialize with fellow riders), appeared.[37] In dense cities, men and women could walk but blocks and find an array of dealers selling scores of bicycles and accessories. In one concentrated area of bicycle retailers in Lower Manhattan, consumers could choose from among more than thirty bicycle shops in an area measuring only about 0.2 square miles (fig. 1.4).

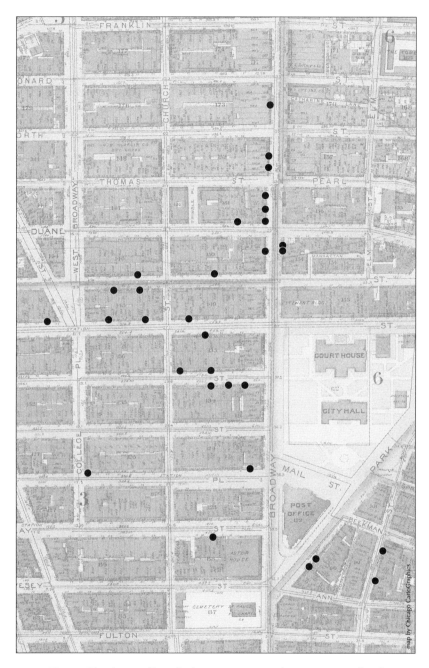

Fig. 1.4. The cluster of bicycle shops in Lower Manhattan in 1896 offered customers an array of choices and a place for enthusiasts to gather.

Stores selling bicycles and shops providing repair and/or rental services filled more than just a single neighborhood. In 1898 Chicago, for example, merchants could be found in nearly every neighborhood of note (fig. 1.5). In all, there were roughly 400 dealers selling or repairing bicycles in Chicago, meaning that there was one bicycle shop per every 4,235 residents. (In 2012, the same ratio in Chicago was closer to one shop per 34,000 residents. Even present-day Amsterdam and Greater Copenhagen have fewer bicycle shops per person today with a ratio of one to 5,571 and one to 4,546, respectively.) With 271 such businesses in 1896, Philadelphia's shops per capita came close to matching Chicago's rate. Smaller cities had equally impressive ratios. Oshkosh, Wisconsin, had 30 shops by 1895 or about one for every 935 people. Detroit in 1899 and Hartford, Connecticut, in 1897 both had about one shop per 3,500 people that either produced, sold, manufactured, or repaired bicycles or parts, while Pittsburgh in 1898 had a slightly less impressive rate at roughly one shop per 5,300 people (still more shops per capita than present-day Amsterdam). Pittsburgh was also home to a half dozen bicycle liveries, renting out bicycles. It was no accident that those rental shops were referred to as liveries, conjuring up a cultural link to horses, the very animal that bicycle salesmen suggested were no longer necessary. Horse liveries and stables that sold and/or boarded horses had much older histories than bicycle shops but were quickly outpaced. According to Detroit's 1899 city directory, bicycle shops outnumbered the old-fashioned liveries by a three-to-one margin. In short, these American cycling cities had more bicycle shops per capita than almost any other major city across time and space.[38]

With bicycle sales escalating, retailers of all varieties looked to profit. It was not uncommon for small shops to stock a handful of machines even if they sold nothing else remotely similar to bicycles. On First and Second Avenue in Seattle, for example, grocers, barbers, gun shops, and cigar stores all sold bicycles.[39] Regardless of the place of sale, someone purchasing a Columbia from any of Pope's 2,000 retail sales agents could expect to pay the list price as printed in the Pope Manufacturing Company's yearly catalog.

Even while Pope and his competitors launched a national retail network, targeted marketing was integral to the bicycle's success. Columbia designed rugged bicycles specifically for commercial functions like delivering mail, messages, and food. It even sold a cold-weatherproof "Yukon" bicycle made for the droves of speculators who joined the Alaskan gold rush. The Colonel also invested mightily (and futilely) in promoting his

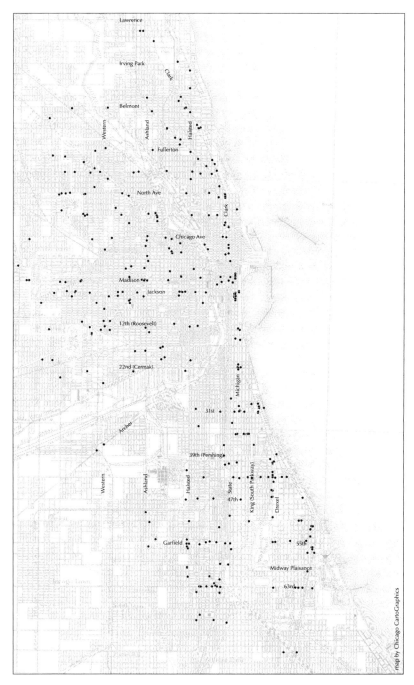

Fig. 1.5. In 1898, Chicago's roughly 400 bicycle shops were spread across the entire city.

bicycles as a potential weapon in war. Yet one untapped market loomed largest: women.

With half of the population at stake, bicycle manufacturers actively targeted the female cyclist. Although some women had ridden tricycles and relatively few had participated in the brief fervor of the velocipede or the high-wheeler, cycling had been a pastime dominated by men. Pope was not simply going to wait for the tides of social mores to shift. He began his own campaign to make female bicycle riding socially acceptable. Believing that most women fretted about learning how to ride in public, Pope established a riding academy that catered to Bostonian women who could experience the trials and tribulations of learning to ride in a private setting. Moreover, he developed machines and accompanying marketing campaigns designed to make bicycles a more attractive purchase for women. He and his competitors launched a series of Lady's Bicycles, many of which featured specially-designed frames and mesh over the rear wheel to ensure that flowing skirts or dresses could hang freely and not be ensnared by any of the machine's moving parts. They often had different gearing too, so that women could turn the pedals with less force than would be needed on a comparable gentlemen's wheel. Pope bragged that his "graceful machines [were] made with such lightness and ease of manipulation even delicate girls [could] cover miles without exhaustive fatigue." While the gendered language was aimed at women and promoted stereotypes about women's frail constitutions, it also indirectly signaled to men that cycling was no longer a dangerous and taxing activity.[40]

Nearly every manufacturer made the same arguments. The 1896 Cleveland Bicycles catalog promoted its "Ladies and misses" models as "calculated to give grace to the rider and avoid any possible feeling of awkwardness. It is a gem of perfection and dainty weight, elegant construction and finish." Unlike automobiles, which were designed for multiple people and necessarily both genders, manufacturers and the cyclists themselves helped to construct a meaning of the bicycle within a gendered context. They all hoped that the bicycle conveyed an appropriate message regarding femininity, even if they did not agree on what appropriate meant. Pope also published and distributed an educational pamphlet entitled "Cycling for Ladies," hoping to lure more women into the market with an extended essay written by a lady cyclist, touting the pleasure and health that comes with riding. For any of the women readers and would-be riders who encountered prejudice, the Pope-sponsored pamphlet boasted that when a woman makes use of her "will and determination," she "removes all ob-

stacles and annihilates every barrier." The design changes and marketing
tactics quickly paid off.[41]

The specially designed bicycles went much further than just offering
two versions, a masculine and feminine bicycle. A cyclist, depending on
his or her budget and taste, could find a wheel with a particular frame
size, wheel size, crank length, gearing, handlebars, hubs, brakes, and finish, not to mention the endless list of accessories. Those sundries, as a
typical catalog from A. G. Spaulding & Bros. in 1890 revealed, offered customers numerous ways to personalize their machines. The single catalog
invited buyers to choose from bicycle lamps (twelve kinds), cyclometers
(five kinds), locks, luggage carriers, home trainers, wrenches, oilers, whis-
tles, bells (and a gong), bicycle stands, oils, cement, tool bags, tire heaters,
saddles, tire tape, cycle brushes, bicycle hoists, rubber tires, badges, bicycle uniforms, bicycle caps, bicycle hoses, bicycle belts, and bicycle shoes.
Without much effort, buyers could find pneumatic pumps, mud guards,
pant guards (designed to keep trousers "neat about the ankle"), weather-
proof jackets, child seats, parcel holders, and repair kits all designed to
make cycling more practical. These add-ons provided the retailer with an
added source of revenue; one historian estimates that almost half of all
money spent on cycling went toward accessories and repairs.[42]

The accessories also provided consumers with more ways to custom-
ize their machines and, in the process, helped construct a popular understanding of what a bicycle was.[43] Although the general shape of the bicycle
became more or less fixed by the dawn of the cycling city, its social meaning was anything but. The same bicycle standing idle looked very different from when it was weaving through the city. Meaning was constructed
and contingent on the type of person who rode the bicycle and the nature
in which he or she rode.[44] In so doing, riders connoted distinct messages
about the activity of cycling and the bicycle itself. A scorcher (the pejo-
rative term for reckless riders who raced around the city) darting around
street corners and brushing shoulders with shrieking pedestrians made
the bicycle seem like a vehicle designed for speed and sport. A wealthy
woman pedaling through a sun-filled city park, moving not much faster
than sauntering pedestrians, appeared to be riding a fancy machine ideally suited for casual recreation. A middle-class professional riding to the
office at a moderate pace looked as if he rode a machine meant for utility.

Of course, the scorcher's, the wealthy woman's, and the office worker's bicycles were, in fact, slightly different. The scorching bicycle might
have had racing-style handlebars that curved downward, the frame of the
woman's wheel would have been crafted especially for ladies, and the

middle-class office worker's bicycle might have been outfitted with an attachment designed to hold his briefcase. The accessories and features of
a particular model enabled individual riders to help construct an identity
as a cyclist and to give their machine an identity as well. Perhaps reflec-
tive or perhaps aspirational, the bicycle and the way in which it was ridden broadcasted messages about its user. Those messages might have been
coded, nuanced, or blatant. Take the 1897 Tiffany bicycle, for example. It
offered its customers machines studded with gold and silver and accessories similarly plated in precious metals. Trendsetters, like the famed
actress and singer Lillian Russell, could be seen riding in a flock of society's who's-who, showcasing the latest fashion atop a set of sparkling
wheels. These bicycles stood in stark contrast to bicycles that catered to
those at the other end of the socioeconomic spectrum. Those machines,
an example of which one manufacturer in France appropriately christened
the *démocratique*, offered a functional no frills alternative. So, while the
invention of the safety bicycle marked a critical stage in the evolution of
bicycle design, the question of what a bicycle was, and who it served, was
one that continued to be asked and answered throughout the 1890s.[45]

The many bicycle accessories also reveal the degree to which at least
some buyers intended to keep their steeds in good health. Locks promised
to fend off thieves; bicycle oils promised to ward off rust. Cycling had become such a big business that advertisers of long-existing products found
ways to market their products for a new use. Procter & Gamble's Ivory
soap was ideally suited to keep a bicycle chain lubricated, or so the company's advertisements claimed in 1896. To maintain their wheels to the
fullest and to get the most out of their repair kits, cyclists would need to
learn about the machine and the technology behind it. While previous experience tinkering with other machines may have endowed cyclists with
the skills to diagnose and repair some of the problems with their bicycles,
parts of their wheels were brand new. In particular, repairing pneumatic
tires often required a close study of the tire repair kit manual. Exasperated
cyclists needed to learn how to change a flat.[46]

When marketing their technological wares, promoters tapped into a
supercharged urban consumer culture. In the 1890s, eager sellers and insa-
tiable buyers incited, as historian William Leach wrote, "the transformation of American society into a society preoccupied with consumption,
with comfort and bodily well-being, with luxury, spending, and acqui-
sition, with more goods this year than last, more next year than this."
Across a broad range of city dwellers, consumption habits expanded as
luxury goods became increasingly affordable for much of the middle class.

Perhaps best characterized by the emergence of the department store in the late nineteenth century, Americans radically altered their patterns of consumption. Hypnotized by the elaborate displays of glistening products, window-shoppers dreamt of a better, and certainly more fashionable, future. Innovative department stores, like the legendary Wanamaker's, marketed, displayed, and sold an array of goods, including bicycles, that catered to shoppers eager to take part in the process of conspicuous consumption.[47]

Just as department stores redefined the "shopping experience," a coalition of bicycle manufacturers sought to display their bicycles in spectacular fashion on their own terms. While most individuals would continue to purchase wheels from local shops, department stores, or acquaintances down the street, bicycle magnates launched a series of carefully curated expositions in order to tantalize the public with style, luxury, and innovation. Local dealers had long adopted the practice of displaying their bicycles, angling their machines, lighting their storerooms, erecting signage, placing price tags, and hanging posters according to the expert advice on "effective window dressing" found in trade magazines. National manufacturers envisioned bicycle shows as something much grander. Staged with dramatic lighting, gleaming bicycles sparkled less as objects of utility, recreation, and pleasure, and more as objects of art, a marvel in their own aesthetic right.[48] Objects, of course, that were meant to be consumed.

The first American bicycle exhibitions in the 1880s followed the practice begun in England at the Stanley Show. They had been relatively small affairs. But in the early 1890s, and especially by mid-decade, bicycle shows became an important channel for marketing and selling machines. In each successive year the exhibitions grew in size, scope, and frequency. In New Orleans, thousands of buyers, sellers, and curious onlookers crowded the electrically illuminated Artillery Hall, which was filled with displays of the latest bicycle models, parts, and accoutrements. Chicago and New York traded hosting duties for the larger cycling exhibitions. In both cities the spectacle grew in tandem with the trade, as the nascent National Board of Trade of Cycle Manufacturers, a collective of the biggest and best-known bicycle makers, invested in these elaborate festivals to celebrate their products. In Madison Square Garden, concerts, trick-riding exhibitions, displays of celebrity-owned bicycles, and elaborate banquets coincided with the hundreds of manufacturer exhibits, lectures on bicycle construction, business meetings, sales orders, and the much-anticipated ceremonies in which the major manufacturers revealed their newest models. Some 120,000 attended the show in 1896 (fig. 1.6).[49]

Fig. 1.6. A scene from the great bicycle show at Madison Square Garden
in 1895. Reprinted from *Scientific American*, February 9, 1895.

Despite a raging blizzard, Chicago's Bicycle Exhibition of 1896 managed to attract more than 10,000 visitors on its very first day (100,000 ultimately paid the half-dollar entrance fee). The fair contained 60,000 square
feet of space devoted to 368 booths operated by 250 separate exhibitors,
displays of bicycle novelties and innovations, and plenty of "handsome
souvenirs" doled out by bicycle manufacturers intending to lure potential
customers over to their booths. After all, selling bicycles was the mission
of these elaborate exhibitions. Local bicycle agents from across the country assembled at these regular shows, visiting the exhibits, meeting and
socializing with manufacturers, and ultimately ordering stock. The one-
week-long show in Chicago was estimated to yield $10,000,000 worth of
goods sold to bicycle agents who hoped to have correctly gauged both the
size of their local market and the tastes of their local consumers for the
upcoming season.[50]

When the agents returned to their respective cities and shops, they
waged their own marketing campaigns. Printed advertisements placed by
local salesmen ran alongside those from national manufacturers, both promoting the same product and both with much to gain from improved sales.
But local agents and dealers devised some unique marketing techniques
as well. One such ploy involved hiring female bicycle models whose job
was to seduce women into a purchase. As one journalist wrote: "She is a

versatile young woman, this bicycle model, and for a fat woman she puts on pads to make her look stout, and she has a way of adapting her own figure . . ."[51] When modeling bicycle suits, the saleswoman would mount a wheel, providing a distorted mirror for the customer. In an in-depth interview, a bicycle model named Helen Ward described the real secret to selling bicycles. Models needed to be "good looking," sport a "good figure," and most importantly be "triggy," which meant "Neat in her waist, long in limb, and of that peculiar build that can wear almost any size clothes." Ward also confessed that a model must be an expert rider, able to ride "without effort." But above all it was the cycling costume that made the sale, she claimed. Consequently, she would try on as many as 100 suits a day for potential customers. To sell the clothes and promote their stores, models would surreptitiously plant themselves in cycling classes for beginners. There, they would inevitably field questions from envious women and intrigued husbands.[52]

Revenues to the schools, commissions to the models, and sales to the bicycle manufacturing firms continued to rise in spite of the economic depression that debilitated American manufacturing and yielded massive unemployment throughout much of the 1890s. As factories stood still and nervous capitalists watched industrial demand sag and prices drop in tandem, bicycles remained such an attractive purchase that production actually increased. In the ten-year span from 1891–1900, domestic producers churned out somewhere between 5,500,000 and 8,000,000 bicycles (fig. 1.7). That amounts to somewhere between a 1,900 and a 2,800 percent increase from the decade prior.[53] The growth was spectacular.

The bicycle economy was so robust in such lean times that contemporaries in other industries blamed the bicycle for their anemic sales. The *Baltimore Sun* calculated that almost $100,000,000 was spent "toward the gratification of cycle fever." As a result, other forms of transportation, instruments of leisure, and luxury goods suffered: liveries lost $20,000,000; saddlery and carriage factories, $25,000,000; jewelers, $10,000,000; tailors, $10,000,000; piano makers, $3,500,000; cigar dealers, $7,000,000; street railways, $3,000,000; and liquor dealers, $2,500,000.[54] While the reporter had few ways to calculate any of these numbers with any certainty and likely exaggerated his case, the bicycle manufacturing industry in 1900 was capitalized at nearly $30,000,000.[55] And that was several years after its peak. The majority of cyclists purchased their vehicles within the 1893–1897 economic maelstrom. The pace of purchases had been so swift that it seemed bicycles had taken over the city. Certainly the noted author Stephen Crane thought so. As he described New York's Boulevard (the

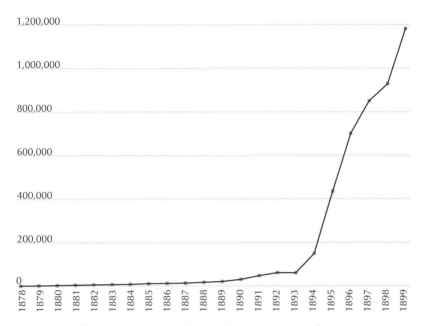

Fig. 1.7. Yearly bicycle production in the United States. Estimates from Bruce Epperson, "How Many Bikes?" in *Cycle History 11*, with minor revisions provided by the author.

Fig. 1.8. Cyclists (including men, women, and at least one African American) near Columbus Circle in New York, 1898. Reproduced with permission from the Museum of the City of New York.

Fig. 1.9. East Main Street in Rochester, New York, 1899. Reproduced with permission from the collection of the Rochester Public Library Local History Division.

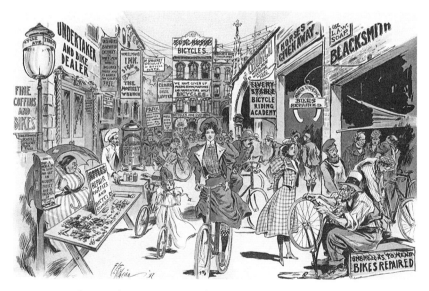

Fig. 1.10. This "Modern Street Scene" from an 1897 issue of the humor magazine the *Judge* caricatures the influence of bicycles on cities. Not only is the intersection of "Cycle Ave." and "Tire St." filled with cyclists, but also every business has begun to cater to them. Reprinted from *Judge*, August 7, 1897.

popular name at the time for the portion of Broadway stretching north of 59th Street):

> [It] has vaulted to a startling prominence, and is now one of the sights of New York. This is caused by the bicycle. Once the boulevard was a quiet avenue . . . Now, however, it is the great thoroughfare for bicycles. On these gorgeous spring days they appear in thousands. All mankind is awheel, apparently, and a person on nothing but legs feels like a strange animal . . . The bicycle crowd has completely subjugated the street. The glittering wheels dominate it from end to end. The cafes and dining rooms of the apartment hotels are occupied mainly by people in bicycle clothes. Even the billboards have surrendered. They advertise wheels and lamps and tires and patent saddles with all the flaming vehemence of circus art . . . Down at the circle, where stands the patient Columbus, the stores are crowded with bicycle goods. There are innumerable repair shops. Everything is bicycle. In the afternoon the parade begins.[56]

It certainly seemed that the bicycle was everything and everywhere. And it did not take long for cyclists to recognize their collective interests and begin to shape the urban world.

CHAPTER TWO

The Cyclists

"The bicycle is the most democratic of machines." "Old and young, rich and poor, men and women, boys and girls—all caught the 'bicycle fever.'" "The bank president and the clerk, the society leader and the shop girl ride side by side." "As a social leveler the bicycle has been unequaled." "Its use is confined to no class." These sentiments, expressed separately from an array of sources across the spectrum of print media in the mid-1890s—*Scribner's Magazine, Munsey's Magazine,* the *Philadelphia Record,* the *Albany Press,* and the *Detroit Free Press*—all sang the praises of the bicycle.[1] That the bicycle was a democratic vehicle, a social leveler, and adopted by nearly everyone was an opinion echoed in newspaper columns, on song sheets and painted canvases, in private diaries, and in public campaigns. While there was some truth to that story, the reality experienced on city streets and inside cycling clubhouses revealed something less perfect.

Nevertheless, as a novel piece of technology that provided both a new form of transportation and a new form of recreation and leisure, bicycles did serve a diverse set of city dwellers who adopted the machines for an equally diverse set of purposes. Affluent urbanites used them to promenade around the city and as a reason to form exclusive social clubs; immigrant groups and blacks tested the boundaries of Americanization and integration on wheels; other less wealthy urbanites mounted their bicycles for their first trip beyond their city's walls. To be sure, the shapes, contours, limits and possibilities of the cycling city were a matter of perspective. Inside the urban kaleidoscope, cyclists equally cherished the possibilities of the bicycle even if with unique and sometimes contradictory motivations. And while not everyone rode, those who did joined a group that was growing quickly and loudly.

How many Americans actually rode bicycles? It is hard to say exactly, but extant reports, commentaries, and select data provide some clues to understanding the prevalence of cycling in the 1890s. In 1897, contemporary estimates put the number of active bicycle riders in the United States as high as five million at a time when the total population amounted to around seventy million and the urban population numbered just thirty million.[2] Considering the number of machines American manufacturers produced, it is certainly possible that five million Americans had ridden a bicycle by the end of the century. Certainly not all of them could be considered active riders, though. In the medium-sized city of Rochester, New York (population of 133,896 in 1890), the city clerk's office reported a total of 21,139 registered bicycles in the summer of 1896. Certainly this was an undercount, as many Rochester cyclists never registered their wheels, but those who did were likely regular riders. Within a few years the number of cyclists totaled more than 40,000 (roughly one quarter of the city's total population in 1900). Considering that there were only 6,000 riders in 1894 and probably no more than a few hundred at any given moment in the 1880s, the growth in Rochester was remarkable.[3]

Rochester was not alone. In 1896, the *Army and Naval Journal* suggested that by a conservative estimate roughly 20 percent of the 1.5 million people living in New York owned bicycles. With others renting their wheels, there were more bicycles than the number of all other vehicles combined.[4] For some sense of comparison, the 300,000 bicycles roaming through the streets of New York in the mid-1890s dwarfs the 13,437 taxis weaving and honking in the city today.[5]

While most cities experienced a dramatic increase in the number of cyclists, few matched New York. According to informal surveys, about 18 percent of people living in Washington, DC were cyclists; in San Francisco, approximately 20 percent. Stated as a matter of fact in legal proceedings, 20 percent of the 50,000 people living in Erie, Pennsylvania, owned bicycles. Riders tended to live in the bigger cities, which often had more paved roads and more people who could afford bicycles, especially at first. Their density made commuting via bicycle more functional, their parks and boulevards were ideal sites for recreation and self-display, and their crowdedness made the thought of cycling far away even more attractive. Larger cities had typical ratios of one bicycle for every five people compared to a country-wide average that was probably somewhere closer to one bicycle for every fourteen people. Smaller cities, especially those in the middle of the country, tended to have fewer riders. Emporia, Kansas, for example, called home by roughly 8,000 people in 1897, had maybe

300 cyclists (one bicycle per twenty-seven people). Still, within cities and around the country, bicycles became the most commonly owned private transportation vehicle of all time. Its closest competitor in 1900 was the horse. In large cities, about four times as many people owned bicycles compared to horses.[6] Contemporaries who witnessed the rapid increase of cyclists quickly endorsed the erroneous idea that nearly everyone owned a bicycle, or soon would.

While the numbers in large cities were impressive, it should be remembered that the number of bicycles owned in the United States never approached the levels reached in the latter decades of the twentieth century or today. Between 1997 and 2007, Americans bought roughly 179 million bicycles and the population totaled just over 300 million (or roughly 1 bicycle for every 1.7 people). Despite the fact that fewer Americans owned a bicycle in the 1890s than in recent history, the bicycle had an outsized presence. A higher percentage of the total population could be found cycling through the city in the 1890s than any time since.[7] Those who owned bicycles in the 1890s were much more likely to ride them than owners of the future. As data from traffic surveys reveal (analyzed later in this chapter and more fully in chapter 7), thousands of riders could be found every day on the busier thoroughfares in America's larger cities. Also, the pace of change was as important as the total number of cyclists. When American manufacturers churned out over a million bicycles in 1899, that was a nearly 6,000 percent increase from 1889, when domestic production had totaled a measly 20,500. A decade before that, in 1878, factories only produced about 50 bicycles.[8] Back then, seeing a bicycle was like spotting a snowy owl. But in a matter of years, bicycles seemed to be commonplace, in part because so many had appeared so quickly. The number of cyclists had increased exponentially and Americans had every reason to believe that the growth would continue, or at least stabilize. Taking that into account, contemporary observations about the popularity of the bicycle are more difficult to dismiss. After all, if the number of cyclists had continued to grow at the same rate, it would not have been long before bicycles overtook the urban landscape.

One traffic count of New York cyclists reveals that cycling attracted a broad set of city dwellers cycling for a variety of purposes. On the section of Broadway north of Columbus Circle (the Boulevard), more than 14,000 riders cycled past a single corner on a seemingly average Thursday in May of 1896. The roadway's reputation as a cyclist's paradise and favorite spot for recreational and leisure riders was well deserved (figs. 2.1 and 2.2). In addition to the numerical data, traffic counters recorded anecdotal

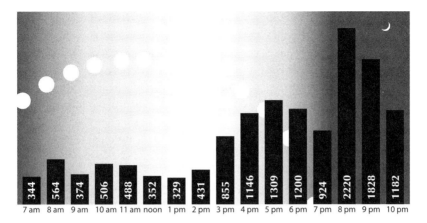

Fig. 2.1. New York City bicycle count, May 1896, 72nd
Street and the Boulevard (Broadway).

Fig. 2.2. This 1898 photograph of Broadway near 64th Street reveals the popularity of the
"Boulevard." Reproduced with permission from the Museum of the City of New York.

observations about the character of the cyclists, which seemed to change with each passing hour. In the early morning, clerks rode to work, then children and teachers on their way to school, followed by businessmen, before a steady stream of daytime leisure riders and then a gush of cyclists, some returning home from work or school, many out for an evening spin. At its busiest hour, between 8:00 p.m. and 9:00 p.m., an average of thirty-seven cyclists wheeled by each minute, a statistic that speaks more to the Boulevard's reputation as a social meeting place after dark than to the many commuters who likely avoided the traffic and ever-present hoopla that made that roadway so famous.[9] Still, on this single street, people rode for transportation, others for exercise or en route to a leisure destination, and some simply to take part in what was a chic activity—cruising down an elegant boulevard, bedecked in fine clothes, and mounted on a device that was itself fashionable.

Far from everyone rode, though; in fact, most did not. Regardless of what it had to offer, the bicycle was still a machine that required human power to function. Long distances and fatigue remained obstacles. Some of those who stood all day, according to a Philadelphia newspaper in 1898, were simply "too weary at the close of the day's work to enjoy riding a bicycle to their homes."[10] Those reluctant to exercise were certainly among the least likely to enjoy cycling, even as others relished the chance to motor themselves around the city. Weather, too, deterred some riders who eschewed the slushy streets, splashing puddles, or extra cold winds produced by cycling. Yet with subways running only on blueprints and with streetcars exposed to the open air (even the earliest automobiles offered little shelter from the elements), there were few perfect options. Nevertheless, the number of active cyclists did vary seasonally.[11] Cyclists on their way to work also needed to find a place to park their wheels, make sure that their clothes stayed clean and dry, and manage to tote their belongings. Even though indoor storage devices, cold-weather cycling suits, and scores of bicycle accessories sought to address nearly every conceivable drawback of cycling and even though many adopted the bicycle because of the exercise that came with it, a group of riders found cycling a hassle and some would never have even considered it as an option. Moreover, a segment of the population did not care much for being fashionable and still others felt well served by their feet, the streetcars, horses, or other transportation options.

Women were also much less likely to become cyclists than men. It is difficult to estimate the exact proportion, but the few traffic counts that differentiated between male and female riders reveal that men vastly outnumbered women, who probably accounted for about a quarter of the total cycling population.[12] Ironically, considering the place of the bicycle in American society today, children also rode at disproportionately low rates in the 1890s. Too short for the high-wheelers, they had rarely participated in the initial enthusiasm for cycling. And even as the safety bicycle came into being, it was generally adults who could be found at riding schools. The 1896 bicycle count on the Boulevard noted that children comprised only 7 percent of the total ridership. In another such survey of the morning commute in Chicago, boys under the age of twelve amounted to less than 1 percent of the total riders. Thanks to steady birth rates and shorter life expectancies, children in the 1890s represented a much greater percentage of the total population than they do today. The 1900 census found that children under the age of fifteen accounted for a massive 34.5 percent of the total population, a far cry from the 5 percent or so of the total cycling population. So the largest group of people who did not become cyclists was certainly the young. In fact, many manufacturers did not even make wheels for children. When Smalley Bicycles of Indiana (appropriately named in that it was a small manufacturer and inappropriately named in that the firm did not cater to small people) issued its 1894 catalog, it lavished readers with great details about its four new models, three for men and one for ladies. Mostly, children did not ride because the bicycle was popularly understood as meant for adults. Of course, this same device would eventually become popularly understood as meant for children, but not until the twentieth century.[13] Although some minorities became cyclists, they were much less likely to do so too, meaning that adult white men constituted the largest contingent of people who cycled not only on an absolute basis, but also relatively. They also tended to be men of some means. Indeed, the biggest impediment to becoming a cyclist, particularly at first, was the matter of price.

As Adna Weber observed in 1899, "the danger of class antagonism is particularly grave in the cities," as "the chasm created by the industrial system yawns widest."[14] Mobility and the ways in which people moved about the city bore the signs of a widening gulf between classes. Moneyed men and women sat on fine upholstery in private cabs pulled by teams of handsome horses, while wage laborers and the under- or unemployed walked. Hardly anyone liked the streetcars. Wealthy types eschewed public vehicles because of the crowds they harbored. Few of the urban poor could afford the fares, and, in certain cities, some minorities, particularly blacks, found that streetcars refused to transport them.[15] Even when they could ride, the level of service was far from equal. The space inside the cars was often reserved for whites; black riders had to stand on the plat-form.[16] For certain strands of the population, streetcars and the elevateds epitomized the limitation of public transportation. Consequently, resi-dents across the socioeconomic spectrum relished the thought of private transportation in general, and the bicycle in particular.

So who could afford a bicycle? In large part, the answer depends on the year in question. In 1890 it would have been impossible to find a wheel for anything close to $10, and by 1900, when the average price of a bicycle fell to $18.91, it would have been nearly impossible to convince someone to pay $100 for a conventional bicycle.[17] Prices varied wildly, de-pending not only on the year but also according to the brand, styling, and accessories of the machine. Early in the 1890s, the average cost of a qual-ity bicycle, which dropped to just below $100, was still relatively prohibi-tive for the average American; nonetheless, in cities across the country, doctors, lawyers, teachers, shopkeepers, ministers, clerks, salespeople, and other professionals readily adopted the bicycle. By mid-decade, $50 roadsters were among the most purchased, and by the turn of the cen-tury, a new, high-end, brand-name bicycle like one of Pope's Columbia bicycles could be had for that same amount. By then, lower quality ma-chines, like those sold through the Sears, Roebuck & Co. catalog, priced for around $10. They may have not been durable, but they were certainly more affordable.[18]

Supplemented by the proliferation of media and advertising, urban con-sumer culture evolved to a point where luxury and high fashion trickled down to those below the urban elite. Bicycles did too, but the evolution was not so simple. While the first cyclists were certainly well-to-do and had enough money to purchase a luxury good, the adventuresome early adopters did not fit neatly among the fashionable set. Mounting and steadying the high-wheelers, bobbing along rough roads, and participating in such an alien activity was not for the majority of those in the upper crust. Early riders, then, represented but a particular subset of the affluent, a fringe element of the moneyed classes and certainly not representative of the Rockefellers or the Goulds who eventually pedaled into the cycling city. In fact, the "society world" was at first, as one writer chronicled, "rather disposed to grumble at [cyclists] as a nuisance, and to silently ap-prove all measures to restrict their privileges." Indeed, it was really not until the mid-1890s that the "fashionable" men and women of American society became cyclists. Partly, at least, their enthusiasm was spurred on by news from abroad, especially from Paris. There, the "best" men and women had begun to ride. The arrival of bicycles in Newport, the upscale summer resort for New Yorkers, signified that the bicycle had arrived for the American elite. From Newport to the cities, wealthy urbanites who often had no day jobs to which to commute and who had long enjoyed relative freedom of mobility found unique ways to enjoy the bicycle.[19]

Thus, society men and women joined, rather than began, the cycling boom that was originally fueled by a small group of young, wealthy, sporting men and eventually turned into a phenomenon by mass participation of the middle class. And until the end of the decade, when prices dropped dramatically, buying a new bicycle was largely an activity confined to the middle and upper classes, even if some of the working class managed to do so. While it was the bicycle men—manufacturers, retailers, and especially advertisers—"who first proved that an article of luxury costing $100 could be sold to the mass," that clearly did not include everybody. In 1895, the typical manufacturing worker earned a paltry twenty cents an hour. Those laborers generally worked ten hours a day, six days a week, netting a $12 weekly wage. Paying $110 for the entry-level Columbia advertised in its 1893 catalog would have cost over nine weeks of wages. There is ample evidence, though, that even in the mid-1890s, large numbers of clerical workers—lower level, white collar workers like bookkeepers and clerks—owned bicycles. In 1890, in Philadelphia the average such male worker earned $925.70 a year in salary (close to $18 per week), evidently enough to fund a bicycle purchase. By 1898, as prices dropped further, the no-frills bicycle sold through Sears, Roebuck, & Co's catalog for $19.75 would require less than two weeks' pay, but this was still a sizable figure totaling almost ninety-nine hours of work. By the turn of the century, new wheels could be had for even less than $10.[20]

For consumers who might not have had the requisite cash for a new bicycle, a robust secondhand market and methods of financing developed, enabling less-affluent urbanites to join the ranks of cyclists. Classified advertisements flooded local papers, announcing used bicycles for sale and potential trades. Desperate city dwellers offered up books, musical instruments, furniture, and even their household pets in exchange for a set of wheels. On a larger scale, bicycle manufacturers openly marketed used bicycles (often alongside newer models) in their annual catalogs and advertisements. One such producer remarked back in 1889 that "the trade in second-hand goods has attained such proportions that . . . special attention is given to this trade, and we buy for cash, take in exchange, or place on sale such machines as our customers have to offer. We have constantly in hand a large stock of second-hand goods from which any rider may select something to suit his fancy or pocket-book." Customers flipping through the forty-nine-page catalog could find more than a hundred different bicycles, ranging from near $30 to around $100, depending on the model and "season" of the bicycle. So even when most new bicycles sold for well more than $100, used machines were available for one third the price. By the late 1890s, that meant some secondhand bicycles could be purchased for just a few dollars.[21]

Additionally, sellers enticed customers unable to afford the upfront costs with installment plans. A. G. Spalding & Bros. offered bicycles for a down payment of only one quarter of the total price, with the remaining payments spread out over six monthly installments. On the local level, dealers in Harrisburg, Pennsylvania, reported that their customers bought most of their machines on an installment plan, while a shop in St. Louis offered its customers payment plans as low as $1.25 per week.[22]

Records from individual riders also show that it was common for riders to trade in an older vehicle for a newer model. One diary from a city cyclist in the 1890s is particularly revealing. In 1893, the eighteen-year-old Arthur Hyde used some of the Christmas money his grandfather had given him to purchase a diary. Over the next four years, Hyde used it as a bicycling notebook, documenting the rides, distances, and bicycle parades in which he took part; his cycling accidents and would-be collisions; the make and model of his bicycles; and even his affection for a woman named Helen (a carnation she gave him in 1896 still sits dried and pressed between the pages). Judging from his notes, Hyde cycled mostly for recreation, touring neighboring towns and cities, but also to run errands and occasionally to work. Like many others, Hyde simply "hired" a wheel at first. For about $1 residents could rent a bicycle for several hours, a popular option for those wanting to try out cycling or for visitors who were without their wheels. But in 1893 Hyde "enjoyed the privilege" of purchasing his first machine. That year he paid $40 for a "Referee cushion tired wheel," the first of what would be many bicycle purchases. The very next spring he traded in his old ride for a new bicycle with only "$20 to boot." In 1895, when Hyde became smitten by the "Bohemian" at Spalding's (he eventually paid $60 for it), he decided to sell his current bicycle, which earned him nearly $45. The following year Hyde returned to Spalding's and traded his "Bohemian," along with "$30 to boot," for the latest Spalding "Model D road racer," which he would sell not too long afterwards.[23]

Hyde's diary illustrates that for at least a segment of urban consumers, eager to have the latest model, selling used bicycles was common. Like many other Americans at the time, Hyde was enraptured by the "cult of the new."[24] His case also illustrates a rapidly growing second-hand market; the old wheels Hyde traded in soon went back on sale. That market, sharply declining prices, and the ability to pay via installments brought bicycles well within the reach of most city dwellers by the end of the decade. As a columnist in 1896 wrote, "It is literally true that the burden of proof is on every man, woman and child to show what physical or financial disability prevents him or her from owning and using a bicycle."[25] The author was certainly overstating his case. After all, journalists at the time made similar statements about the supposed democratization of yachting: "There is really no excuse for anyone who seriously thinks of going into yachting being stopped by the expense, for it is a sport that is open to practically everyone."[26] But the sentiment about cycling did begin to ring truer and truer as the calendar marched toward the new century.

By the end of the 1890s, the bicycle became the first truly independent vehicle available to large segments of the urban population. For the near entirety of human history, feet served as the primary mode of transportation. Animals had long been utilized as means to transport cargo or people, but nothing afforded the same mobility, independence, and accessibility as did the bicycle. Sedan chairs required the help of at least two other (strong) people. Horses could provide door-to-door service, but that service came at a great expense, limiting it to a choice clientele. Even after the initial purchase, maintenance expenses (e.g., food and shelter) never ended. In fact, it not only cost more to buy a horse than a bicycle, it generally cost more to maintain a horse for a year than to purchase a brand new bicycle. Writing in 1896, an author concluded that "for the medium classes who are unable to keep horses with the accompaniment of coachmen, footmen, and other expensive auxiliaries, the invention of the silent steed has been a boon indeed." Aside from cost, many urbanites found bicycles superior to horses in other ways. Horse fatigue could prematurely end a trip. And death was far more absolute when it came to an animal compared to a machine. Summed up by a writer in an 1895 article published in *Scribner's Magazine*, "A bicycle is better than a horse to ninety-nine men and women out of a hundred, because it costs almost nothing to keep, and it is never tired." Consequently, for those whose aspiration to own a horse was but "a wistful dream," purchasing a bicycle was a very real possibility. It needed "only to be stabled in a passageway, and fed on oil and air." Bicycles, which offered the flexibility of walking, speeds greater than a horse's trot, reliability, and affordability, began to replace horses for some consumers in American cities. And manufacturers quickly picked up on the trend, targeting potential customers with advertisements (fig. 2.3) suggesting that would-be buyers replace their horses with two wheels.[27]

Fig. 2.3. An 1896 advertisement for Columbia Bicycles. Reprinted from *Exhibit of Columbia Bicycle Art Poster Designs* (Hartford: Pope Manufacturing Co., 1896).

Surely, most of those who bought bicycles had never owned a horse and, therefore, took possession of their very first vehicle. Of course, buyers were more likely using bicycles to replace or complement trips made by walking or streetcar than trips via horse. But even then, advocates liked to remind riders of the significant potential cost savings—actual and implied—accrued by owning a bicycle: "The average rider saves 20 cents a day in carfare . . . this is exclusive of all doctor's bills." Others estimated that cycling saved them as much as $100 a year and that purchasing a bicycle would pay for itself in the course of weeks, not years. Some of this talk reflects the booster-prone media more than reality, as most streetcar trips cost only five cents and those who spent twenty cents a day transferring were considerably wealthier than the working classes, who often walked to work. For workers who did ride the streetcars, assuming the traveler rode to and from work each workday and paid the nickel fare without any transfers, he or she would accumulate a yearly transportation bill of around thirty dollars. For that price, the worker could have purchased a used bicycle at almost any time in the 1890s or a new model towards the end of the decade. The very poor were priced out of both streetcars and bicycles; for workers who did ride the streetcars, the bicycle offered a legitimate alternative.[28]

Bicycles offered the promise of democratizing urban mobility, even if not to the degree that those overzealous cheerleaders had reported. One investigation into the "Tenement House Problem" revealed that cycling enabled workers to travel with "great ease and celerity" around the entire city. Thanks to the robust secondhand bicycle market there, the report specifically noted that for Buffalo, New York, "the bicycle plays a larger share in the comfort and convenience of the working-man in Buffalo than in any other city in America."[29] While that was likely an exaggeration, in snowy Buffalo and cities around the country, the bicycle indeed enabled increased mobility for classes that were historically confined. Accident reports, diary entries, and newspaper articles reveal that it was not just doctors and lawyers riding around town. Sales clerks, seamstresses, barbers, and janitors did too.[30] But most tenement dwellers on New York's Lower East Side or the families living on the blocks surrounding the Hull House in Chicago did not.[31]

As part of a larger revolution in transportation technology, men and women adopted bicycles alongside other public transit options, bringing them to regions that had previously only been accessible to more-mobile urbanites. Within the cities, leisure activities had long been formed along class lines. Theaters, for example, had sections catering to different classes of patrons or, more commonly, the entire theater catered to a particular group of city folk. Other forms of recreation followed similar paths. In late nineteenth-century America, "the different social classes intermingled as little as possible in their sporting pleasures." Even as spectators, relatively homogenous socioeconomic crowds patronized events and when the crowd was more diverse, ticket prices served to segregate the spectators into cordoned off sections. In theaters, arenas, and on city streets, the urban world was a stratified one. "In the evening as well as during the workday, the city was sorting its classes of people into increasingly distinct institutions and spaces." And even as cities became increasingly diverse, wealthier classes found ways to distance themselves from the general population.

Moving "uptown," and eventually to the suburbs, provided a comfortable space, but with transportation technology advancing, such separation grew harder and harder to maintain.[32]

With bicycles, the countryside, parks, beaches, and suburban enclaves that had once been walled off by fences of wealth, power, and prestige became destinations for more, while certainly not all, of the urban population. Of course, many urban cyclists could not suddenly afford suburban homes. Nor did they have the leisure time to meander through the park at the fashionable hour. But on bicycles, cyclists could ride through the neighboring suburbs and take a spin in an urban park in the evening, on the weekends, or on their way to work. While the leisure class enjoyed recreation and exercise, bicycles enabled more urban dwellers to indulge in these activities, particularly the middling classes.[33]

That cycling democratized private transportation and that certain city spaces evolved into destinations for urbanites representative of a wider range of the socioeconomic spectrum was certainly true, well noticed, broadly praised, and oft exaggerated in the 1890s. Medical authorities heralded the bicycle for bringing middle-class workers out of doors, while others welcomed the thought that the middle class could enjoy the "pleasures and amusements of life" once reserved for the wealthier sort. As described in the *Philadelphia Record*, the city's Fairmount Park was transformed by the troops of a cycling army "made up of all classes." The paper continued that "as one watches the almost endless procession that pass[es] along the drives of Fairmount Park he is struck by the unconventionality and democracy of it all," with riders from various classes "each feeling equal to the other for the time being" and commingling seamlessly. Many commentators went so far as to claim that the bicycle was the single greatest mechanism to remove class distinction. One writer in *Forum* magazine certainly thought so: ". . . there is no leveler like the wheel. Every rider feels at liberty to accost or converse with every other rider, not only bound but willing to give him aid in distress or accident, and in various ways to treat the bicycle as the badge of equality among all its possessors." As much premised on hope and exaggeration as reality, this claim and the hundreds of others expressed in cities across the country were predicated on the fact that since so many Americans could now afford bicycles (used models, at least), the social barriers between classes would tumble.[34]

Reality did not stop mostly middle-class journalists, like this one in 1896, who wishfully imagined that the transition from expensive horses to cheap bicycles had profound effects on the nature of private transporta-

tion, making freedom of movement available to anyone: "What are Dec-
larations of Independence and universal equality, and what are paltry
muskets in the hands of insurgents, before the insinuating democracy of
a cheap horse, that is swift, yet tractable, for any one of any age or either
sex; that requires no feeding, no attendance, and no stable room? Verily,
the pursuit of happiness is most reasonably attempted if the pursuer is
mounted on the swiftness and comfort of a bicycle."[35] These "pursuits of
happiness," the worlds of leisure and touring, exercise and recreation that
had once been in the domain of only the well-to-do, did become more fea-
sible for more of the urban population, even if the bicycle failed to erase
the markings of class. The fact that so many contemporaries thought (or at
least hoped) that the bicycle was accomplishing that very goal reveals an
acute awareness of a growing rift among urban Americans and a desire to
bridge the ever-widening gap between classes. The urban elite had a different perspective.

CYCLING CLUBS

Promenading down grand boulevards or through city parks at the fashionable hour was common practice for the city's elite. The parks were places
where the leisure classes found solace in the open space and comfort in
the company of their fellow park-goers. Often designed as segregated
spaces for the wealthier tier of the urban populace, the parks quickly became playgrounds for riders who could only afford to rent a bicycle by the
hour. The bicycle was no longer the standalone symbol of wealth that it
once was, as some young men scouting for wealthy wives complained. Of
course, clothes, manners, and the make of the bicycle might serve to distinguish riders, but affluent cyclists found an easier way to differentiate
themselves.

Aside from cruising gently through well-manicured parks, flaunting
their stylized bicycles and chic clothes, and literally moving away from
the lower classes, wealthy and upper-middle-class urbanites also used the
bicycle as an impetus to create new exclusive social networks.[36] In general, voluntary associations first gained widespread popularity in the early
nineteenth century. Societies devoted to religion, temperance, and abolition joined dozens of clubs centered on books, sport, and other interests.[37]
Toward the end of the nineteenth century, club life expanded significantly.
As cities grew into impersonal webs of traffic and bureaucracy, residents
hungered for ways to create more personal, social communities. Clubs did

just that. They provided members a way to identify themselves as part of a distinct group and a way to classify themselves amid millions of human beings, a way to nest in the chaotic forest of urbanity. In the latter decades of the nineteenth century, societies formed to accommodate the growing number of disciples of America's newest fascination: bicycles. The story behind the bicycle clubs and their evolution reveals much about the expanding base of urban cyclists, as well as the opportunities and limitations that bicycles provided for their owners.

Formed by early adopters of the high-wheel bicycle, the first clubs represented a select group of mostly young, well-to-do white men. Since essentially all of the early cyclists in the 1880s came from the wealthier classes, the composition of their membership necessarily reflected as much. As a spokesman from such a club in New Orleans described, "The fundamental principle, that personal ownership of a wheel is a requisite for membership, acts in itself as a sort of check against indiscriminate applications for admission." Like those that would follow, many of these early clubs adopted a formal set of procedures for inviting new members, electing officers, selecting uniforms, governing behavior inside official clubhouses, and plotting social events and rides. The mostly bachelors who joined these organizations bound themselves to military-like rules and structure. The earliest organization, the Boston Bicycle Club, formed in 1878. Within several years, most major American cities claimed multiple cycling clubs. Cycling clubs organized century runs (100 mile rides) and printed touring maps detailed with favored routes, road conditions, and the locations of bicycle-friendly hotels. Social events off the bicycle were just as common. At one such meeting, a dinner hosted by the Harvard University Bicycle Club on March 7, 1881, members sang songs, talked bicycles, and feasted on an eight-course meal featuring larded grouse, black duck, and walnut pudding. Outside of universities, local cycling clubs emerged in the nation's leading cities and often organized to improve local cycling conditions and laws. While still in their nascent stages and when the most prominent clubs boasted only hundreds of members, they managed to exert political influence. As local club membership increased, savvy riders recognized the potential for collective action.[38]

On the breezy shore of Newport, Rhode Island in 1880, representatives from thirty-one separate bicycle clubs united to form the League of American Wheelmen (LAW). The LAW, a fitting acronym, quickly began to fulfill its mission to "ascertain, defend and protect the rights of wheelmen."[39] It would ultimately develop into the most powerful voice for American cyclists. At the local level, individual bicycle manufacturers subsidized the largest clubs, realizing that the organizations might serve at the center of a grassroots procycling campaign. When the Massachusetts Bicycle Club erected its headquarters in Boston, Colonel Pope helped pay for its construction. With Pope's dollars and input, the concrete ramp inviting club members to wheel through the front door opened to traffic in 1885. The members, who shared stories, drinks, and weekend rides, joined as much for the camaraderie as for any hope of wielding political power.

As the high-wheelers disappeared and as the safety bicycle found its way into the mainstream, a new set of clubs emerged. By 1896, the island of Manhattan claimed more than fifty clubs, Chicago had fifty-four, and in Denver, a dumbfounding 18-plus percent of city residents called themselves members of the Denver Wheelmen. Nationally, membership in the LAW climbed to over 100,000 in 1897.[40] These clubs catered to groups not quite as diverse as the cities themselves, but close.

In general, the vast majority of bicycle clubs organized in the 1890s were almost always formed along class lines and, to a lesser extent, according to ethnicity, race, and gender. Club organizers devised an application process designed to weed out any potential undesirables. Even the LAW, which often bragged about its ever-swelling membership rolls, had its limitations. "The league wants members in large numbers, but it does not want everybody," the membership office warned. The LAW reminded its supporters that the organization's solid reputation must be kept intact by keeping uncouth applicants at bay. Recruiting for city clubs was a delicate process since membership in a particular organization often connoted a certain reputation. Applications generally required candidates to list their occupation, membership fees could be used to dissuade lower-class members from joining (one exclusive club, for example, charged a $100 initiation fee), and clubs mandated that all new members be vouched for by an existing member (current members often had significant veto power to deny membership).[41]

Since these voluntary associations were designed to bring people together around a common interest, and since it was the commonalities that provided the initial attraction to join a club, it is not particularly surprising that the members came from similar ethnic groups and social milieus. As an article about local cycling clubs in *Outing* magazine reported, "Their center of attraction arises from the similarity of the individuals in personal aims, in social instincts, in opinion . . ."[42] To codify the sameness, organizations often required their members to don club uniforms.

One early club explained to its members that there would be little leeway
when it came to appearance:

> [The uniform] shall be a Norfolk Jacket and Knee Breeches of Citizens
> Club Clot, gray Flannel Shirt, navy blue Necktie with white polka dot,
> citizens Club Stockings, black low Shoes, and a regulation navy Cap, of
> same clothes suit, with turn down visor and a black silk cord (except
> in the case of the Captain and lieutenants, who shall wear silver) and
> the Club Badge of silver . . . The summer hat shall be a white Helmet
> with the Club Badge affixed to the front . . . Each active member shall,
> within thirty days after his election, provide himself with a complete
> Uniform, which must be inspected and approved by the Captain.[43]

Selecting the official uniform was often the thing club members fought
about the most.[44]

The urban elite quickly formed their own clubs. Primarily, these
riders used the bicycle as a means of social engagement and as yet another way to cement their membership in high society. The most obvious outcomes of these efforts came in the form of dozens of exclusive
bicycle clubs dotting America's leading cities. Their clubhouses surely
included rooms to store, clean, and repair bicycles, but the rest of the
building generally had few overt signs of its bicycle heritage. Libraries,
card rooms, and billiard tables kept members busy while dumbwaiters
shuttled food from kitchen hands to hungry cyclists. One of the more
palatial headquarters even included a barber shop, a writing room, several bowling alleys, steward's quarters, executive offices, a gymnasium,
and plenty of "cozy nooks." Bicycle clubhouses offered much more
than just a starting point for a Sunday "run" to the country or a table
for a postride meal; they were sites for social interaction and display,
settings for elaborate "stag smokers," midnight galas, and tea parties.
They were also places governed by strict rules. Like most other clubs
(bicycle and otherwise) that sought to create clubhouses reflecting the
desired reputation of the group, the Illinois Cycling Club forbade members from gambling or drinking on the premises and engaging in any
kind of "ungentlemanly conduct." Members were specifically asked to
exercise caution when bringing guests to the clubhouse who might de-
tract from the "respectable crowd that make up our audience." To foster a greater sense of exclusivity, such clubs commonly limited guests'
access.[45]

At a time when cycling had peaked in popularity, these elite riders insisted that cycling was much more than just a mode of transportation. For everyday cyclists, riding may have been just that—the easiest way to get from A to B—but these cyclists used bicycles for different purposes entirely. With so many people riding bicycles, it became more important to advertise club members as recreational and/or social riders, not the utilitarian or irresponsible sort, like the scorcher. Scorchers, who sped around the city with hunched backs, represented everything elite riders hoped to avoid. They had a well-deserved bad reputation for recklessness and audacity. In the eyes of critics, they had taken over the city. Speeding through traffic and riding on sidewalks, the worst variety of riders became emblematic of the entire group. In an 1896 article, originally published in the *Buffalo Evening Enquirer*, a journalist explained that the scorchers who ignored traffic regulations were already beginning to threaten the bicycle's place in the city: "There has of late years flooded the ranks of bicycle riders a large number of the rougher sort, who unschooled by the adversities and trials through which the originals had to pass, value lightly and abuse those present privileges they enjoy and for which they toiled not."[46]

Some unruly cyclists did pedal through the city in a destructive manner. At a conference on municipal improvements in 1897, one speaker declared that "the greatest enemy to the cyclist in moulding public opinion, is the scorcher, whose sins are visited on all wheelmen, and they are held responsible for his misdemeanors . . ."[47] Their actions, at least theoretically, threatened to endanger the reputation of cyclists as a whole. So it is not surprising that so many elite riders spoke so ardently against these "lesser" riders. "It is most unfortunate that so many ruffians should have been attracted to this charming exercise, and should degrade it by reckless riding and insolent indifference to the comfort of other users of the road," one rider complained. "The young men who race along our public streets and country lanes in insufficient clothing at something over fifteen miles an hour should be promptly dealt with and suppressed, as some noxious parasite that has taken lodging in a fair flower. . . ."[48] Sometimes cyclists took it upon themselves to deal with the "scorcher" issue. In 1895, the Associated Cycling Clubs of Philadelphia offered to pay for a new corps of officers charged with keeping rogue cyclists in check.[49] Nonetheless, pedestrians, carriage drivers, and others often cited these sorts of riders when they argued against wheelmen-friendly laws or infrastructure.

As cities and their populations grew, it became more and more important for the urban elite to find new ways to differentiate themselves from others, including scorchers. To that end, many bicycle clubs published their own magazines, disseminating news not only about upcoming bicycle-related events but, even more so, about the social affairs of the club and its members.[50] Perhaps best epitomizing the elite class of cycling clubs was New York's Michaux Cycle Club, for which membership was widely sought and rarely given (fig. 2.4). Named after the French inventor credited with adding pedals to bicycles, the club counted military officers, captains of industry, and their wives as members. They could enjoy a morning riding class, bicycle dances in the afternoon (elaborately planned events in which riders pedaled about a ringed floor in concert with live orchestras), or extravagant teas held inside the club's elaborate headquarters.

Fig. 2.4. Members of the exclusive Michaux Cycle Club in New York typically rode (or spectated) indoors at the club's glamorous academy located at Broadway and 52nd Street. Reprinted from *Scribner's Magazine*, June 1895.

They could also take pride in knowing that they had won entrance into an exclusive club that brought with it what one reporter called "social cachet of the most authoritative sort."[51] Other elite organizations, athletically oriented or otherwise, began catering to their cycling members. The well-known New York Athletic Club and Boston Athletic Club each spawned auxiliary bicycle groups, and New York's ultra-exclusive Metropolitan Club, organized without an athletic bent, housed some 200 bicycles for its aristocratic membership.[52]

For these well-heeled cyclists, the bicycle served as a means of identification—a status symbol. They lived in a world "where classes distinguished themselves by the clothes they wore, the shops they frequented, the parks they strolled in, and the houses they inhabited . . ." With bicycles enjoyed by an increasing number of people, upper-class riders found exclusive cycling clubs a convenient way to differentiate their cycling activities from those of the larger urban community. Wealthy urbanites might join several clubs, each devoted to a group that shared a similar ancestry, political bent, cultural taste, social philosophy, or interest in sport. In fact, they had many sporting choices. Hunting, yachting, and golf had become popular pastimes among the elite and also offered recreation and exposure to nature. Yachting clubs offered many of the same opportunities as the leading cycling clubs. They often mandated that club members wear uniforms, sponsored regattas, and maintained sprawling clubhouses governed by strict rules and filled with endless diversions. Golf experienced a similar wave of popularity in the 1890s (the first course opened in 1885 and by 1900 there were 1,000), leading to the creation of new clubs that offered members a number of sporting activities and attracted many of the same kinds of people who joined the elite cycling clubs.[53]

Elites were not the only ones who joined bicycle clubs. All sorts of cyclists who could never have attained membership in their city's most august organizations started their own groups of like-minded riders. Sometimes they sought to distance themselves from certain kinds of people; other times they were the ones unwelcomed. In such cases, they had few options other than to start their own associations with cyclists just like them. Consequently, clubs for bicycle enthusiasts began to cater to nearly every age, ethnicity, and gender, albeit most often in homogenous groups. While some of the clubs invited both men and women to join, most catered just to men. A select group of organizations contained exclusively female cyclists who, at first, often borrowed club facilities from men. In Chicago, female riders eventually formed three clubs of their own, while many of the larger, exclusively male clubs included auxiliary units just for women. Other groups opened their doors to those who lacked the pedigree and wealth to join the most exclusive clubs.[54]

While bicycles still remained a luxury good for the working class and while club membership was certainly not something that those without a modicum of discretionary income and leisure time would seek, many alternative bicycle clubs had a far more inviting application process than the most prestigious clubs. The Century Cycle Club, in Washington, DC, only charged its members fifty cents in dues, a far cry from the $50 that some others required.[55] Emulating the behavior and recreation patterns of wealthier folk was certainly a part of clubs like the Peirce Alumni Cyclers in Philadelphia. The group catered to riders who had not quite yet joined the ranks of the middle class. The coed group of clerical workers invited graduates of the Peirce School, a technical college for future clerks, to join. Profession-related clubs, including groups of police officers, firefighters, letter carriers, and newspapermen, appeared in major cities throughout the decade. In Philadelphia, the nearly 100-strong group of clerks provided its members many of the same opportunities and performed many of the same functions as other organizations that were decidedly middle class. They maintained a clubhouse, organized rides and social functions, and lobbied the city government for improved cycling conditions.[56]

Groups organized around a shared ethnic identity proliferated as well. In New York, the cycling city encompassed Chinatown, which had its own riding school and a growing number of cyclists. As early as 1892, a small group of Chinese American riders in New York organized themselves into the New York Mongolians. The riders took recreational tours of the city and its nearby environs. Likewise, in 1895, a group of Chinese cycling enthusiasts formed the aptly named First Chinese Bicycle Club of Philadelphia, which maintained its own club headquarters and riding academy. In New York, the Hinode Bicycle Club consisted of Japanese American businessmen who participated in citywide cycling parades and who earned the distinction of being one of the "best uniformed" clubs. In Brooklyn, the Norsemen's Cycle Club invited all children of "Harold the Fair-Haired" to join. Together with the Danish and the Monitor Cycle Club, they formed the Scandinavian Associated Cycling Club. Groups of Italian Americans in Boston's North End and New York's Little Italy formed their own clubs. And in Chicago, the German Wheelmen maintained an active presence. There, too, Polish American and Cuban American cyclists joined thousands of other riders in an 1898 lantern-lit bicycle parade that was filled with pageantry, led by the city's cycling mayor, and watched by President McKinley.[57]

In one respect, ethnically-oriented bicycle clubs provided immigrants with an opportunity to participate in overtly public activities and a national phenomenon. In purpose and form, their clubs mimicked the hundreds of other bicycle clubs. When taking a group ride around the city or participating in a local bicycle race, Chinese American wheelmen, Polish American wheelmen, and every other kind of wheelmen were riders much like any other. Clearly, certain ethnic groups, like a cohort of Chinese riders who advertised that its members would dress according to the prevailing fashion, hoped that cycling would provide something of an assimilative experience. After all, these groups employed bicycles for more than commuting—they were also a medium of social engagement, a way to participate in a cultural phenomenon, and a means to be included in mainstream civic events and public demonstrations. The *Los Angeles Times* even pronounced "The Wheel a Splendid Factor in Developing Citizenship." To be sure, participating in popular forms of recreation and leisure was a common way for immigrant groups to experience Americanization. But this was certainly not a case of simple assimilation. Ethnic groups could purchase mass-market items and still find ways to endow "their own meaning to new possessions."[58]

The large-scale urban cycling parades were emblematic of the kinds of opportunities (and limitations) that cycling offered immigrant groups. In these grand parades, cyclists would wheel their way through the city, organized in distinct groups according to their club affiliation. On the one hand, this might mean that the Norsemen's Cycle Club or the New York Mongolians would be riding alongside tens of thousands of other riders, mostly from the white, urban middle class, and in some ways, as parades often do, this might serve as an expression of community solidarity. On the other hand, they would also be doing so within a segregated group: in other words, dozens and dozens of relatively segregated, homogenous groups were embedded within a much larger, heterogeneous parade.[59] The parades reflected the city itself, a remarkably diverse place, but a world in which neighborhoods continued to segregate the population.

Similarly, in the bicycle races in which many cycling clubs participated, individual heats or races were often segregated along ethnic or racial lines. And although spectators largely enjoyed watching, and the press regularly enjoyed reporting about, "colored" or "Chinese" racers, their reactions frequently focused on the physical differences among the riders.

Few of the press reports on such events failed to point out the stereotypical physical differences of ethnic riders, such as a characteristic 1894 *Los Angeles Times* article that promised readers a titillating race between the "almond-eyed wheelmen."[60]

That cycling was an important feature of ethnic communities is also revealed in specialty newspapers and magazines. In the *American Hebrew*, advertisements for bicycles ran comfortably alongside those for kosher meat.[61] Readers could also expect a steady dose of bicycle-related news, fiction, humor, and editorial comment. Likewise, the *American Jewess*, an 1890s periodical written for Jewish women, printed ads for "bicycle corsets" and joined the national debates about whether and how women should ride.[62]

Other media outlets followed a similar model. Spanish-language newspapers in Las Cruces, Los Angeles, New York, El Paso, and Albuquerque featured scores of bicycle advertisements, articles about the effects of "ciclomania," and stories that extolled the bicycle as a means to escape the city, as a social leveler, as a tool for practical transportation, as a way to enjoy healthful exercise, and as one of the most promising inventions ever created. German-language newspapers, too, could hardly ignore the craze. Cycling had truly become an American phenomenon, which meant, by the end of the nineteenth century, as more than half of the population in the country's twelve largest cities were either foreign born or the children of foreign born parents, that it included a broad set of ethnic communities and recent immigrants.[63]

Often excluded from local clubs, black cyclists formed their own organizations. Baltimore's Uptown Cycle Club; Louisville's Union Cycle Club; Washington, DC's Capital League Wheelmen, the Hannibals, and the Ideal; Boise's Thompson Street Colored Bicycle Club; New York's Calumet Cyclers; Boston's Riverside Cycle Club, and Los Angeles's Nonpareils represented just some of the "Colored Wheelmen" of their respective cities. When the League of American Wheelmen officially barred blacks from joining by adding the word "white" to the list of requirements for membership in 1894, black members found that their membership badges no longer afforded them access to LAW meetings and events and aspiring members found their applications denied. Black cyclists who had been members of the LAW pled with the organization's northern members to reverse their decision. The Captain of New York's largest all-black cycling club contended that "none but colored men of the best class ride bicycles, and they are no more objectionable than German or Irish wheelmen." Class should trump race, Spencer unsuccessfully argued. Likewise, the cycling publication read across Northern cities, the *American Wheelmen*, questioned the drawing of the color line: "Why they should be so treated does not appear since they pay the same annual dues and are entitled to all the privileges the others enjoy. The action of the meet promoters shows an animosity or bigotry that is ill befitting this lightened age." Regardless of the mixed northern opinion, local chapters of the LAW in the South simply would not compromise when it came to "forcing obnoxious company upon southern wheelmen," as the delegation from Louisiana characterized it.[64]

As Jim Crow laws swept across Southern cities and as the Supreme Court in *Plessy v. Ferguson* endorsed the constitutionality of racial segregation, so too did the LAW exclude black cyclists. This act belied the suggestion that the bicycle welcomed a new order of inclusiveness. Not everyone took the news so easily. Disconcerted black cyclists from several large cities banded together to form the District Associated Wheelmen. Although this group did not quite achieve its original lofty goal to create a parallel, national organization, the formation of a new Colored League of American Wheelmen (or a "LAW unto Themselves" as the *Los Angeles Times* termed it) was reason enough to celebrate. Following the passage of a resolution that forbade black cyclists from participating in the LAW parade, members of the newly formed association for "colored" riders planned their own parade. White wheelmen, the *Washington Post* reported, "may save themselves lots of trouble" by not attending. And so on an October night in 1896 several hundred black wheelmen rode on a five-mile route around the nation's capital. Most carried Chinese lanterns, many wore elaborate costumes, and a good number were decked out as "Uncle Sam." The black cyclists who dressed as Uncle Sam—the personification of the United States—and participated in a parade at once protesting their exclusion and celebrating their resolve might have been mocking the hypocrisy of American liberty or perhaps reveling in that very promise. Either way, they did so in what was becoming a ritualized American activity—cycling.[65]

Though lacking the glare of Chinese lanterns or dazzling costumes, black cyclists rode to work and for pleasure without much fanfare in many cities. An 1898 survey in Chicago counted 134 "colored" riders among the morning commuters.[66] Surely the total number of Chicago's black cyclists was many times larger. And although it is impossible to ascertain the veracity, one cycling club captain counted 2,000 black riders among New York City's army of wheelmen.[67] Even so, with a total black population of around 60,000 it is clear (as photographic evidence further suggests) that blacks and other minority groups rode at a rate far less than that of whites.[68] Yet black women and men, old and young, could be seen riding through Chicago, Boston, Washington, DC, or any other sizable city. The *New York Herald* recorded that black cyclists maintained a regular presence in New York and especially its main cycling thoroughfare, the Boulevard:

> Where can one find a more picturesque sight than the array of colored men on wheels? There is a vast army of them. Where on earth they come from nobody knows, but there they are, by scores and hundreds. Colored women, too, abound. They wheel as well and dress as tastefully as their white sisters. The men are usually altogether past criticism. . . . Truly they are all that, and if any philosopher feels dismal over the future of the Afro-American race let him visit the Boulevard and see its representatives as they whiz past.[69]

Certainly the ways in which black riders adopted the bicycle and the degree to which black cyclists were accepted varied greatly from region to region and from city to city. It was not completely unusual, for example, for a contingent of black riders to participate in a citywide parade filled with cyclists of varied ethnic and racial backgrounds. Like other leisure cyclists, black riders would also take tours of the neighboring countryside or longer trips to other cities. When one group of black riders from New York finished a 100-mile ride that ended with a tour through Philadelphia's Fairmount Park, they reported of having been treated well, in what was presented as less than striking news. Nor was it unusual for mainstream city papers, like the *Washington Post*, to regularly report on the activities of black cyclists in the same manner as general cycling-related issues. Cycling among urban blacks must have been commonplace enough not to warrant special attention. News reports about "Negro" or "Colored" cyclists almost never remarked that such riders were a rarity or a phenomenon, but rather messengers, commuters, racers, club members, and leisure riders like everyone else.[70] Black newspapers maintained coverage about all things bicycle and regularly featured advertisements for bicycles and bicycle accessories.[71]

Nevertheless, prejudice abounded. The majority of newspaper articles that contained any reference to everyday black cyclists highlighted traffic accidents. Typical headlines read "Negro Cyclist Ran into Lady"; "More 'Scorcher' Victims: A Fast-Riding Negro Cyclist Ran down Two Children Yesterday Afternoon"; "Run over by a Colored Bicyclist"; and "Reckless Negro Bicyclist . . . under Arrest for Running down Mrs. Robinson." In the press, "colored bicyclists" disproportionately ran down whites. Undoubtedly it went both ways on the streets, even as some people wondered about why "negroes" caused so many cycling collisions. And when white cyclists were involved in accidents, reporters decided that their race was irrelevant. More than occasionally, newspapers also caricatured black cyclists along the lines of dominant negative stereotypes. Outside of the press, blacks found few clubs (the LAW or otherwise) willing to welcome them and few cycling races that did not bar or segregate black riders.[72] In some ways participants and in other ways pariahs in the broader phenomenon of cycling, black riders used bicycles like the rest of the urban population, but there were some ways in which black riders used bicycles to demonstrate and celebrate in their own way.

On Emancipation Day, marking the anniversary of Lincoln's famous proclamation, legions of "colored wheelmen" assembled near the nation's capital and in Springfield, Illinois, to celebrate by parading on their bicycles.[73] Riders marched in jubilee on top of a machine whose devotees were mostly white and, until relatively recently, mostly wealthy. That they chose to remember the emancipation of slavery with vehicles so often cited as emancipating was probably no accident. For onlookers, nothing was more American than bicycles, and perhaps it served as an appropriate way to commemorate an important American milestone, yet the parades likely meant less to the observers than to the participants, who, through their festival, were creating a narrative. Borrowing a phrase from Clifford Geertz, they were creating a "story they tell themselves about themselves."[74] Addressing social or racial issues through a parade was nothing new and neither was the story they were narrating.[75] For those riders used to prejudice and railing against it, the cycling city represented yet another moment in history where reality clouded, but could not deter, the promises of hope. In all, the bicycle represented more than just a way to move about. For certain urban inhabitants it seemed to hold the potential, whether realizable or not, to be a social leveler. As one prominent writer rosily predicted, ". . . the bicycle promise[s] to fulfill for us the Declaration of Independence . . . the black and the Chinaman speed . . . across the pleasant levels of Democracy."[76]

The American cycling city, lost in time, grew by virtue of its people. The cycling community came to include more than just young white men of means. As bicycles cruised through parks and sat outside office buildings, the meaning of those trips and the functions those wheels served depended, to a great degree, on the cyclists themselves. Social class affected not only the kind of bicycle a cyclist purchased but also the way in which he or she used it. The wealthiest fretted about how their wheels looked and which of their friends had taken to the sport; the very poor saw bicycles as great tools, greatly too expensive; and the many in between who worked in shops, offices, banks, and schools and who eventually bought wheels did so for both practical and social reasons. Those middle-class riders constituted the majority of riders—they had the means to afford bicycles and the desire to appear modern and leisured. They, and to a lesser extent recent immigrants and African Americans, formed their own bicycle clubs, as did the urban elite. These largely homogenous groups—in terms of race, class, and gender—belied the idea extolled by middle-class journalists that the bicycle spawned classlessness. That notion was more of an aspiration than reality, voiced most often by those who wanted to live in such a world. In the end, cyclists included a host of people riding for a host of reasons, prompting city officials to ask a new question: How do we manage all of those cyclists?

CHAPTER THREE

Rules of the Road

As the bicycle peaked in popularity, cyclists moved within a complex web of urban infrastructure. In the final decade of the nineteenth century, cable cars, elevated trains, street railways, omnibuses, horse cabs, carriages, and remnant horsecars offered urbanites a variety of ways to move about. Nearly everyone, though, traveled via the street. The elevated trains and subways represented obvious attempts to reduce street traffic, but the elevateds came with a host of problems—construction expense, noise, shadows—and the days of comprehensive subway systems in the United States were still years away.

Making matters worse, urban population densities had skyrocketed by the turn of the twentieth century. Streets that were once playgrounds for children, open-air shopping markets, or de facto front porches became closer to the streets as we know them today.[1] Governed by municipal law, streets were meant to circulate traffic in and around the city. Pedestrians continued to use the streets, but at great peril and amid a hodgepodge of individual carriage drivers, cyclists, and an eclectic mix of privately-managed public transit options.

So with the number of cyclists growing rapidly, cities began to wrestle with how to accommodate them. "It is plain that the bicycle, in its sudden popularity, has given rise to new questions in municipal administration," a Philadelphian opined in 1896. "The streets were originally constructed for the use of pedestrians and ordinary vehicles. The omnibus, and tram-car, drawn by horses, and the electric streetcar in turn required special regulation; but they made no radical difference in the general use of the streets. The bicycle introduces a new element. It is a vehicle of a different kind that requires different regulations."[2] In reality it was not just all of the new bicycles but also the general increase in traffic and the

sheer diversity of vehicles that created havoc.[3] Without traffic signals or
a coordinated system to regulate traffic flow, bicycles posed their share
of unique problems. Unlike horses and streetcars, bicycles moved nearly
silently through the city, at a quickened pace (before bicycles, traffic typically moved at a walking pace), and with the power to accelerate and turn
quickly.

No consensus existed (even among cyclists) about how to regulate bicycles because no consensus existed about the bicycle itself. How people
thought bicycles should be classified not only related to the way bicycles
moved about the city but also depended on what people thought the primary function of bicycles was. In what ways were bicycles like pedestrians, horses, carriages, and streetcars and how did they differ? Were they
vehicles? Did they belong in the parks? Should they be required to have
lights, bells, and brakes? Should they be licensed and taxed? Although
comprehensive traffic codes, traffic lights, and traffic signs were largely an
invention of the twentieth century, cyclists in the 1890s forced municipal
governments to rewrite (or create) traffic laws, alter traffic patterns, and
rethink the transportation network.[4] The ways in which these ordinances

Fig. 3.1. The corner of Bedford and Atlantic Avenues in Brooklyn, New York,
1896. Reproduced with permission from the Edgar S. Thompson Photograph
Collection, Brooklyn Museum/Brooklyn Public Library, Brooklyn Collection.

Fig. 3.2. This photograph from Los Angeles near the turn of the century shows a realistic mix of traffic—two bicycles, two streetcars, four horse-drawn carriages, and lots of pedestrians. Courtesy of the University of Southern California, on behalf of the USC Libraries Special Collections.

were designed, debated, and applied reveals an obvious need to accommodate bicycles, but it also provides a lens through which to explore how urban Americans thought about their cities and their traffic. Before automobiles, it was bicycles that brought rules, regulations, and bureaucracy to the streets.

Although cyclists would soon disappear from city streets, their impact on municipal law was long lasting. Their sudden arrival forced city officials to reconceptualize the role of government in restricting movement on the streets, which would continue to influence how cities regulated traffic long after cycling faded in popularity. In enacting laws, local politicians not only determined how vehicles moved but also created a landscape that acknowledged and promoted bicycle use. After all, it is people and politics rather than technology that shape cities.[5]

Initially, the urban environment was rather inhospitable to cyclists. In the waning years of the 1870s, major metropolises like Boston, Providence, and Brooklyn closed their streets to bicycle traffic. Other cities lacked comprehensive bans on cycling, but often circumscribed the city, prohibiting bicycles from traveling in parks, on boulevards, or through certain neighborhoods.[6] The hostility had multiple births. Relatively few owned bicycles and relatively few could realistically become cyclists. For the most part, women, the elderly, children, and the less-than-affluent found that bicycles were either not designed for them, too difficult to ride, or too expensive. Others saw bicycles as a silly novelty, certainly not worthy of sharing space with legitimate vehicles. Attuned to the hoofed alarms which warned of coming traffic, pedestrians quickly judged the silent yet speedy bicycles a hazard; carriage drivers and teamsters were less than happy to share the road with machines that allegedly made their horses skittish and that often moved at a faster clip than them.[7] Thus the lone cyclist who dared to challenge the restrictions rode at the mercy of the police, the courts, and the horse driver.

With mixed success throughout the 1880s, riders challenged city ordinances restricting their access to city streets and parks. In San Francisco, Hartford, Newport, Brooklyn, and elsewhere, anticycling ordinances originated from the notion that bicycles (or velocipedes, as many of these restrictions remained from an earlier era) were playthings, not vehicles. In each of these cities, riders successfully overturned the bans. Cyclists in Philadelphia and Chicago won access to their city's parks, places from which they had long been barred. Cities tended to have more usable roadways (compared to the surrounding country), but it was the urban parks in particular that boasted the most passable and scenic routes. To a certain degree, cycling's popularity depended on the ability of cyclists to attain the legal rights to ride through the city and its parks. Getting this key to the city was no easy task.[8]

No battle was more important in the war between organized cyclists and city officials than that which concerned New York's finest prize, Central Park. In 1880, angry patrons complained about bicycles wheeling through their park. In response, the Commissioners of Central Park outlawed cyclists from enjoying the 843-acre oasis of rolling hills, smooth paths, shaded knolls, and imported vegetation. The purported rationale for the prohibition was simple: bicycles frightened horses. The ensuing fight over the ban raised significant questions, not only about bicycles in the Park, but also about the bicycle's place in the city.[9]

On July 2, 1881, three cycling enthusiasts violated the antibicycle ordinance. It was a deliberate act aimed to test the constitutionality of the ban. One man rode a bicycle, two others mounted tricycles, and each was affiliated with a local cycling club. Since tricycles (often used by women) might have been more easily characterized as "pleasure carriages" along the lines of horse-drawn carriages, the tricycling agitators thought they would have a better chance of winning their case. Tipped off by the violators themselves, the police made the arrest and solicited the five-dollar fine. The cyclists resisted. Saved from prison by their lawyers, the three men were placed on parole and a flurry of widely watched legal battles ensued.[10]

Bicycle manufacturers and clubs rallied behind the cyclists in hopes of using the case as a means to challenge the validity of anticycling ordinances outside parks and in other cities. With a legal precedent held in the balance, the burgeoning LAW joined forces with Colonel Pope. A savvy entrepreneur, Pope emerged as a powerful champion of cyclists' rights. With the public support of the LAW and a reported eight thousand dollars from the Pope Manufacturing Company, the campaign for unfettered access to the city mobilized around the Central Park case.[11]

In the courtroom, the park commissioners continued to defend the ban on cycling as a mechanism to protect horses and their owners. Prosecutors led witness after witness into the courtroom, each one recounting an instance in which his horses became "crazy at the sight of a bicycle." The cycling advocates' attorney could do little more than mock the absurdity of the prosecution's central argument. After documenting that most horses can, in fact, ride safely alongside bicycles, the defense counselor satirized the park commissioners' attitude toward the cyclists in a crayon drawing that featured a calm cyclist wheeling through the park surrounded by "horses standing on their heads, others running away, men and women knocked down, and children run over." The finer details of the drawing revealed that the cyclist "carried a knife and revolver" and was "determined to kill all he could not run over." The sarcastic approach failed. The cyclists lost their case and after several appeals, cycling remained a prohibited activity in the city's most treasured park.[12]

In the spring of 1883, New York cyclists launched a reinvigorated campaign for access to Central Park. This time their tactics focused on demonstrating the bicycle's innocuousness. A group of wheelmen presented the park commissioners with a petition requesting the use of Central Park and Riverside Drive (which also remained unavailable for cycling) for a massive cycling parade. The commissioners approved the parade route, which had been carefully laid out by the organizers. Not coincidentally, the plans called for the participants to wheel directly past the residence of Egbert Viele, a commissioner of Central Park. The publicity for the LAW-sponsored parade included this noteworthy detail, likely to ensure that the hundreds of cyclists cruising by Commissioner Viele's home would do so in proper form. In the end, the 1883 Central Park parade served not only to galvanize the spirit of the city's cyclists but, more importantly, also to alter public opinion.[13]

Newspapers estimated that anywhere between 750 and 2,000 cyclists participated in the League of American Wheelmen's fourth annual "meet" in May of 1883. The morning session was dedicated to club business; in the afternoon, cyclists took to the streets for the grand parade. Hailing from more than six states, the members lined Fifth Avenue and began their exhibition, riding past Commissioner Viele's property and ultimately through Central Park. About 10,000 New Yorkers stood out in the sun while packs of riders stormed by. The festivities culminated in a banquet later that same night. Hundreds of LAW members, an ex-mayor, local clergymen, the commissioner of public works and, most notably, several Central Park commissioners filled the great hall inside the Metropolitan Hotel. The swanky, six-story, brownstone-fronted hotel contained rooms for up to 1,000 guests, some 250 servants, and had an opulence that attracted fat wallets and the dapperly dressed to its lower Broadway location.[14] Following some opening toasts and a procession of jocular speakers, the organizers asked several of the prominent guests to offer their thoughts on the festivities of the day and on the bicycle in general. No attendee was more important than Parks Commissioner Viele, a Mexican-American War veteran and a future congressman. Sporting a weighty moustache, he stood in the oversized, sun-lit room crowded with rosewood furniture and addressed the boisterous crowd. Impressed by the massive exhibition, Viele declared that "if there ever was a manly exercise, a manly enjoyment, it is . . . the steel horse." He continued by predicting that the peaceful parade (the commissioner cited "hearing no reports of skittish horses") "would be the signal for a thorough acceptance of the bicycle as an ordinary vehicle of locomotion."[15] The support of at least one park commissioner was secure.

The banquet lasted well into the night, as most of the speakers ignored the suggested five-minute time limit. The League of American Wheelmen members gleefully recounted the marvelous parade and anticipated that their demonstration would open the gates of Central Park and all of the roads of the city to cyclists. After all, the strategy had worked before. In 1881, the Wheelmen held a parade in Boston and the following year a similar exhibition in Chicago. Like the meet held in New York, both sought to demonstrate the bicycle's ability to coexist with other urban inhabitants, including horses. And in both cases, city officials lifted certain anticycling restrictions.[16]

The effects of the New York parade were similarly immediate but more limited. Within weeks of the meet, the park commissioners redefined the rules of the park to accommodate some cycling but fell short of allowing full access. The commissioners decided to allow "efficient riders" (defined as members of the organized cycling clubs) to use the West Drive of the park from sunrise to 9:00 a.m. Cycling enthusiasts welcomed the concessions (the Citizens Bicycle Club of the City of New York even decided to name Commissioner Egbert Viele as its first and only honorary member), but the limitations were severe.[17] Since only those cyclists belonging to official organizations gained access to the park, casual riders remained barred. It was only days before the Central Park Commissioners granted the LAW exclusive, albeit selective, admission to the park, that some of those same commissioners had dined alongside club members at the annual banquet. Perhaps the wheelmen had convinced the commissioners that club cyclists differed from the less sophisticated variety that sped by horses and crashed into pedestrians.

To be sure, the park commissioners' persistent regulations revealed their desires to keep Central Park an attractive destination for the city's elite. Even though the law-testers and high-wheel riders in general represented a segment of the elite, their taste for bicycles and adventure generally put them at odds with values of Victorian culture. Often bachelors, many of these earliest riders indulged in a sporting male culture that lived most comfortably in urban pool halls and saloons, a world that not everyone welcomed. Thus, the ultimate accommodation of cyclists was crafted within the confines of a strict set of rules governing appearance and behavior. While many of the city's wealthy, horse-owning populace may have objected to *any* bicycle use in the park, New York's most prominent citizens probably gave begrudging approval to the clause that restricted park use to club members and required that even those cyclists wear an appropriate uniform. In neighboring Brooklyn, Prospect Park commissioners applied equally selective admission requirements. After adopting a set of rules regulating bicycle use in the park that was "approved by the most experienced riders" and "suggested by the organized clubs of this city, with the view to avoid all possible opposition from the public," only approved riders, donning a numbered badge could access Olmsted & Vaux's other famed creation.[18]

When city officials refused to loosen any comprehensive anticycling ordinances, cyclists eyed the state government. In the spring of 1887, Governor David Hill of New York considered a bill that would afford bicycles the same privileges as any pleasure carriage on all highways and parks in the state of New York. The principal opponent of the measure was Central Park Commissioner Crimmins. At a hearing on the bill, Crimmins apparently submitted "several yards of petitions" from some 7,000 carriage-owning New Yorkers who opposed the law. John D. Crimmins had come to the commission with a solid reputation as a city builder. A prominent Irish Catholic and Democrat, Crimmins was the president of a construction company that built much of the city's infrastructure, helping usher it into its modern and industrial form. Among these varied projects were many of the city's elevated railways, which perhaps informed his perspective on transportation and the role of bicycles. Regardless, Crimmins and the other park commissioners expressed greater concern over retaining their own authority than any of the particular details of the bicycle bill. After all, the commissioners had crafted their own ordinance regulating bicycle use in the parks, an ordinance that was now in jeopardy. The bicycle bill threatened to establish a precedent of permitting the state legislature to shape the contours of city space. The park commissioners sought to preserve their power.[19]

With the prospect of ordinances that might outlaw cycling in any of New York's parks and streets, the cycling lobby united in support of the bill. The two mainstays of the lobby, the LAW and the bicycle manufacturers, once again captained the effort. At the same hearing that Commissioner Crimmins decried the bill, Isaac Potter, an executive member of the LAW, and Charles Pratt, a cycling enthusiast and an attorney for Colonel Pope, joined nearly a hundred cyclists in Albany to show their support. Without a dissenting vote in the Assembly, and but two in the Senate, Governor Hill endorsed the bicycle bill. Referred to as the "Liberty Bill" among cyclists, it recognized the bicycle as a legitimate vehicle and granted cyclists all of the same rights as the buggy-driver.[20]

The passage of the "Liberty Bill" established the bicycle lobby as a legitimate political force. A cycling advocate wrote the bill, local cyclists lobbied their representatives, and scores rode their bicycles to Albany for the official hearing. As local papers reported in 1887, anyone seeking public office had to consider the "bicycle vote." "The fraternity of wheelmen is said to control 20,000 votes here," the *Brooklyn Daily Eagle* added. Thus it was no surprise that the Governor "considered it discreet to sign" the "Liberty Bill."[21] In reality, it would be a few more years until politicians had to account for the bicycle vote. Through statutory law, first in New York and then soon after in other states, bicycles had garnered legal status to use the road. Even before cycling had entered the mainstream, the high-wheeler pioneers helped lay much of the groundwork for the widespread adoption of bicycles. Because of their efforts, prejudice against the bicycle, as one such rider recalled, "has subsided, opposition been quelled, [and] restrictions removed."[22]

Even before legislatures enacted bicycle ordinances, judges began to define the bicycle's place on the road through common law. Just as the "Liberty Bill" did, judges established the bicycle's privileges and responsibilities as equal to those of "any other vehicle or carriage." For example, in Topeka, Kansas, the state's Supreme Court heard a case involving a cyclist who was ticketed for violating a city ordinance that prohibited cyclists from traveling across a particular bridge. The court ruled "that there can be no question but that a citizen riding on a bicycle in that part of a street devoted to the passage of vehicles, was but exercising his legal right to its use, and a city ordinance that attempted to forbid such use of that part of a public street would be held void as against common right." Bicycles were now numerous enough and their supporters vocal enough that the old notion of simply banning bicycle use was no longer viable.[23] The question was no longer *if* bicycles could ride in the city but rather *how* bicycles would ride in the city.

More often than not, lawmakers passed municipal legislation in piecemeal fashion. Oftentimes, the acts were meant to calm the chaos on the streets. As one journalist dramatized, "streams of bicyclists pass each other with bewildering rapidity and mingled in the throng are heavy truck teams, carriages and all sorts of vehicles which insure a broken and dismembered corpse to the venturesome person who dares venture in." Hyperbole aside, the increasing popularity of cycling and the dangerous amalgamation of traffic could no longer be ignored. In Rochester, New York, local police reported almost 100 accidents a day. In a plea to its city's common council, the *Detroit Free Press* summarized the problem: with so few regulations and with "this appliance of civilization" being used so widely, the people of Detroit traveled through the city in great peril. A series of bicycle ordinances, the newspaper suggested, was long overdue.[24]

While many of the standard rules of the road (e.g., keep to the right) were established by tradition, increased demand for access to the street necessitated a more formal code. Mayors, city councils, judges, and other officials routinely recognized the uptick in bicycle traffic and the associated headaches. As the Common Council of Philadelphia described, the "great increase" in bicycle traffic created a "grave problem" for the city and its streets.[25] In response, they enacted what was often common sense legislation, targeting particular problems.

Eventually, most municipal governments responded with a series of ordinances. By 1895, in Michigan, lawmakers in nineteen out of the twenty-two largest cities felt compelled to draft specific regulations governing the bicycle. As cyclists took to the streets at night, officials required that they carry lamps. Speed limits and alarm bells were meant to slow the rising number of accidents. In response to those vexatious children who tripped cyclists by covering potholes with paper or sprinkling the street with obstacles, cyclists in several cities secured passage of legislation that made the throwing of glass, tacks, nails, or other impediments meant to tumble cyclists onto the street illegal. Bans on sidewalk riding sought to protect pedestrians as did prohibitions against reckless driving, trick or "fancy" riding, and coasting—the practice of riding downhill with one's feet off the pedals. (Famously, the Duke of Marlborough was one of the first cyclists arrested for "coasting." He was in New York to marry Miss Consuelo Vanderbilt and was caught cruising through Central Park with his feet casually resting on the handlebars.[26])

But these laws were often isolated and enacted in a singular fashion. Nonetheless, these smaller ordinances caused city governments to think more broadly about the ways in which people and vehicles moved about the city. It would not be long before the increase in cyclists, the traffic they created, and the competition for road space between cyclists, pedestrians (who they sometimes ran over), and streetcars (with which they competed) prompted broader and longer lasting municipal reforms. Typically these more comprehensive approaches were born from relatively narrow debates about city traffic that were symptomatic of a larger problem. One such instance, surrounding the Boulevard in New York, was emblematic of both the problems and the possibilities of the bicycle. The debate over traffic on the Boulevard led to a far-reaching series of traffic guidelines that restructured traffic not only in New York but in many other American cities as well.

New York's Boulevard developed into such an attraction that the once ghostly street became the city's most trafficked, and contested, cycling thoroughfare. Thousands of riders wheeled along each day and night. In 1896, the New York Board of Aldermen decided that it could no longer ignore the Boulevard's traffic problems. For months, individual aldermen, city newspapers, carriage drivers, and cycling clubs participated in a public debate about the bicycle's place on the Boulevard and on city streets in general.

While the bicycle had an acknowledged right to the road by the second half of the 1890s, the burden of ensuring safe and efficient traffic circulation grew in proportion to the number of riders. In "the interest of bicyclists," an alderman introduced a resolution barring all heavy vehicles from the Boulevard for the three-plus mile span of roadway extending northward from 59th Street. The alderman proposed that only bicycles and other light vehicles be allowed, arguing that the Boulevard's "heavy traffic" was dangerous to bicycles. The threat to cyclists included more than just an inadvertent act. Alderman Robinson explained, "It is known that drivers of heavy vehicles take pleasure in running into bicycle riders, with the object of annoying them, and frequently causing serious accidents." The accidents on the Boulevard, he continued, "[were] not accidents at all, but the deliberate results of drivers attempting to break the wheels of riders." In light of these malicious attacks (which were much less common than the Alderman suggested) and an urgent "city demand," the alderman sought to transform the Boulevard into a bicycle thoroughfare. In the process he incited a debate that reverberated around the nation. All the way in Tennessee, readers perusing the *Memphis Commercial Appeal* could keep up with the Boulevard saga in New York.[27]

In New York the proposed resolution appeared popular. An informal poll of more than 2,500 *New York Herald* readers found that nearly all of its respondents favored restricting commercial and heavy vehicles from the Boulevard.[28] Nevertheless, opposition quickly surfaced. Ironically, it was the very group that seemed to gain the most that most adamantly opposed restricting heavy vehicles from the Boulevard. Organized cyclists under the umbrella of the LAW sent a public letter to the Board of Aldermen insisting that the LAW and other cycling clubs had not conceived of the measure and were, in fact, "unalterably opposed to it." The letter highlighted that the LAW was "delighted to find that not a single wheelman or wheelman's organization appeared before your Honorable Body to ask for such a special privilege as the exclusive use of a street on this island." Since cyclists, and the LAW in particular, had been the primary advocates for open-access roads and having themselves been barred from the parks and the streets, the LAW admitted that it would be unprincipled to now ask that other vehicles be excluded from the roads. It vigorously opposed any kind of regulation that would restrict any vehicle from public streets. The LAW acknowledged the mounting traffic problems on the Boulevard (like many other city streets around the country) and maintained that safety concerns necessitated intervention. In lieu of the Boulevard restriction ordinance, the LAW pleaded with the Board of Aldermen to give riders a roadway "free from the perils of death and maiming" and to provide cyclists with the "privilege of riding in any and all the streets without menace of life and limb which now exists," in what the LAW referred to as the "most dangerous [city] on the continent for a cyclist." The nation's leading body of organized cyclists reiterated its demand that wagon drivers be required to carry lamps and be subject to speed limits. If roads were safe, "the cry for a restricted thoroughfare [would] cease," the LAW concluded.[29] Regulation trumped restriction.

The LAW continued to lobby against the initial proposal barring heavy vehicles, in addition to the many alternative resolutions floated in the fall of 1896. One compromise called for restricting heavy traffic for only certain hours. The mayor suggested his own plan to divide the Boulevard into separate parts, one of which would be devoted to wheelmen. General C. H. T. Collis, the commissioner of public works, and New York Alderman Goodman both suggested a forward-looking plan to "stripe" the Boulevard. Both halves would be asphalted, one side black for trucks and the other white for bicycles. The radical plan to segregate traffic with colored lane markers represented an obvious need to reconsider and formalize traffic flow. Ultimately the aldermen agreed to segregate traffic, albeit without the colored lane markers. One side was for heavy vehicles, the other for light (fig. 3.3). Making sure everyone kept to his or her own side was one of the new duties for a corps of policemen, monitoring the street from atop their own bicycles. But these measures were merely temporary, as the Boulevard debate ignited a broader discussion. Ultimately it prompted a new plan to govern traffic across the entire city.[30]

In 1897, New York became the first city in the nation to pass a comprehensive set of traffic ordinances. The ordinances of 1897 marked a shift from a largely de facto system of governing traffic to one that actively sought to define movement on the streets. The new system had widespread implications, as many other municipalities looked to New York as a model. Moreover, the ordinances explicitly acknowledged the bicycle as a legitimate urban vehicle, classing it alongside traditional vehicles. Most remarkable of all, however, was the fact that the new guidelines governing New York's traffic, and ultimately those enacted in other major cities, were crafted and proposed by the cyclists themselves.[31]

The New York Division of the LAW drafted a series of traffic guidelines, knowing that it was only a matter of time before the city would recognize the need for traffic governance. To prevent any future, unfriendly legislation, the wheelmen thought it wise to introduce their own comprehensive ordinance to ease city traffic and reduce the number of accidents. At a meeting of New York's Law Committee of the Board of Aldermen in 1897 a group of well-known citizens and prominent cyclists convened to propose a new set of ordinances to govern city traffic. The cyclists might

Fig. 3.3. This image of the Boulevard in 1898 reveals the (rather unsuccessful) efforts to separate traffic on New York's Broadway. The sign that is seen hanging over the street reads: "pleasure traffic keep over to the left, business traffic keep over to the curb." Reproduced with permission from the Museum of the City of New York.

have feigned latitude and flexibility, but they made sure their ideas were imprinted in the final draft. The wheelmen formally introduced numerous suggestions, including regulations that required slower moving vehicles to keep to the right, drivers to use hand signals to indicate turns, and all vehicles to display lights after dark. It also prohibited vehicles from suddenly stopping or parking in the middle of the street and established a minimum age (sixteen) to operate commercial vehicles.[32]

After weeks of deliberation and on the last day of August 1897, the Board of Aldermen concurred. The new set of "rules of the road" finally established a thorough set of traffic guidelines, repealing the barely extant vestiges of ordinances written way back in 1811 when a triumvirate of New Yorkers famously decided to turn their island into a rectangular grid of intersecting streets and avenues. The vast majority of the codified rules mirrored the suggestions originally made by the city's wheelmen, including the sections requiring hand signaling, bells, and lights; defining the methods of passing; establishing rights of way; and setting a minimum driving age. To be sure, many of these measures merely cemented traditional practice, but other components—requiring hand signals and establishing a legal driving age—were radically new. Certain elements failed to gain traction. Cyclists regularly rode more than two abreast despite its prohibition. Most importantly, though, the revised ordinances helped confirm the bicycle's status as a recognized vehicle to be classed in the same category as a carriage, an omnibus, and the like.[33]

More than simply granting cyclists equal access to the roads as the "Liberty Bill" had done, city officials defined appropriate cycling behavior in some bicycle-specific manners, but more often in universal traffic codes. Bicycles *and* carriages could only pass on the left. Cyclists *and* carriage drivers were forced to use hand signals when turning a corner. Even though it was the bicycle that prompted the new traffic laws, the ordinances sought to regulate all vehicles on all public streets.[34]

These restrictive laws promoted the notion of bicycles as legitimate urban vehicles, subject to legitimate, official regulation. In fact, the most common complaint from cyclists about proposed ordinances in American cities was that the proposed rules did not apply to everyone. Requiring lamps and enforcing speed limits annoyed cyclists, but riders often found such measures palatable and ultimately supported reform so long as the restrictions applied to all vehicles. When laws singled out cyclists, the reaction was much less favorable. Following an ordinance which required cyclists to carry lights and warning bells, local riders in Oakland joined in a parade distinguished by the cacophonous sounds of bells and horns intended to mock the new restriction. Cyclists in Topeka, Kansas, did the same thing. To protest against a new ordinance that imposed a speed limit and mandated that riders carry alarms or bells and lights after sunset, cyclists gathered together for a mass ride. Cruising along at a snail's pace, they rang cowbells and gongs. Angry marchers on wheels made sure to stop in front of the residences of the aldermen responsible for the ordinance, making as much noise and trouble as they could. Police suddenly stopped enforcing the law.[35]

Not every city was so cyclist friendly. Some cities enacted and enforced laws over the objections of cyclists. Often defended as measures to promote safety, the ordinances irked cyclists, who liked to complain about the regulations almost as much as they liked to ride their bicycles.[36] In many cities, though, the cyclists defined, and city officials approved, essential guidelines concerning how bicycles should maneuver through the city. And in so doing, cyclists provided the framework to accommodate not only the rising number of bicycles but also other (and future) modes of transportation.[37]

Still, not everyone was happy. Citing the increased danger that cycling added to the dynamic of traffic, a reporter from the nation's capital in 1896 noted:

> A spirited warfare is growing, developing between the bicyclists of Washington on the one side and the pedestrians and riders and drivers of horses on the other. The bicyclists are demanding entire control of every road and pathway. They have asked the commissioners for the enforcement of a set of regulations that would practically place all others at the mercy of the rider of the bicycle. Their appeal to the commissioners is the very pinnacle of insolence. The bicycle organizations want the right of way everywhere.[38]

The increase of cyclists, the ways in which they seemed to be taking over the city, and their control over new traffic legislation appalled a growing number of city dwellers. Objectors complained that the riders wanted it both ways, that when it suited their best interests, cyclists differentiated themselves from other drivers. When turnpikes began to demand tolls from cyclists, suddenly their machines seemed much less like other vehicles.[39] As riders toted their wheels on the railroads, their vehicles miraculously became mere luggage.

On the streets they wanted their bicycles to be considered legitimate vehicles and on the sidewalks anything but. In reference to the sidewalk issue, and the then-pending 1897 legislation defining the bicycle's place in New York, one angry citizen wrote:

> I desire to enter a protest to the so-called rights of the bicyclist population, and while the Board of Aldermen are considering an ordinance for regulating their rights let them insert a clause prohibiting bicycles from being wheeled on the sidewalks at any time. In order to get the right to wheel in our parks, if I remember correctly, the bicycle was decided to be a vehicle . . . and what will they want next? It is indeed a great nuisance to have these wheelmen, with their so-called vehicles, walking down Broadway, on the sidewalk, when this thoroughfare is crowded. Let us have a plain definition of a "byck" and then make it take its place. If a vehicle it has no rights on the sidewalks whatever.[40]

The Board of Aldermen in New York heeded the complaints, at least to a degree, prohibiting cycling on the sidewalks so long as the abutting street was well paved.[41]

Truthfully, when it came to lobbying for procycling rules and regulations, cyclists often asked for special privileges (despite publicly and repeatedly arguing [as the LAW often did] that they wanted vehicle equality). To the dismay of others, they seemed to almost always succeed. On the West Coast, the *Argonaut*, a local San Francisco paper, editorialized, "Bicycle riders must be taught that not the entire earth and the fullness thereof are theirs."[42]

Cyclists did perpetually lobby against legislation that would have required that their wheels be licensed, registered, or taxed. As cyclists began to lay claim to more of the city, some municipal governments saw a potential new source of revenue. The idea of a bicycle tax was floated in several cities to help offset the costs of accommodating bicycles. In other cities it was the cyclists themselves who, through their direct financial contributions, hoped to gain greater control in shaping the city. In New York, authorities proposed a bicycle tax plan under the guise of protecting both cyclists and pedestrians. The tax failed. In Pittsburgh, city officials reasoned that "anything that puts the country and the city in easy reach of each other is a benefactor greater than can be measured in dollars" and so, quite obviously, warranted a half-dollar tax. The one dollar, half dollar, or thirty-five cent registration fee (depending on the city) was used for a variety of purposes. In Seattle the cyclists proposed the tax themselves in order to fund bicycle path construction. In Chicago the briefly implemented tax amassed the "Bicycle Tax Fund," which was allotted for general cycling-related improvements. The would-be tax in New York was earmarked to pay down the city debt.[43]

In the cities in which a tax was levied on cyclists, the law mandated that cyclists secure a bicycle license and attach a corresponding plate to their wheels. Riding without a license was cause for a fine. Most municipal governments, including New York, ultimately balked at imposing such taxes because of protests about "unwarranted discrimination" and "class legislation," since other vehicles were not taxed. As a sign of the bicycle's indeterminacy, some thought a bicycle tax should be considered as part of a broader vehicle tax, while others thought of a bicycle tax more along the lines of a tax on hunting rifles. Either way, in Seattle, Rochester, Pittsburgh, and elsewhere, the bicycle tax signaled that bicycles had officially arrived and warranted the regulation and bureaucracy that came with licensing and taxing. The taxes also provided an opportunity (or perhaps a missed opportunity) to rebut the Buffalo city engineer who remarked that because cyclists "do not pay the bills," they do not control the city plan. Although the vast majority of cyclists, including organized groups such as the LAW, opposed such measures, a few perceptive cyclists realized that by licensing and taxing their wheels there would be a permanent and ongoing source of funds dedicated to building bicycle-related infrastructure. In the end, few cities levied direct taxes on their cyclists (even those that did often repealed the measures rather quickly because of protests), meaning that municipalities did not usually have dedicated funds to improve the city for the growing numbers of cyclists.[44]

While bicycle taxes often failed to become law, cities around the country followed New York's lead in enacting comprehensive traffic and bicycle codes. Later in 1897, Washington, DC, passed its own set of rules governing traffic. Like New York, the nation's capital required cyclists to carry bells and lights. Because of public protest and cries of vehicular discrimination, the Commissioners of the District of Columbia quickly rewrote the original ordinance and mandated that "all public vehicles" display lighted lamps. It also instituted a speed limit—six miles an hour on streets with tracks for streetcars, twelve miles an hour on most others, and fifteen miles an hour on streets outside the dense city center. One feature of Washington, DC's new traffic laws was quite unique. With the stated goal of improving safety, section thirty of the new ordinance outlawed bicycles featuring handlebars that dipped more than four inches below the top of the saddle and mandated that riders keep their heads fully upright. Essentially, this ordinance sought to prevent scorchers from racing on DC streets, as those downwardly curved handlebars were traditionally paired with riders focused on speed. The ban, which met a flurry of protests and legal challenges from cyclists, expressed a sentiment shared by a growing group who considered cyclists a hazard.[45]

At roughly the same time, the city of New Orleans enacted a series of bicycle ordinances regulating traffic by limiting cyclists' speed, prohibiting sidewalk riding, and requiring lights at night. To prevent reckless driving, the city mandated that riders keep at least one hand on the bars, while Chicago forbade its cyclists from turning corners at speeds in excess of four miles per hour.[46] Other cities mandated that bicycles be outfitted with brakes. These measures to curb speed and irresponsible driving met a mixed fate. Cycling organizations often blocked brake requirements, claiming that they were an "infringement upon their personal property" and "utterly unnecessary." They argued that cyclists should maintain the right to decide if the convenience and safety of brakes offset their expense and added weight.[47] That cyclists were powerful enough to prevent commonsense legislation from becoming law was at the heart of one New Yorker's complaint:

> When the League of American Wheelmen makes a requisition upon a legislative body it is respected. The league decided that railroads in New York State ought to transport the vehicles of bicyclists who travel by rail without charge, and the Legislature of New York has ordered it done. It was held in New York City that pedestrians would be safer in the street if the bicyclists were compelled to have brakes on their machines. The league thought brakes unnecessary, and the Common Council refused to require them.[48]

New York was far from the only city in which cyclists played a central role in enacting such ordinances. As the members of Detroit's Common Council acknowledged, "a large number of bicycle riders, including the presidents and others representing the several bicycle organizations" had signed off on that city's traffic ordinance.[49]

By their very nature, bicycles caused confusion about how they should be classified. Unlike other forms of transportation, the bicycle was portable. Bicycles not only rode alongside streetcars and railroads but could also be carried by them. Moreover, bicycles functioned as a means of travel and as a means of recreation and sport. Scorchers enjoyed speed for its own sake. Touring cyclists wanted to explore, not commute. In dealing with such a variety of cyclists, municipal governments faced the challenge of drafting universal traffic ordinances and cycling-specific ordinances, which promoted certain bicycle functions and curbed others. Ordinances banning racing-style handlebars, for example, targeted merely one segment of the cycling population. Yet cyclists as a whole resented the notion of any government-imposed restriction. As a result, many logical proposals often failed to become law. Lumping together all cyclists for purposes of regulation had its rewards for riders but also its perils. The speeding scorchers, albeit a minority, eventually became the symbol of the worst that cycling had to offer.

While city ordinances regulating bicycle use often contained a few central elements, municipal governments varied in how they crafted and applied the law. The number of city ordinances and the disparity of rules between cities frustrated many riders who asked for a more universal approach. Without such uniformity, cyclists and cycling organizations often developed an unofficial code to ensure safe and efficient movement.

In particular, cyclists relied on warning bells to negotiate urban space. As the *Boston Herald* reported, the system was quite convoluted: "When approaching two people from the rear, three rings, 'I will pass between you.' When approaching from opposite direction, one ring, 'I will pass to the right.' Two rings, 'I will pass to the left.' . . . 'I want to talk to you' is conveyed by some riders by three long bells."[50] Even though some of these signals were common knowledge, many were not. Thus city officials across the country enacted ordinances like the one passed in New York in 1897. The wave of regulations came so fast, were applied so unevenly in different cities, and covered so many different facets of bicycle riding that the subject lent itself to great parody. One critic suggested that it would not be long before heavy breathing induced by a long ride "can only be indulged in by special permit from the police department." He further joked that in order to hear oncoming cyclists, bicycles would come with drums and gongs. In order to see cyclists at night, riders would have to "fire rockets and burn red, white and black fire continuously." On top of all that, cyclists would need to carry signs that read: "this is a bicycle; don't let it run you over."[51] At the other end of the spectrum, some city dwellers did not think that the ordinances went far enough. The bell ordinance in Wilmington, North Carolina, irked at least one citizen who thought the statute empowered cyclists and put the burden on pedestrians to get out of the way. (He not so seriously suggested that pedestrians carry lanterns to make themselves more visible to cyclists and revolvers in case the lanterns failed.)[52] Despite the local variations, cities across the country recognized the need to think more deeply about governing bicycle traffic.

By the mid-1890s, no visitor to a major American city could spend a weekend without noticing the bicycle's presence. Along the roads, in the parks, and across the bridges, cyclists cruised through the city. No longer restricted from certain spaces, bicycles merged with other forms of urban transportation, subjected to the same traffic regulations. After more than a decade of legal battles and public protests, cyclists had gained access to the city, but the nature of that access was continually redefined. City after city began to legislate narrowly passing laws that sought to control a particular problem that bicycle traffic created. Over time, these merged into comprehensive ordinances that often went beyond dictating how bicycles moved, into how all traffic moved.

It was, however, not just the traffic on the streets that concerned cyclists. So too, did the streets themselves.

CHAPTER FOUR

Good Roads

In the 1890s, American cities were in the midst of a great transformation. Immigrants poured in. Populations swelled. And public infrastructure was forced to catch up. How would clean, potable water be delivered
to the masses? How could a city of acres house a population of millions?
How could people, cargo, and commerce circulate most efficiently? All of
these questions, and the ways in which American cities answered them,
had significant consequences for the built environment. Of critical importance was the question of transportation. With horse-drawn vehicles came
piles of manure and a foul stench that became inextricably linked with
urban living. Elevated trains added mechanical noise and cast shadows
over the city. Eventually, subways rattled buildings and real estate values.
Today's cities owe much of their shape to the automobile. The parking
meters, garages, gas stations, honking horns, and asthmatic population are
hard to miss. But before automobiles dominated private transportation, bicycles and their advocates had a chance to shape the city.

Facing a series of complex and strikingly modern transportation problems (and an equal number of potential solutions), Americans in the 1890s
lacked professional planners to which they could turn. The future of the
city was up for grabs. It is not surprising, then, that the right to draw
the blueprint for urban transportation was so hotly contested among private capitalists, elected officials, reformers of all stripes, and, of course,
cyclists.

While various forms of transportation had redirected urban travel for
decades, at the precipice of the twentieth century city transportation un-
derwent its most sweeping changes yet. An important piece of the transformation of travel, bicycles left a physical footprint on American cities
and prompted new discussions about city design. Included in that discus-

sion was the laying and paving of new roads. Few could appreciate the promise of smooth asphalt better than cyclists. With more force and more success than anyone else, cyclists fought for new and improved roads—so much so that a new wave of politicians could ill afford to ignore the "bicycle vote." The new roads were supposed to be merely one part of a new city designed by and for cyclists. As one asked in 1896, "Has anybody, we wonder, thoroughly realized the change that will come over the appearance of our cities when everybody uses a bicycle?" His answer: "The changes that will ensue are so many and so great as to be unimaginable yet. A revolution is coming—may it be soon!"[1] The ways in which cities adapted in order to accommodate cycling were "so many and so radical as to amount virtually to making the world over again . . ."[2] While he was certainly exaggerating, it is true that the American city of the 1890s was, more than ever before or after, a cycling city.

On the eve of America's bicycle era, public roadways had a well-deserved bad reputation. As an 1888 US government report outlined, American roads were among the very worst. "They are deficient in every necessary qualification that is an attribute to a good road; in direction, in slope, in shape and service, and most of all, in want of repair."[3] In comparison to railroad and canal construction in the early to mid nineteenth century, roadways had fewer supporters and received even fewer investments. The early turnpike roads, like the Pennsylvania Turnpike built in 1794, almost always failed to win public monies. Well into the nineteenth century, road improvement projects continued to be underfunded and provincially controlled. Part of the problem was that "public roads themselves barely registered on the public consciousness as transportation improvements. State maps from this era depict railroads, canals, and rivers, but not local roads."[4] With internal improvement money earmarked for other projects and with a dearth of trained engineers, little public support, and a decentralized system of road construction and maintenance, public roads suffered mightily.[5] Poor roads wreaked havoc in American cities. One journalist, surveying the cycling environment across some of the country's largest cities, wrote: ". . . in Chicago [riders] scurry over wooden blocks, and also perpetually dodge cable cars engineered by maniacs; in Cincinnati and Kansas City they pedal up altitudinous hills over stony streets and muddy paths; in Boston and Philadelphia and San Francisco their spines are daily impaired by rattling over the deadly cobblestone."[6] The prospect of good roads and bicycles, however, promised a retooled transportation system and a new conception of mobility. As one professional clergyman, who moonlighted as a good roads advocate preached, residents living in a city with smooth streets "will be emancipated from the tyranny of the inconvenient elevated and the deliberate trolley." Cyclists "will lightly spin from place to place in comfort, speed, and rare delight."[7]

Far and away, cyclists emerged as the most powerful agent of change in reforming American roads in the late nineteenth century. As early as 1881, observers noted the bicycle's growing influence on the development of road construction, and by the end of the decade, cyclists unequivocally asserted themselves as the chief advocates of the "good roads" campaign. With limited shock-absorbing technology, nineteenth-century bicycles rode most comfortably on paved streets. While other forms of transportation moved across the same streets, the quality of those surfaces was in many ways less important to their function. Streetcars and elevateds rolled along tracks. Uneven surfaces certainly bothered horse drivers, but not to the same degree as the teetering, narrow-wheeled bicycle. Horses themselves had the most to complain about, but they had some difficulty articulating their frustration. The future and popularity of the bicycle, however, corre-lated with the quantity and quality of smooth surfaces. To be sure, cyclists could, and often did, ride on unpaved surfaces. While stubborn cyclists would ride anywhere, anytime, not everyone was interested in bumping along, inhaling dust. Few among the urban population could truly under-stand the disastrous nature of America's roads better than cyclists. "By be-coming at once rider and horse," cyclists knew the roads intimately. "No one knows the disadvantages of bad streets and roads so well as those who ride the wheel," the *Richmond Times* commented in 1896. It further pre-dicted that "the great army of wheelmen and wheelwomen" would ensure that the dreadful roads were a thing of the past.[8]

Cycling road books from the 1890s illuminate early cyclists' almost obsessive concern with good roads. The guides offered maps, suggested routes, and detailed notes about the type and quality of road surfaces for touring cyclists (fig. 4.1). In a typical road book, seasoned riders publicized their favorite routes, some on "fine macadam," others over "rough mac-adam," "across [a] stony hollow," down "a dirt road," through a "sandy, narrow side path," and still others atop asphalt. Favored routes almost always corresponded to the best paved (and least hilly) streets. Contem-porary diaries from individual riders also reveal that cyclists maintained a keen awareness of road quality and regularly recorded not only their routes and distances but also the road conditions.[9]

To the benefit of cyclists, the science of roadmaking was in the midst of its own transformation. For much of the nineteenth century, cities had

Fig. 4.1. On this 1896 "Map of California Roads for Cyclers," each road is labeled by color and number, indicating the type of road (e.g., "Bicycle Road"), the condition (e.g., "G" = "Good"), and the grade (e.g., "R" = "Rolling").

experimented with a wide array of paving materials. Combinations of wood, gravel, sand, bricks, granite blocks, macadam, coal tar, and all sorts of stone had been used to lay roads. Asphalt changed everything. In the 1880s, a discovery of a vast, Trinidadian asphalt deposit (a natural mixture of stone, sand, and other minerals) supplied American cities with a quality, and seemingly interminable, supply. That, coupled with the budding crop of professional municipal engineers in the 1890s, resulted in a wave of asphalting in those cities that could afford it and where citizens and cyclists demanded it.[10]

The degree to which local cyclists influenced local street construction reflected the structure of the prefederal system of road building. Until the turn of the twentieth century, road construction was largely governed by local authorities. Since abutting property owners had traditionally been responsible for their neighboring streets, the kinds of materials and quality of construction varied widely from neighborhood to neighborhood. "The character of the pavement on a given street has depended on chance," a member of Chicago's Committee on Street Paving reported in 1895, or "the whim of an Alderman or the importunity of a contractor." Therefore, local interest groups, like cyclists, could lobby, pay, and labor for new roads, while a single wheelmen-friendly alderman could move projects forward. Officials at the meetings of the city council or the Board of Aldermen made many of the most important decisions regarding public works and the city in general. These local officials, often representing a small neighborhood and a narrow set of interests, decided which roads should be paved and by what means.[11]

As cyclists moved to the forefront of the incipient "good roads" movement, they joined a rather limited constituency. To varying degrees, municipal engineers, sanitation and health experts, carriage producers, and manufacturers of paving materials and equipment supported investment in public roads. Economists touted the financial benefits of improved roads, citing potential efficiencies and increased commercial intercourse. Even though cyclists often publicized the economic benefits of road construction and improvement, their primary motivation was transparent: to extend the range of bicycle travel. To that end, cyclists worked to replace old roads with paved surfaces on which they could freely roam the city and its adjacent countryside.[12]

In 1888, organized cyclists, particularly the League of American Wheelmen, began to take up the "good roads" effort in earnest. The timing of the LAW's involvement was no accident. Initially cyclists had focused their efforts on gaining the right to use public roads and parks, essentially to legitimize the bicycle as an urban vehicle. But once courts and lawmakers endowed cyclists with the legal right to ride in the late 1880s, the cyclists' efforts moved, quite literally, onto a different terrain. The LAW reallocated its resources from emphasizing the *right* to the road to the *quality* of the road. It amended its constitution to include road improvement as a central tenet of its mission and simultaneously established an executive committee for the improvement of highways. After its initial attempts to introduce road bills (mainly to centralize and fund road-building projects) failed, the LAW and its supporters launched a publicity campaign to alter public opinion. From 1890 to 1895 alone, the LAW spent more than $120,000 to print and disseminate pamphlets intended to "excite a public interest in behalf of better roads and streets." Promoting good roads became so important that the LAW even started publishing its own magazine, *Good Roads*, devoted to the subject. By 1898 the League printed approximately 1,250,000 copies of the then six-year-old monthly magazine and distributed them to its members, politicians, libraries, and anyone who would read it.[13]

In addition to the LAW, the most outspoken proponent of road improvement was Colonel Albert Pope, the bushy-faced bicycle tycoon. In a series of speeches, his baritone voice sang the praises of good roads and all that they promised. He almost never mentioned the bicycle in these rather insipid lectures, preferring instead to cite the economic treasure that lay waiting in the streets of asphalt. As the principal owner of the nation's leading bicycle company, his stake in the good roads campaign was obvious. He endowed the first ever professorship in road engineering at MIT, successfully lobbied for the creation of a Massachusetts State Highway Commission (its membership consisted exclusively of LAW members), published a series of speeches and letters on the subject, paved a portion of Boston's Columbus Avenue with his own money, and pleaded with the organizers of the 1893 World's Columbian Exposition to include an exhibit on road making (again at his own expense).[14]

Pope, the LAW, and ordinary cyclists also used the political arena to advance their agenda. In the 1896 presidential election, the LAW contacted every delegate of both the Republican and Democratic conventions, insisting that a "good roads plank" be folded into the official platform. That same year, *Munsey's Magazine* remarked on the LAW's political involvement that "It has not yet launched into politics as a new 'third party,' nor has it nominated a candidate for the Presidency, but these things may come later." Actually, the LAW was too smart for that. Remaining nonpartisan was key to the organization's success in representing the interests of a large and growing population, many of whom would switch from party to party based on a particular candidate's "cycling record."[15]

Year after year the LAW's political organization strengthened as it lobbied and introduced new legislation to not only create and improve roads but also to benefit cyclists more broadly. Outside of the LAW, everyday cyclists banded together, flexing their political muscle in the name of bicycle-centric cities in general and "good roads" in particular. Unabash-edly, the Viking Cycling Club in Chicago signaled in its prospectus that "this club and its associates control 1,800 political votes and will sup-port those candidates favorable to wheelmen and wheeling."[16] Politicians needed no such reminder.

It was not just the cyclists themselves or newspaper men who recog-nized the influence of the wheelmen. In his annual report, the Commis-sioner of Public Roads in New Jersey said what had become obvious: "So great has become the number of wheelmen in all the States of the Union that their influence will, as in the past, be more strongly felt in the [State] Legislatures."[17] Statewide politicians often wrote to cycling clubs and local papers pledging their allegiance to the wheelmen. In 1897 San Francisco's mayor thought it wise to join the LAW, and in Chicago's mayoral race of the same year, Carter Harrison began his election bid by riding a "cen-tury" (a 100-mile ride) to prove his loyalty to the city's wheelmen.

Harrison was well aware of Chicago's powerful "wheelmen vote" and how to manipulate it. As an avid cyclist who credited riding with provid-ing a mental "sedative" and as a member of a local cycling club, Harri-son was reminiscent of many of the voters he sought to win over—a simi-larity that the son of a five-term Chicago mayor highlighted throughout his campaign. To launch his mayoral campaign, Harrison orchestrated a posed photograph, designed more to confer his reputation as a legiti-mate cyclist than to normalize his naturally narrow-set eyes or flaunt his well-groomed, pyramidal moustache (fig. 4.2). As Harrison later recalled, "What with the rakish cap, the old gray sweater and the string of eighteen pendant bars, I looked like a professional, a picture which I knew would carry weight with the vast army of Chicago wheelmen." Each of the pen-dant bars (likely engraved with details) represented a completed, long ride. Supporters proudly sported buttons featuring the photograph and hardly anyone could ignore the posters that were hung in store windows and plas-tered on walls across the city. Underneath the image of the mayoral candi-date ran the text of his campaign slogan: "Not the Champion Cyclist; But the Cyclists' Champion." Ultimately, Harrison won the election. To thank his cycling supporters, whom he credited with his victory, he fulfilled a campaign promise to lay a much-desired bicycle path.[18]

Throughout his five-term tenure, Harrison promoted cycling and the interests of cyclists, a fact that he reminded his cycling comrades of each election season. "I understand that among the candidates for the may-oralty I am the only wheelman," Harrison wooed. "Being a wheelman myself, I am cognizant of all the wheelmen's needs, and a glance back at

Fig. 4.2. Carter Harrison. Reproduced with permission from the Newberry Library, Chicago, Midwest MS Harrison, Carter H. Harrison IV Papers, box 17, folder 827.

the past two years during my occupancy of the mayor's chair will show that the wheelmen's interest have not suffered at my hands." He proceeded to list his accomplishments: improved roads (he listed road improvement as one of his favorite "hobbies"), road extensions, dry strips of asphalt (unsprinkled with water) for the cyclists' benefit, new cycle paths, and an epic battle with the streetcar operators that resulted in requiring new, more bicycle-friendly, rails to be used. His cycling supporters loved him for it. He is, one Chicago rider boasted, a "friend of the boys who wear knickerbockers." Another wrote, "Harrison.—May his tire never be punctured."[19]

Cyclists not only lobbied for road improvement; they also played a critical role in the road construction process itself. Oftentimes the cyclists proposed the paving of particular roads, found creative ways to fund the projects, and nearly always supervised (and often complained about) the construction. In July of 1897, the Roads Committee of the Associated Cycle Clubs of New York issued a map of the city's streets. The guide de-

Fig. 4.3. The role of the bicycle vote in Harrison's election even received the attention of satirists. The cartoon at the very top features Mayor Harrison and his bicycle surrounded by his two mayoral opponents who are desperately trying to learn how to ride, apparently a prerequisite for victory. The second cartoon features the three mayoral candidates racing toward the finish line of the "Mayor's Race." "With An Eye to the Wheelmen's Vote," *Chicago Wheelman*, March 29, 1899. Reproduced with permission from the Chicago History Museum.

tailed which streets had been paved and outlined the optimal routes for intracity travel. At least implicitly, the map also served as a trophy; the miles of smooth streets symbolized the cyclists' influence. According to a *New York Times* reporter, the Commissioner of the Department of Street Improvement "made nearly every improvement suggested by the [cycling] committee," rendering the city's wheelmen the "most constant and the most important factor" in road improvement. The list of public works projects ran several paragraphs long and cut across a giant swath of the city. The sudden increase in road-improvement construction derived from both city officials and city cyclists, who often coplanned future projects. As reported in New York in 1897, "improvements for cyclists in this city are scheduled on a large scale by the New York Consulate of the League of American Wheelmen." In concert with the city's Department of Public Works, the LAW's Committee on Streets and Highways outlined the necessary road improvement projects and jointly monitored road conditions. Even without an official role in the planning of public works, cyclists formed a boisterous body of street inspectors that civic leaders could hardly ignore.[20] One protest in 1896 highlighted the growing influence that cyclists exerted over the city's design, and its roads in particular.

Despite its trademark hills and cobblestone streets, San Francisco boasted a sizable bicycle population. Like cyclists in other cities, San Francisco's riders demanded that their city be redesigned according to their needs. Thoroughfares and parks, they petitioned, needed to be illuminated, traffic regulated, and streets widened, paved, and beautified. Perhaps most importantly, cable cars needed to be put in their place. The nemesis of many San Franciscan cyclists, cable cars imprinted onto the city a number of physical obstacles detrimental to cycling. Moving cable cars forced cyclists to dodge their way through the city, while miles of tracks made for unnavigable trips, frequent accidents, and plenty of ill will. In particular, cyclists rallied against the river of dormant tracks that remained only as a monument to a long-gone cable car franchise. Even though the tracks were no longer in use, if a company still owned the franchise, it still owned the tracks. More than a few cyclists believed that the cable car operators purposefully left the tracks on the streets in order to discourage cycling. Indeed, the remnant tracks, the space between the rails (often left unpaved), and "the slot" (the space in the road where an underground cable meets the grip of a cable car) caused perpetual headaches for cyclists and sometimes even serious accidents.[21]

In response, cyclists urged the city to remove the abandoned rail tracks and to pave or repave the most deplorable streets as part of an 1896 citywide campaign. For the cyclists, the two measures were one in the same since the cable car operators had been the chief impediment to the urban, "good roads" effort. The main battle in the war between San Francisco's transportation alternatives centered on Market Street, a primary artery and crowded thoroughfare in the heart of the fog-filled city. Cyclists argued that the Market Street Railway was to blame for the street's miserable condition. Pitted against their rival, San Francisco riders gathered together for a massive parade to protest against the encroaching cable car corporations, to demand better roads, and to demonstrate their growing might.

There may not have been another spectacle more prevalent in late-nineteenth-century urban America than the parade. Although parades had long been used as a way to visually express a set of ideas—be it patriotism, solidarity, or disgust—the frequency and scale of these urban street spectacles increased dramatically toward the end of the nineteenth century. Groups small and large in cities throughout the country coalesced along lines of mutual interest to put on imaginative performances designed to entertain as much as anything else. As cycling advocates used the public theater of the streets to dramatize their cause, bicycles became a conspicuous object in 1890s parades. Taking advantage of dramatic lighting, wheelmen and wheelwomen often favored parading through the moonlit city, celebrating an achievement, honoring an individual, or demonstrating their political will. Thousands of Chicagoans participated in three separate torchlight parades designed to express their dual support for the presidential candidate William McKinley and the principle of "sound money." In Brooklyn, riders communed for a celebratory procession thanking the City of Churches for finally paving a long-deteriorated street. And in Hartford, Connecticut, cycling paraders paid homage to their true hero: a steam street roller. Serving as the Grand Marshal of the 1896 Hartford parade, an illuminated "baby" steam street roller covered in red, white, and blue led a battalion of city cyclists in a triumphant march, celebrating the newly asphalted Main Street.[22]

Back in California, thousands of wheelmen and wheelwomen pedaled their way through downtown San Francisco with lanterns lighting their path, cruising past an estimated 100,000 spectators. The Union Iron Works Wheelmen, the Bay City Wheelmen, the Mail-Carriers' Cycling Club, the Ladies' Alpha Cycling Club, and about twenty-five other clubs joined an unwieldy group of "unattached" cyclists who managed to stay together despite the persistent interruption of oncoming cable cars. On the way to Market Street, the parade's final destination, bonfires raged, house lights flickered, and orators preached. Fireworks boomed in the distance. Despite its carnival atmosphere, the parade was about something much more. It was politics.

Funeral dirges played as the cycling paraders walked their machines across Market Street in protest to "mourn" the street's dilapidated condition. One float featured a hanging dummy and a verbal threat to any anti-good-roads politician. Another banner that read "We are looking for the man who objects to the repaving of Market Street" flapped above a collection of hearses. A few determined participants nearly started an all-out riot when they ripped up patches of wooden block pavement (widely acknowledged as a subpar paving material). Some of the wood found its way onto the cable car tracks, as did angry demonstrators determined to block traffic. According to reporters, when the cable cars approached the various obstacles, the mob engaged in "warfare." Protestors hurled objects through the windows and (unsuccessfully) attempted to flip the cars.[23]

Tensions finally simmered when a series of speakers addressed the raucous crowd. The president of the Cycle Board of Trade took the podium and recapped the rationale for the protest and the expected results:

> The objects of our demonstration as wheelmen are three-fold. Primarily, to educate us all to a realizing sense of our own strength and possible influence. Secondly, to rejoice with our South Side friends over the improvement of Folsom street; and lastly, to protest most vigorously against the condition of San Francisco pavements in general and Market street in particular. Similar demonstrations in sister cities have resulted in such an awakening of the public mind to public action that to-day the bicycle is conceded to be the greatest boon of modern invention, if for nothing more than for its accomplishments in the betterment of city streets and country roads. I trust that the objects of this demonstration are accomplished and that from to-night we may date a new era for San Francisco and her pavements.[24]

The speaker was right. Concessions to the cyclists came quickly. Market Street was repaved and the city launched new boulevard and bicycle path projects. San Francisco's cycling community had proven its fortitude.

Mass-transit operators and city cyclists clashed in other cities as well. In Philadelphia, streetcar operators responsible for paving and maintaining the streets surrounding their tracks often did so poorly in order to damage their "most formidable rival," critics surmised. In rare instances, streetcar companies actually did encourage paving projects—only when it hurt competing streetcar companies. Operators joined cyclists in championing asphalt paths, so long as they ran alongside their competitors' tracks and threatened only their businesses, a professor in 1897 reported.[25] In Chicago, too, cyclists and a streetcar operator fought over city space when a rail franchise sought the rights to place tracks on Jackson Street, a popular city street and cycling thoroughfare. In a sweeping protest, city cyclists demanded not only that Chicago aldermen table the plan to lay streetcar tracks but that they also transform Jackson Street into a bicycle-only boulevard. Protesters donned yellow ribbons inscribed with their demand: "Jackson Street must be boulevarded." City officials bowed to the masses and enacted the "yellow ribbon ordinance," transforming Jackson Street into a wheeling paradise. Cyclists in Buffalo did not fare so well. There city officials replaced asphalt with stone blocks on the space between the railway track and its periphery. When a Buffalo city engineer was asked whether or not the city's cyclists approved of such a seemingly anticycling measure he responded, "They do not pay the bills, so we do not allow them to dictate."[26]

Undeniably, most cyclists contributed nothing directly to the city budget. As independent vehicles, bicycles required no leases from the city but also no special infrastructure. The smooth asphalt that cyclists preferred benefitted other users of the street (although it could be slippery for horses). On the other hand, streetcar corporations paid handsome license fees in exchange for a lease on city roads and the freedom to operate with relatively few regulations. While the rise of the automobile is often seen as the driving force behind the decline of public transportation in the twentieth century—partly as a result of public policy that favored private transportation—it appears that in the 1890s, municipal governments often promoted privately run public transportation.[27]

Aside from changing the character of the road, street paving and construction remapped the city with promises of physical expansion and progress. As the cyclists helped lay the asphalt, they also laid the foundation for municipal growth. One illustrative example involved the development of the area surrounding New York's "Boulevard." As one contemporary described, the history of the Boulevard epitomized the development that came with paving:

> A few years ago Broadway disappeared in a kind of morass at Fifty-Ninth Street. From that point the "Boulevard" trailed its slimy length northward to nobody but the map-makers knew where, and, as far as the average New-Yorker was concerned, the Boulevard was a place of outer darkness. A few blocks of asphalt laid above Fifty-Ninth Street attracted the wheel-men, little shops began to appear, and people who came to watch the wheel-folk thronged the sidewalks . . . Then came the wonderful craze for the bicycle, which attacked rich and poor alike, and made the completion of the Boulevard pavement a public necessity. The rag-weed had to go, and from a howling wilderness the Boule-

vard in two years has become a beautiful parkway, with grass-plots and
flowers and gravelled [sic] walks.[28]

New roads precipitated changes in the city's physical structure and had
lasting effects that extended far beyond the smooth surfaces.

Paving and improving streets also served to boost civic pride. At a time
when the City Beautiful movement was in its nascent stages, Americans
recognized the value of beautifying the city, which in many cases started
with paving the streets. One contemporary commentator equated picturesque roads with a healthy city: "the sight of a smooth, even road that
winds along like a golden ribbon . . . brings the comforting thought to a
native that his people are happy and prosperous, that there is well being
where the road begins, where it ends and all along where it serpentines its
way." Likewise, in a sermon on the value of cycling, a clergyman averred
that "by laboring for good streets and roads" wheelmen can "contribute directly to the happiness of our fellow-men." Asphalt stretching across and
beyond the city center was to beautify both the city and its people. With
noiseless bicycles marching along silky roads "municipal greatness" and
"civic well being" awaited. As a municipal street engineer summed up,
"there is nothing which goes further to make a city attractive as a place
of residence, to foster a healthy public spirit and municipal pride . . . than
well paved streets." Or, put in even simpler terms, "mean streets make
mean people."[29]

Even after the creation of new roads, cyclists sought to ensure that
existing roads stayed in useable condition. When pavement deteriorated,
cyclists launched public campaigns demanding that their city's commissioner of public works repair roadways.[30] The Associated Cycle Club maintained such an influence inside Chicago's city hall that the Superintendent
of Streets gave them specially crafted postal cards. Each one contained a
printed form on which cyclists could record spots in need of repair. When
the postcards came in, municipal workers made the repairs *at once*," according to at least one wheelman.[31]

When a dearth of funds obviated a full-scale paving project, cyclists
succeeded in convincing city officials to develop imaginative mechanisms
to make the streets more accommodating to bicycles. Some engineers
carved street corners to round their hard edges, promoting easier travel for
cyclists. And in many cities, riders ensured that at least strips of asphalt
be laid on the roads. Running alongside the gutter (occasionally down the
center of the street), the ribbons of asphalt essentially served as bicycle
lanes; they provided a smooth shoulder on which cyclists could traverse

otherwise rocky streets. Cyclists glided along their narrow paths, their smooth mini street within the larger street, as the rest of traffic bobbed along the underfunded portion of the road. Cyclists would frequently determine the exact location of the strategically placed strips, including on Philadelphia's Broad Street and New York's Madison Avenue. They selected these specific locations in order to create as long a continuous path as possible, allowing cyclists to move around the city without ever having to ride on an unpaved surface. This network of asphalt proved so popular among cyclists in its city that the *Philadelphia Ledger* declared Broad Street nearly impossible for pedestrians to navigate. The LAW and the city's cycling community met relatively little resistance in their quest for these improvements, which were designed exclusively for cyclists. Like their brethren in Chicago, the New York wheelmen exercised such power that they even convinced the Health Board to restrict the Street Sprinkling Association from hosing down entire streets, which created a slick surface. Instead the board agreed to leave a three foot swath of asphalt dry for the safety and pleasure of cyclists.[32]

While wheelmen gained power within city halls, animosity towards cyclists lingered. Some city residents feared that by smoothing streets, their residential blocks would turn into cycling thoroughfares. Gone were the days of quiet blocks ideally suited for children playing in the afternoon sun or neighbors loitering under the cool moonlight, they feared. In one particular case in 1895, a group of panicked neighbors from Brooklyn petitioned the city's common council against laying asphalt on what had been a lightly trafficked street. "For the safety of our children who would not be menaced by additional travel of bicycles," they begged the city to leave the uneven cobblestones alone.[33]

On the whole, however, procycling advocates in the 1890s exhibited sizable influence. Thanks to the evolution of the science of road making, the availability of asphalt, and the voices of cyclists, nearly every city's roads improved in the 1890s; to be sure, the nature of that improvement varied from city to city and it is impossible to quantify how many of those roads would have been paved without the cyclists demanding them. Nevertheless, contemporaries saw a clear link between the increase of cyclists and the number of paved roads. Around the country, outside observers and government officials cited cyclists as the foremost source of the increase in road building and improvement. The *Milwaukee Journal* noted that the bicycle "has done and is doing a greater work for good common roads than any other agency, ancient or modern." It was not just cheerleading cyclists or exuberant journalists who gave cyclists credit. The San

Francisco Board of Supervisors acknowledged that it was the great army of cyclists that prompted the city to "provide the streets with smooth surfaces . . . ." Councilmen, aldermen, and supervisors in countless cities similarly credited the persistent demands of wheelmen as reasons to fund paving projects. For the Commissioner of City Works in Brooklyn, the link was so strong that when his office created a map detailing the city's as-phalted and macadamized roadways he titled the guide "Brooklyn's Bicy-cle Streets." Although the map symbolized much progress, he spelled out a number of future construction projects as part of his promise to improve the conditions for cycling in the city.[34]

By 1902, the paved roads in New York covered almost 1,800 miles, and within just the boroughs of Manhattan and the Bronx, the stretch of as-phalt roads increased by nearly 1,000 percent from 1890 to 1900. Washing-ton, DC, was commonly lauded as a "Paradise for Wheelmen" thanks to sharp improvements in road quality. Perhaps it is not surprising that the capital city, which would become the paragon for America's City Beau-tiful designs, boasted an impressive number of flat, tree-lined, asphalted streets. From 1884 to 1904 in Philadelphia, the percentage of roads quilted with cobblestones dropped from ninety-three to six, a statistic that reveals not only the preference for asphalt but also the sheer number of newly paved streets.[35]

When it came to improving highways outside of the city (a chief con-cern of touring cyclists), activists adopted a broader approach. For the LAW, Colonel Albert Pope, and others, improving city streets was central, but so was improving the roadways between major cities. Highways prom-ised to link a network of cities and to offer urban cyclists an escape to the countryside through rural, and previously disconnected, spaces. In the 1890s, recreational bicycle touring became a popular pastime and those riders depended on roads that extended outward from city centers. Hence it was cyclists who, the *Atlantic Monthly* noted, had incited a sudden "in-terest in the construction of highways which characterizes our time."[36]

Organized cyclists also formed a potent political lobby in the name of highway improvement. Starting in 1889, the LAW introduced a series of bills in the New York Legislature, calling for the creation of a state high-way commission and an appropriation of state monies to fund road build-ing and improvement. Despite selective support, including a State Senator who conducted his re-election campaign on a platform of road improve-ment, most of the measures failed. But after several attempts, the New York Legislature finally passed the Higbie-Armstrong Act in 1898, which created a framework for funding and building new roads. The bill laid the institutional groundwork to construct highways on a massive scale and was copied by cyclists in other states. The chief counsel of the LAW helped draft the bill and an assemblyman, whose only other bill mandated that railroads carry bicycles for free, introduced it.[37]

Throughout the 1890s the LAW also lobbied state legislatures to establish road-building agencies; at the national level it pushed for a federal highway system. Reluctant farmers often opposed such measures, fearing excessive taxes and loss of local authority. As one stubborn farmer put it, "It is them bicycle fellers that want the roads . . . you can't poke any of your newfangled notions into us farmers."[38] To convince the skeptical agrarians, the LAW launched a massive publicity campaign, promising their rural counterparts a healthier environment, faster delivery services, and a place on an ever-expanding cultural network.[39]

The allies of the good roads campaign began to see measurable results. Heeding a suggestion from Colonel Pope, the federal government established the Office of Road Inquiry (ORI) within the Department of Agriculture. Headed by an engineer and a noted cyclist, the ORI focused mainly on improving rural roads, conducting research regarding paving materials and road management, working with agricultural institutions, and publishing an array of materials regarding road construction. The LAW's influence on the ORI was remarkable. The LAW furnished the federal bureau with funding to promote the good roads campaign. It lent expertise in the science of road building, submitted examples of model legislation, and promised the backing of a powerful political lobby. The private organization of cyclists even paid for almost all of the costs to publish and disseminate the literature created under the public auspices of the ORI and the Department of Agriculture.[40]

On a smaller scale, the LAW continued to impact highway development by advocating for signposts. Cyclists anticipated that guide boards warning of dangerous conditions and identifying roads, directions, and distances between towns would ease intercity travel. At no cost to the state, the LAW offered to measure and certify the distances between towns. In several New England states the LAW secured laws mandating that townships erect signs at all major crossroads. With pride, wheelmen put up most of the signs themselves.[41] While the ORI and the efforts to improve highways constituted a campaign to reform rural roads for long-distance, touring cyclists, the good roads movement contained an important urban dimension. Members of the LAW and local cycling clubs, readers of *Good Roads* magazine, and the majority of those cyclists lobbying for better roads lived inside American cities. Surely they did not focus solely on improving roads dozens or hundreds of miles away from their homes.[42] Moreover, while a small portion of cyclists ventured across the country mounted on wheels, most did not. For the majority, the goal was simple: to make the city (and its immediate surroundings) friendlier to bicycles.

As the columns of trade magazines like *Municipal Engineering* revealed, large-scale public works projects or long-term plans to build for the future had to reckon with bicycles.[43] Nevertheless, the paving of highways and the large-scale transformation of urban streets, save the bicycle-friendly strips of asphalt, would have eventually occurred even without the vigorous army of cyclists. After all, massive road construction projects continued well after the bicycle's decline in popularity and influence. But the individual paving projects, the particular timing, the immense scope, and the specific streets chosen were shaped by the pleas of cyclists. Municipal improvement was an ongoing process and one that had to account for cyclists and their demands. It was no coincidence that as American cyclists gathered strength (both in numbers and political clout), street improvement projects redoubled. The truth is that bicycle ownership and the number of good roads rose in tandem; in part because of one another and, in part, not. Although not preferable, cyclists could travel over ill-paved terrain. Smooth asphalted streets came into being even in places where cyclists had not been the driving force. But once the roads were laid, they invited even more cyclists, who then began to demand even more improvements.

A recent book argues that Americans developed a dependence on cars because "the built environment all but require[d] them to do so."[44] The case for bicycles is much less clear. The relationship between the popularity of cycling and the infrastructure that promoted it was, on the whole, more symbiotic than causal. The ultimate reality was that bicycle traffic increased and more streets were paved. In the process, roads became roads—arteries for traffic.[45] Consequently, an old question resurfaced: Where should the cyclists ride?

CHAPTER FIVE

The Bicycle Paths (Not) Taken

Bicycle paths forever changed the landscape of the city and the bicycle's place within it. The then-radical notion of creating separate roadways just for cyclists signified the bicycle's growing footprint on the city map. Municipal governments considered the pathways as merely one element of a larger scheme to regulate and accommodate bicycles. In 1895 *Century Magazine* even predicted that such paths were the sign of a new era in city planning. In the future, "we may see in all our great cities lines of streets reserved for bicycles."[1]

Not everyone hoped for such an outcome. Not even all cyclists. The laying of bicycle paths caused sharp debate and hinted at some fundamental and long-lasting problems of trying to incorporate bicycles into (or in this case segregate them from) general traffic. The potential negative outcomes of creating "off road" spaces worried traditionalists, who reminded their fellow riders that bicycles were vehicles and belonged on the streets. Others jumped at the chance to build a network of convenient and safe bicycle roadways. The debate fractured the emergent bicycle coalition in the 1890s and, in some ways, continues to do so even today.[2]

The bicycle path movement emerged in the context of a turning point in urban transportation. With city streets carrying a diverse group of vehicles and with urban populations growing steadily, municipal governments reconceived how traffic should flow, often resulting in the separation of vehicles. By the middle of the nineteenth century, sidewalks facilitating urban pedestrianism were commonplace. And by the late nineteenth century, cities experimented with one-way boulevards, regulations designed to isolate heavy and light traffic, and trains that rode above or below the street. Bicycle paths represented yet another way to restructure traffic. In

Fig. 5.1. The narrow Exchange Street Bridge in Rochester, New York, could not accommodate cyclists, who were relegated to walking their machines on the footpath. Reproduced with permission from the collection of the Rochester Public Library Local History Division.

some cities bicycle paths came before comprehensive traffic regulation; in other cities they followed the reforms.

The "wheelways" served different functions in different cities. In dense, urban centers bicycle paths minimized traffic and offered a safer, alternative thoroughfare. Accidents involving bicycles, wagons, and pedestrians had become all too common.[3] In poorly paved cities, bicycle paths might have served as the only passable way between two points of interest. In other instances, the pathways performed the role of an expressway by which riders could escape the city center, often with an enticing natural landmark (a lake, a beach, a mountaintop vista, etc.) as its final destination. Not uncommonly, the paths ran inside city parks and on portions of existing boulevards, while others served as country roads for cyclists in rural areas.

Within and outside the city, paths occupied unique spaces. Sometimes they ran along the side of the road (thus commonly referred to as sidepaths) either between the sidewalks and the main road, beyond the sidewalks, or in place of sidewalks altogether. Some cities laid paths in the center of the roadway or in what may have been a grassy strip between two boulevards. In other places, the paths went where streets did not. They stretched across grass, dirt, and hills, charting new routes through and beyond the city. The paving surfaces ranged considerably and included asphalt, vitrified brick, stone, cinders, dirt, and gravel.[4]

The most significant bicycle path of the nineteenth century, the Coney Island Cycle Path in New York, epitomized the development of bicycle path construction and how cities came to accommodate their cyclists.[5] When plans for the path were finalized in 1894, the *New York Times* reported that "Brooklyn will probably have the first long stretch of wheelway ever built for the exclusive use of cyclists . . . Its natural advantages should make it the most attractive path in the world." The five-and-one-half-mile roadway, stretching from Brooklyn's Prospect Park to Coney Island, provided a majestic "straight run to the sea" and ran parallel to the existing Ocean Parkway, which suffered from spotty paving and catered to heavier vehicles. For the exclusive use of wheelmen, the new tree-shaded path connected two of Brooklyn's most prized treasures: its greatest park and the most famous seaside resort in the country (fig. 5.2).[6]

Desperate for what was (erroneously) heralded as America's first bicycle path, cyclists not only lobbied for the path's construction but also helped pay for it. At a meeting in which a Superintendent of the Parks expressed concerns about the estimated $1,000 per mile cost to lay the compacted gravel path, a group of leading cyclists huddled together and pledged to

Fig. 5.2. The Coney Island Cycle Path and Ocean Parkway, ca. 1894, before the path was complete. *Thirty-Fourth Annual Report of the Department of Parks of the City of Brooklyn* (1895), 9. Reproduced with permission from the Brooklyn Museum/Brooklyn Public Library, Brooklyn Collection.

raise $3,500. The wheelmen launched a frenzied campaign soliciting support throughout Brooklyn. With fundraising theater parties, and through the patronage of local cycling clubs, newspapers, and individual donors, the Coney Island Cycle Path Fund swelled well past its original goal. Construction commenced quickly. On a glorious Saturday afternoon in June 1895 an estimated twenty-five thousand cyclists wheeled their way across the country's newest attraction. The path enjoyed such great initial popularity that cyclists and city officials immediately began planning more paths in and around the city. Complaints about the dangers of riding over the Brooklyn Bridge led to a proposal for a separate bicycle path over the East River, and the New York Legislature seriously considered paving a forty mile bicycle route that would have hugged the old Croton aqueduct, from Croton Lake to the edges of Northern Manhattan. The mayor of Boston not only backed a plan to cut a bicycle path through Boston Common for commuting cyclists but also hoped to build his own version of the Coney Island Path. While some of these grand ideas never materialized, the network of bicycle paths that carpeted American cities in the 1890s would stand as the largest system of paths for many decades to come.[7]

By the late 1890s, Seattle's twelve miles of attractive, winding bicycle paths made it the envy of a group of city engineers from Oakland who wondered if they could build something similar. A city engineer in Seattle responded by explaining, in detail, how so many of the picturesque paths had been built. But the short answer was easy to understand: "private enterprise." One of Seattle's prominent cycling organizations, the Queen City Good Roads Club, footed most of the bill. The remaining portion came from the license fee levied on, and proposed by, the city's cyclists. The license fee, or bicycle tax, required all riders to register their vehicles and secure a license before accessing the paths. After covering the cost of license tags (to be conspicuously attached to the bicycle's front fork) and registration, all of the remaining money from the $1 per year bicycle tax was earmarked for the paths. Local cyclists in St. Paul and Minneapolis similarly spearheaded a successful movement to lay bicycle paths in and around the Twin Cities. Individual riders from St. Paul funded the majority of the seventeen miles of pathway that extended outward from its city. The network of paths reached Minneapolis, where that city's riders had laid their own bicycle path, thus creating an intercity network. They managed to do so with little municipal support.[8]

While many of the paths were used for intracity travel, a few connected neighboring cities. Certain activists called for a more regional approach to planning. One such proposal would have connected Baltimore to Washington, DC, via a forty-mile-long bicycle highway. The toll road backed by private money never materialized. Another project sought to link Chicago and Minneapolis with a 530-mile path, while yet another proposal included designs of a Manhattan to Ohio (via Buffalo) bicycle route. Even bolder proponents of bicycle paths championed a transcontinental bicycle road connecting San Francisco and New York. These visionaries planned well into the future, selecting routes based on population growth rates and modeling their profits on the ever-increasing populace of cyclists. In some regions, networks actually began to appear. In a single county in upstate New York, some 150 miles of paths were laid in just a few years, and by 1902 the entire state could claim roughly 2,000 miles of cycle paths.[9]

Advocates of these paths participated in an early form of regional planning at a time when such comprehensive schemes were few and far between. To facilitate tourism between cities and to accommodate adventurous cyclists, these bicycle superpaths promised speedier and safer travel; in some cases they simply made it possible to travel within a network of cities. Local organizations would be responsible for building paths extending outward from their city center until meeting up with a neighboring city's path. On a magnified scale, cyclists and city engineers dreamt of a national bicycle path system similar to the national highway system inaugurated in the 1950s. Crisscrossing paths would enable cyclists with the time, endurance, and will to access any major city in the country. They could easily tote their luggage with one of the many specially designed attachments on the market. In what was likely the world's first bicycle path convention, local groups from various cities sent representatives to Rochester, New York, to plan for such a network.[10]

An innovation largely unknown in the 1880s, bicycle paths began to unspool across American cities and were quickly projected to become as common as sidewalks and, soon, to even float in the air. In Chicago in 1897, cyclists tired of traffic and poor road conditions likely relished the proposal of an electrically illuminated "aerial bicycle highway." The elevated path was to stretch over existing elevated train tracks and to be paid for by the riders themselves. Supporters imagined it would provide speed, safety, and comfort to the ever-growing population of cyclists who could follow a continuous network of boulevards on the ground and paths in the sky, separated only by a quick ride in an elevator. Another group of investors in Chicago planned its own eight-mile elevated cycleway. Perched sixteen feet above the city's busy streets, the path was conceived especially for commuting cyclists. Regular riders would be given a discount on the proposed ten-cent fare. New Yorkers likewise talked about the prospect of an elevated cycle path, spanning the length of Manhattan.[11]

These grand designs for bicycle infrastructure might seem fantastic and, in reality, these futuristic structures that would cart wheelmen from one edge of the city to another rarely left the realm of imagination. One exception was an elevated bicycle path that sought to connect two cities on the West Coast. Anchored by Pasadena and Los Angeles, the nine miles of planked Oregon pine promised the tens of thousands of cyclists who lived in the two cities an easy escape to the country or a fast commute to their neighboring city. The originator of the elevated bicycle path idea, Horace Dobbins, a millionaire and cycling enthusiast, originally found little support for his implausible pet project. But the pace with which Californians adopted the bicycle convinced state legislators that interurban traffic, as much as intraurban traffic, demanded a more modern approach to planning. With estimates that Pasadena and Los Angeles would together house 100,000 cyclists in just a few years, a California state senator in 1897 acknowledged that "locomotion by bicycle is getting to be so general that it seems some provision must be made for the people who resort to it, and who are becoming more and more numerous." Consequently, he warned that the state needed to think proactively and "look forward to the time when we must prepare all our public roads and streets for the use of bicycles." In the interim, he supported the construction of the elevated path and championed a bill that allowed the California Cycle-Way to acquire property through eminent domain. Promoters of the Cycle-Way boasted that the first elevated bicycle path on Earth would spur commercial intercourse and function as a paragon for other metropolises grappling with an abundance of bicycles. They were wrong.[12]

On the first day of 1900, 1,000 cyclists celebrated the new century and the opening of a section of the Cycle-Way by forking over the ten-cent fare. Perched fifty feet above the ground at its apex and supposedly "strong enough to bear a service of trolley-cars," the path was built wide enough to accommodate four cyclists abreast; was illuminated by electric lights at 100-foot intervals; offered an expressway that was free of horses, dogs, and wagons; and provided unparalleled views of the scenic countryside. The Moorish-inspired terminal in Pasadena provided rental, repair, and storage services, while the Merlemont Park Casino, to be built midway and surrounded by lavish gardens, was to house cafes, reception rooms, a ladies' reading room, and a Swiss dairy. This luxurious rest stop promised cyclists a bucolic respite on their journey between the two cities or simply a destination for those wishing to escape the fog of urban life.[13]

Fig. 5.3. The California Cycle-Way, ca. 1900. Courtesy of the University of Southern California, on behalf of the USC Libraries Special Collections.

Fig. 5.4. Unlike California's Cycle-Way, which linked two urban centers, the proposed elevated bicycle path in New York was designed to serve cyclists within that city. The blueprint called for streecars on the ground level, elevated railroads above, and a bicycle-only path on the very top. Reprinted from *Review of Reviews*, June 1896.

Even though the path enjoyed an initial popularity, Dobbins began floating alternative, and more lucrative, uses for the right-of-way connecting Pasadena to Los Angeles. Within a few short years it became obvious that the pathway would never be finished. Railroad company executives, concerned about losing their customers to the Cycle-Way, brokered a deal

Fig. 5.5. A "Suggestion for Rapid Transit." Reprinted
from *Munsey's Magazine*, May 1896.

with Dobbins, killing the innovative project that was once dubbed a certain success. By 1907, with the speedway remaining only half built, a campaign to raze the existing portion began. In language signaling that the cycling city had died even faster than it was born, the Pasadena City Council
announced that the unpleasant "old landmark" would be removed.[14]

While the California Cycle-Way never fully materialized, many bicycle
paths on the ground did. The paths attracted new users but also caused fear
and dissention within the bicycle coalition. Some fretted that the bicycle
paths would lead to the bicycle's demise as a legitimate urban vehicle. Even
before the advent of the safety bicycle, cyclists had fought for the right to
use the street. Once successful, cyclists joined omnibuses and trolley cars
in transforming urban streets. Aside from being thruways, the streets had
once functioned as open-air markets, as places for pushcarts, as meeting
places, as walking paths for pedestrians, and as front yards in which to enjoy precious urban commodities: light and air. But by the end of the nineteenth century, city traffic, exacerbated by bicycles, put an end to the everyday street carnivals. The previously multifunctional street had become
more one dimensional, serving primarily as an artery for transportation.[15]

With the redefinition of the street, cyclists recognized the need to
classify bicycles as vehicles. Around the country cyclists succeeded and
secured their right to the road. But the issue of bicycle paths created a
double-edged sword that endangered the future of urban cycling. On one

hand, smooth pathways isolated from city traffic provided a safe and easy way to move about the city (and in the long run proved to be the most effective way to promote safety and encourage cycling). Yet other cyclists worried that the proliferation of cycling paths threatened the bicycle's legitimacy. These contrasting views erupted in an 1896 battle over Brooklyn's Ocean Parkway and the adjacent Coney Island Cycle Path.

Brooklyn park commissioner Timothy Woodruff expected a warm welcome from the city's wheelmen. After all, he had proposed adding to and improving the splendid path that brought Coney Island within easy reach of the city's riders. In less than a year after its completion, the greatest bicycle path in the world proved inadequate. With the original path well worn by a regular "human panorama" of riders, the initial expectation that the path would last at least a decade dimmed. One traffic count showed 32,000 riders used the path on a single day and contemporary accounts often estimated that between 25,000 and 30,000 riders regularly used the path, meaning close to three percent of the borough's entire population could be found on this single stretch. (The per capita equivalent in Brooklyn today would amount to roughly 75,000 riders.) To alleviate congestion on the path, Woodruff agreed to pave a "return path," which promised cyclists two separate one-way paths to and from the shore. But his proposal came with a caveat. It stipulated that cyclists must ride exclusively on the pathway and not on the adjacent parkway. Brooklyn cyclists lauded the path as a great asset and the vast majority of riders used the pathway instead of the crowded street anyway. However, a few cyclists looked past the promise of a new cycle path. A senior member of the LAW denounced the ordinance as illegal and "absurd," and the LAW's Rights and Privileges Committee put out an official statement lambasting Woodruff for setting "a bad precedent" by violating "the plain intent and meaning of the Liberty bill, which is the greatest safeguard of the wheelmen." According to that bill, no local authority could exclude cyclists from any roadway in the state, the LAW reminded Woodruff.[16]

Similar debates arose in San Francisco where the Golden Gate Park Commissioners authorized the construction of bicycle paths simultaneous to issuing a mandate that riders use only the paths and avoid the main drives. The local LAW division in San Francisco followed their East Coast brethren in protest on the grounds that bicycles, defined as vehicles, could not be prohibited from the streets. In Cleveland, too, cyclists lobbied against a new bicycle path that would have rendered an adjacent mixed-use boulevard a bicycle-prohibited roadway. And in Manhattan, certain cy-

Fig. 5.6. This illustration reveals how traffic was separated on Riverside Drive in
Manhattan, before the cycle path was built. Pedestrians walked on the outer edges,
others lingered on the generous bridle path (second from the left), saddled horses
trotted on their own path (third from the left), and bicycles and carriages rode
on a boulevard split for traffic heading north and south. In 1897 the bridle path
was turned into a cycle path. Reprinted from *Munsey's Magazine*, May 1896.

clists criticized the cycle path on Riverside Drive because it crowded out
pedestrians (and the many who enjoying sitting with "bicycles rolling by
at [their] feet"), ran counter to the principles of the good roads movement,
and was unnecessary since the boulevard was ample enough to accommodate everyone (fig. 5.6).[17]

Across the river in Brooklyn, Commissioner Woodruff defended the
two bicycle paths adjacent to the road, sixteen and eighteen feet wide respectively, as mere extensions of the roadway. Woodruff maintained that
he was simply separating traffic, with lighter vehicles relegated to the
far right (the paths).[18] Considering that a row of trees and a bed of grass
separated the pathway from the main boulevard, people had good reason
to construe the park commissioner's plan as either smartly progressive or
very illogical.

Most critically, the Ocean Parkway/Coney Island Cycle Path debate
began to splinter the once-unified political coalition of wheelmen. Most
cyclists supported the path. The prospect of more wide, paved pathways
exclusively for their use was certainly an attractive one. Some, including
members of the LAW, were so appreciative that they not only supported

the measure but also agreed to serve as part of a special cycling police corps charged with enforcing the new ordinance. But selective opposition reverberated inside the Litchfield Mansion where Commissioner Woodruff later swore in the rookie mounted policemen. Alex Schwalbach, an outspoken doyen of the wheelmen, denounced the ordinance as illegal. In a confrontation with the park commissioner, Schwalbach praised the bicycle path but emphasized that cyclists had a right to the highway, regardless of whether any paths existed. In a testy battle of words, the commissioner insinuated that the bicycle path improvements might be called off if wheelmen persisted to protest the ban on parkway riding. The crowd screamed "No, no." Schwalbach could not be persuaded. "Wheelmen have a right to the main driveway and we will have the privilege of going there even if we have to give up the cycle path," he insisted. For Schwalbach the issue was not about comfort or safety. It was about legitimacy. He contended that the bicycle had a right to the road and any attempts to separate bicycle traffic, even those ordinances packaged as procycling, endangered the bicycle's future.[19]

The Good Roads Association, of which Schwalbach was the first vice president, took immediate action to distance itself from its renegade leader. Members decided to relocate their upcoming executive meeting somewhere other than Schwalbach's popular riding academy. The organization, which counted Brooklyn's mayor, comptroller, and commissioner of public works as members, effectively boycotted one of its leading members in what the cycling community saw as a clear "slap" to the man who jeopardized the glorious pathway. In addition, the Good Roads Association president, Albert Angell, publicly diverged from Schwalbach and backed the Brooklyn park commissioner's decision to bar bicycles from the main drive. As he saw it, "If [the commissioner] has the right to give us the exclusive use of the cycle paths, he has the right to give other pleasure vehicles the exclusive use of the main driveway. If one is illegal, both are, and I doubt if the wheelmen generally will approve the action of any one who attacks the legality of the cycle paths, and that's just what it amounts to."[20]

Despite the support of the Good Roads Association, opposition to the Woodruff proposal intensified. The Committee on Streets and Highways of the LAW's New York Division warned that granting exclusive rights to a road (or path) was something that it had fought hard against and, on ideological grounds, refused to support. Isaac Potter, an officer and future president of the LAW who had once authored a lengthy treatise on the mechanics of planning, building, and maintaining bicycle paths, now became one of the path's most tireless opponents.[21]

The road to legitimacy required that bicycles be classed and regulated like all other urban vehicles, cyclists had once argued. The LAW, Colonel Pope, and countless organized and unattached cyclists had focused their efforts on lobbying lawmakers to define the bicycle as a vehicle, in the same manner as the carriage. They then opposed city ordinances requiring cyclists to carry lamps, bells, or register their vehicles, not on the grounds that the restrictions were too prohibitive but rather because they were not equally applied to all types of vehicles. Emblematic of the hypocrisy evident in the push for bicycle paths, a band of cyclists instigated a campaign to replace the horse bridle path in Central Park with a cycle path.[22] It was not too long before when cyclists were altogether barred from those same grounds. The seemingly endless, and sometimes conflicting, demands of the wheelmen did not go unnoticed. An 1899 news article declared:

> By constantly demanding they (wheelmen) make not only themselves but their cause unpopular . . . At first it was against the law to ride it in the streets at all . . . then its use was restricted in the parks, at the request of the horsemen, who are now in a ridiculous minority as compared to the wheelmen . . . when these restraints were removed and the same right to the streets and roadways was given to the bicycles that is given to other vehicles, the wheelmen requested still further privileges; they wanted special paths, and they wanted to ride on the sidewalks.[23]

Cyclists had as difficult a time figuring out the bicycle's rightful place in the city as anybody else.

In the end, and despite the selected opposition, Commissioner Woodruff enacted a comprehensive set of eighteen ordinances regulating vehicular traffic in Prospect Park and on the Coney Island Cycle Path. Rule number eight dictated that cyclists use the bicycle path exclusively. Riding on the parkway was cause for arrest.

While this path and others gave urban cyclists exclusive roads for travel in and out of the city, they began to further separate, physically and conceptually, bicycles from other traffic. Once considered a toy for childish adults (and which would ultimately become a plaything for children), the bicycle enjoyed, for a brief period in the 1890s, multiple constructions. Among them was the status of legitimate vehicle, moving through the city, serving commercial functions, and providing a primary mode of transportation for city residents. In 1896, a reporter for *Scientific American* jubilantly, but mistakenly, proclaimed that the bicycle had "once and forever" moved "out of the arena of mere pastime, and [had] established its economic value as a reliable means of transportation."[24] But by offering riders a separate path, the city and its cyclists accepted the fact that perhaps bicycles did not belong on the streets and, at least implicitly, endorsed the idea that bicycles belonged on the isolated pleasure paths where casual riders could enjoy their toys. The championship of bicycle-only roads also undermined the legal doctrine at the very heart of the rationale that cyclists applied over and over again: bicycles are just like any other urban vehicle. Yet on the pathways the men and women who cruised atop their light frames validated the theory that bicycles were somehow different from the assortment of vehicles that traversed the roads. As one avid cyclist predicted in an 1896 editorial, bicycle paths "will be the means of segregating the wheelmen into an exclusive, and I fear odious, class."[25] Cyclists had good reason to be worried, as cycling would indeed regain its pastime status.

Others grew concerned that the bicycle path movement disenchanted important allies. In the campaign for good roads, cyclists boasted about the universal benefits of smooth pavements. Since teamsters, farmers, merchants, consumers, urbanites, and country folk all stood to gain from improving road conditions, cyclists solicited these interest groups to join the good roads coalition. Indeed, by advocating for improved road conditions, cycling advocates made friends more easily (although still not that easily) than they did by pushing for standalone bicycle paths. With their demands echoing louder than ever, noncyclists moaned "that the wheelmen want the earth." Even some procycling organizations argued that the bicycle path movement cannibalized the good roads movement and was "essentially selfish in motive." When a division of the LAW spoke out against bicycle paths, it lobbied instead for "good roads, which must prove a benefit alike to all classes of citizens." But they faced an uphill battle, considering that the majority of riders pushed the LAW to focus on laying bicycle paths, which could be laid cheaply and for their exclusive use.[26] Fragmenting the delicate and—what would prove to be—ephemeral alliance of cyclists and those noncyclists who supported good roads proved costly in the near term.

Regardless of politics, back in Brooklyn, the bulk of local cyclists welcomed the new path, along with the 108 linear feet of bicycle racks; 460 linear feet of benches, shelters, and bathrooms; shaded rendezvous points;

and water fountains all built just for them. Wheelmen and wheelwomen could enjoy the Flower Garden Shelter by parking their machines anywhere along the abutting thirty-foot bicycle rack. In the summer, riders visiting the music pavilion could valet their wheels, and in the winter, park officials enclosed one of the open-air cycling shelters to provide a cozy space for riders. No matter the season, adjacent roadhouses and taverns offered cyclists food, drink, and a boy to look after their wheels. In fact, so many riders enjoyed the path that tens of thousands of local wheelmen participated in a parade thanking the commissioner, who was tapped as the Republican candidate for lieutenant governor (he would serve three terms in this role, including under Theodore Roosevelt) for his work on behalf of cyclists.

With the total spectators numbering upwards of 100,000, the *New York Journal*, in its usual hyperbolic tone, reported that "all the wheelmen in Brooklyn, or nearly all, passed in review before him and cheered him until those who loved him doubted that they had ever done him full justice." Quite simply, the splendor of the paths overshadowed the ban on parkway riding.[27]

Despite all of the debates, many cyclists continued to lobby and pay for additional paths, and many delighted in their accomplishments and the city's accommodation of their wheels. Voices of protest, including those from within the LAW, which by 1900 devoted considerable resources toward the bicycle path movement, quietly ebbed. From 1895 (when the Coney Island Cycle Path opened) to the turn of the century, Chicago, San Francisco, Los Angeles, Seattle, St. Louis, and nearly every other city of considerable size built bicycle paths. In Minneapolis, the city engineer measured thirty-five miles of bicycle paths within the city limits by 1900; Denver was home to a fifty-mile path leading out of the city; Portland claimed an impressive fifty-nine miles inside its boundaries; and by 1902, St. Paul's cyclists found 115 miles of paths on which to ride. By then the paths emanating outward from Rochester gave its wheelmen and wheelwomen access to rolling hills, nearby towns, and suburbs, and totaled an impressive 205 miles. That number is not quite what Amsterdam or Copenhagen boast today (roughly 280 miles and 220 miles, respectively), but, at the time, the bicycle path networks in these American cities were among the largest in the world. Today Amsterdam is widely known as having among the best bicycle infrastructure of any city. It has about one mile of bicycle path for every 2,900 people—a ratio that fits in between that of 1900 Portland (one mile for every 1,500 people) and 1900 Minneapolis (one mile for every 5,800 people). There are, of course, other factors. Population density and the shape and size of the city affect the need for and layout of paths. But the fact that even some American cities in the 1890s can compare favorably to current cycling meccas is noteworthy.[28]

As impressive as bicycle-path building was, it could have gone a lot further. Ample evidence suggests that municipal governments did not go far enough to secure these paths and, therefore, the future of urban cycling. Although city governments legitimized the bicycle as a vehicle in the 1890s, many of the reforms stemmed from an era in which local interest groups and private citizens exerted significant influence in municipal planning. "The city was neither ruled by a single power elite, nor by a genteel, patrician, or merely rich upper class." The middle classes "influenced decisions directly, through a variety of increasingly effective organizations, including several political machines and a variety of special-interest groups, and indirectly, through their votes, petitions, demonstrations, strikes, and boycotts."[29] As just one example, the League of American Wheelmen, in concert with local cycling clubs, emerged as a powerful political coalition and as one of the most vocal lobbying groups in American cities. Even though their voices have since gone unheard by most historians, they represented a viable and potent political faction in the 1890s. Mayors, aldermen, and even the president of the country recognized the growing army of cyclists, who effectively lobbied for better roads, friendlier traffic laws, and municipal ordinances. When local governments failed to go far enough, cyclists, perhaps to their own detriment, often took matters into their own hands.

In the 1890s and early 1900s, municipal governments often saw transportation as an avenue for profit, and their plans were as much about making money as improving transportation. Streetcars and trolleys, which paid for their rights to operate, expanded their reach at the invitation of municipal governments. Bicycles offered municipalities few potential revenue streams. Cyclists had spearheaded the two movements to pave and/or build new roads and to lay bicycle paths. The former benefitted the entire urban population, while the latter served only cyclists. Both had their benefits, though neither yielded direct monies for the city.[30]

So the bicycle paths that sprouted across the nation, promising to bring the country closer to the city, to make the city more navigable, and to connect distant cities, were more often paved by groups of cyclists or private capitalists than by local government. Even when the government, city or state, became involved, it was still a model that depended on significant private investment. America's first significant bicycle path linking Coney Island and Prospect Park in Brooklyn was originally funded by donations from cyclists. Riders in Seattle, St. Paul, and Minneapolis raised money for, oversaw the construction of, and helped to police their own paths. In St. Louis the daily paper sponsored its city's bicycle path in 1896 by collecting subscriptions from its readers. And the quixotic plan for an elevated bicycle path connecting Pasadena with Los Angeles, just like the would-be bicycle highway between Baltimore and Washington, DC, foundered in the hands of individual capitalists. Bicycle paths remained in the hands of private enterprise and, as one reporter noted in 1900, "received so little recognition by highway authorities." Local cyclists and their city governments brokered deals and forged compromises to lay paths and asphalt specific streets. But the results were patchwork. In certain cities, or in certain parts of cities (where wheelmen exerted the greatest influence), they could promise votes or simply pay for the improvements themselves. The consequence was often half-baked projects like the California Cycle-Way. With its true mission to produce dividends and not to improve transportation or facilitate recreation, the California Cycle-Way, like so many other grand proposals, failed. When bicycle interest waned, capitalists lost interest, and the projects suffered mightily.[31]

In the nineteenth century, to accommodate the growing population of urban cyclists, cities engaged in bicycle-friendly urban planning (at least relatively), in an age when terms like "greenways" and "eco-friendly" were still decades away and at a time when the word "green" almost always simply referred to the color. They also did so at a time in which a motley collection of engineers, politicians, reformers, businessmen, and laypeople planned and reshaped America's cities. Modern urban planning was a twentieth-century invention. By all accounts, there were no professional planners. There were no trade journals. No one held a professional degree in urban planning.[32] Consequently, with a hodgepodge of competing interests and urban infrastructure developing in piecemeal fashion, particular interest groups, including cyclists, often exerted disproportionate influence over a singular set of planning concerns. Representing a wide range of interests, urban power brokers wrestled for control in city after city.

Perhaps the truest picture of the distribution of power rests in the historical city itself. By examining its concrete elements, we can discover abounding evidence about its builders. The landscape of the late nineteenth-century American city provides a historical canvas that can reveal its context.[33] The newly paved roads and boulevards, the small strips of asphalt laid for cyclists, the bicycle-only pathways, and the rewritten traffic laws represented only the most tangible monuments of the cyclists' efforts. With populations numbering the tens of thousands in many cities and the hundreds of thousands in the largest cities, with strong organizational support and leadership, with a powerful political lobby, and with the pluck to protest, parade, and boycott, urban cyclists were responsible for these physical changes. Without professional urban planners, individual riders, cycling entrepreneurs, and cycling clubs coalesced into a powerful special-interest group that influenced the design of American cities and, in the process, crafted a city that came to accommodate and promote cycling. But with the debate about bicycle paths, the long campaign to promote bicycles as legitimate urban vehicles suddenly took a step backwards and fractured the newly formed bicycle coalition. Certainly, even more paths would have been built had it not been for the strong opposition within the ranks of cyclists. While those cyclists who predicted the problems of segregating bicycle traffic were spot on, in the grand scheme they were misguided. What they did not know was that it would be the paths that would literally pave the way for future cycling cities. The paths, not the streets, came to define the cities that cyclists called home in the twentieth and twenty-first centuries.[34]

In all, though, the paths served as but one piece of a larger network designed by activists to accommodate and promote bicycle use. These visionaries had only begun (or so they thought) to reconceive the city along these lines. Their vision of the future city, shared by a legion of enthusiasts, everyday riders, lawmakers, and engineers, was nothing short of utopian. And dead wrong.

CHAPTER SIX

Riding for Recreation and Health

Honestly, the bicycle has done more for the good of the human race than all the medicines compounded since the days of Hippocrates.
—*The Journal of Hygiene*, November 1896

Biffers—Do you think bicycle riding conducive to health?
Whiffers—Most assuredly. My health has improved wonderfully.
   "But you don't ride a bicycle."
   "Who said I did?"
   "But you said bicycle riding improved your health."
   "Yes; get so much exercise you, know."
   "Exercise? How?"
   "Dodging the bicycles."
—*New-York Weekly*, 1894

In the 1890s, the American city was a promised land. Millions flocked to urban centers, leaving Europe, the Jim Crow South, and the American countryside in their dust for a world supposedly filled with jobs, absent of discrimination, and infused with vitality. In the final three decades of the nineteenth century alone, the urban population living within the ten largest US cities doubled. Upon arrival, however, urban transplants often experienced something short of a fairy tale. Cities stank and rang with noise. Ugly buildings sat sandwiched between fouled streets and polluted skies. People squashed into tenements, neighborhoods, and entire cities, even as population growth and metropolitan consolidation pushed municipal boundaries farther from the urban nucleus. Urban life offered the best and worst of humanity. Millions of inhabitants living and working in an area circumscribed by mere miles created a culture that promoted efficiencies

of economy and capital, enhanced social opportunities, and fostered inge-
nuity, as easily as it invited vice and pollution. As the twentieth century
approached, it was the evils of urban living that earned American cities
their reputation for chaos and disorder; for dirtiness and dangerousness;
and for their impoverished, uneducated, and uncouth inhabitants who
seemed to comprise an ever-growing proportion of the population.[1]

Reformers imagined a different kind of city. Libraries would educate
and welfare institutions would reform the troubled population. Political
corruption would be rooted out by a new system of municipal management defined by efficiency and run by disinterested experts. Perhaps no
issue, though, was more important than improving the health of the city
and its residents. Towards the end of the nineteenth century, professional
health departments finally became an official organ of municipal governments. Journals and national associations devoted to the rising number of
sanitarians grew in numbers and prominence. They, along with engineers,
doctors, and city improvers, exposed the dangers of urban living and began
to espouse a number of remedies. Armed by a new philosophy of moral
environmentalism, reformers sought to recast America's cities into beautiful, ordered spaces that would promote harmony. Most famously, supporters of the "City Beautiful" movement, as it later came to be known,
favored Beaux-Arts architecture, classical design, and civic monuments
meant to inspire. The grand, tree-lined boulevards that urban cyclists
enjoyed symbolized this powerful new dogma. Supporters assumed that
the boulevards, like the obelisks, monuments, oversized civic spaces, and
arresting architecture that embodied the movement, would awe and uplift city dwellers, but, for a growing group of reformers, it was nature that
could provide the cure-all for the ugliest of urban behaviors.[2]

Reformers also celebrated science, machines, innovation, and modernization. They turned to modern technology for answers to modern
problems.[3] To cast the utopian blueprint of the twentieth-century city
into reality, bicycles—perhaps the most representative symbol of the new
middle-class obsession with nature, exercise, and recreation—played a
vital part. By bringing nature squarely within the urban realm, by promoting physical exercise, and by contributing to broader environmental
reform, bicycles appeared to solve one of the biggest problems affecting
American cities and the people who filled them.

Recreational cyclists included an array of people cycling for a variety of
reasons. Many of those who joined cycling clubs did so for the leisure opportunities and social status that came with it. Whether a club member or

not, cyclists enjoyed roaming through the parks and down the boulevards for pleasure, an excuse to get outside and to promenade. Not everyone, though, participated equally. Doctors and reformers tended to be far more worried about the toll that urban life took on middle-class professionals who spent their workdays holed up in offices. They lacked access to the outdoors and needed exercise and a mental break in ways that manual laborers supposedly did not. As a poem published in 1896 (as part of a 150-page compendium of poems all devoted to cycling) highlighted, it was the "white-faced office boys" and "care-worn city clerks" who fled the city on bicycles.[4] These riders constituted the majority of cyclists, and while they rode for many reasons, perhaps none was more important than health— physical and mental.

ESCAPE

Nineteenth-century Americans were well aware of the seemingly impenetrable boundaries that separated urbanity and rurality. In 1880 the American psychologist G. Stanley Hall found that the majority of Boston's primary-school-age students had "never seen a plow or spade, a robin, squirrel, snail or sheep; they had never observed peaches on a tree or growing grain and could not distinguish an oak tree from a willow or poplar." That the majority of urban residents, children and adults, had become alienated from nature and that the city environment seemed to lack all of the salutary features of a pastoral life—wildlife, clean air and water, ample space, and natural beauty—signaled alarm. In response, certain school administrators touted the bicycle as an educational tool and as a way to broaden the limited experiences of the urban population. For the kinds of students whom Hall had surveyed, there was "no better way of teaching how wide and varied the world is, than to let them begin their exploration and investigation near their homes" atop a bicycle. Bicycle trips for school-age children and, even more so for adults, brought an environment antithetical to that of the city within convenient reach.[5]

Much earlier in the nineteenth century, and long before bicycles arrived in serious numbers, Americans had participated in recreation and physical activities within the urban core. The walking city had ample room for sporting activities and even the hinterlands were not so distant. Yet, by the end of the nineteenth century, the largest American cities housed more than a million densely packed people, buildings that reached toward the sky, and fringes that seemed to be continually swallowed up by ever-expanding metropolises. The previously "empty spaces were filled in [and] the countryside became less accessible to the masses . . . making sporting options unevenly available to urban populations."[6]

Urban Americans surrounded by artificialities, machines, and industrial order developed a new appreciation for nature in the late nineteenth century. In 1896, a writer articulated this new perspective: "It will be admitted that the conditions of life in cities are not conducive to health or morality; that rest and recreation must be found outside; that we, as people are getting too far away from Nature and her teachings and live too much in the forced atmosphere of a social hothouse."[7] Thus meadows, mountains, rivers, and rocks could provide therapeutic solace and simple pleasure wholly absent from the urban sphere.

The popularity of the back-to-nature movement evinced itself in various ways. Toward the end of the nineteenth century, Britain's Sir Ebenezer Howard found an eager and transnational audience for his version of a utopian community—"the Garden City." The most distinguishing feature of these planned, self-sufficient, small-scale communities was that rings of nature (or green belts) would surround the "garden city" and reconnect its residents with the natural world. Novelists and journalists glorified the country too, as magazines and newspapers devoted to out-of-door activities flooded urban newsstands. In 1890, Congress established Yosemite and Sequoia National Parks. Rural America developed into a kind of mental and physical "playground," offering space for the body to ramble and the mind to roam. While some of the curative attributes of nature and recreation had long been lauded as valuable and had already served as the impetus for the rural cemetery movement and the expansion of urban parks, the back-to-nature movement intensified in the late nineteenth century. More importantly, it moved out of the exclusive domain of the wealthy and became an obsession for many in the urban middle class. The countryside was glorified. And it was atop bicycles that crowds of urban worshippers flocked to the temple of nature.[8]

Contemporary cyclists and writers marveled at the machine's ability to shrink what had been a vast gap between two diverse worlds. Described in an 1895 article published in the *Century Magazine*, the cycling phenomenon promised to "bring the city and the country into closer relations." Urban wheelmen and wheelwomen exploring the countryside toted with them "modern ideas and modern ways of living, and . . . gentle distillations of city wealth," while the natural beauty of the countryside returned a set of calmer, healthier, and rejuvenated riders back to the city. In 1896, another advocate described the bicycle as "a distance destroyer. It brings city and country close together and places 'green fields and running brooks' where once there were but smoky walls and a heavy atmosphere." The two worlds of city and country no longer seemed so distant or distinct. Once outside the city, cyclists could enjoy all of the sights so noticeably absent from their quotidian routine. In particular, cyclists sought out the vistas and scents, the flowers and wildlife, the most natural of wonders that could no longer be found inside manmade cities.[9] One cyclist described these goals and the unparalleled experiences of venturing out of the city atop two wheels:

> Just now, while the primeval woods are looking for the coming leaf-time, when the brooks that have been long hidden are gleaming in the light, when the cattle are lowing in the meadows, and glad with the first day of liberty my wheel and I have beautiful times together. We are at home in our world. And when we are off together, miles and miles from town, and the air is crisp and tonic, the sunlight a genial friend, when I am spinning over the rough country road with the blood bounding through my veins, with every pore of the skin alert, and with the heart alive; when the swift motion carries me on like a thing of wings, and the exhilaration fills me with a sense of exultant power, then it seems that the wheel is well worth living for, and makes all life richer.[10]

In short, by promising to bring down the invisible walls that encased most American cities, bicycles attracted the masses, while reconfiguring the ever-changing dynamic between crowded cities and the relatively open spaces that surrounded them.

Although the bicycle afforded a new kind of independence and mobility unrivaled by other forms of transportation, many cyclists depended on several forms of transportation for longer trips. Cyclists might take a ferry or railroad to a distant location where they could then ride around an exotic place that might have been unreachable by bicycle.[11] Since bicycles were relatively lightweight, riders could easily carry them on boats and trains. This practice was so popular that on one Sunday in 1896 some 38,000 cyclists boarded ferries leaving Manhattan for a ride out in the country. Over the course of a three-and-one-half-hour window on a Saturday in July 1897, the Long Island Railroad reported that it carried 20,000 New Yorkers out to Long Island, 25 percent of whom brought their bicycles.[12]

Of course, railroads and other modes of public transportation connected the city to the country, but the bicycle provided a unique form of spatial flexibility. With a map in hand and with no fixed schedule or special fare, an individual cyclist or a small group of riders could leave the city with few preparations and even fewer plans. Late-nineteenth-century cyclists repeatedly referred to the "liberation" and "freedom" provided by the bicycle. Others had similarly praised the railroad for promoting liberty by enhancing mobility, but the nature and size of the railroads, the mega-corporations behind the operations, and the fixed tracks and schedules made users feel more like dependents. Writing in 1900, one urban cyclist recounted, "there is something incomparably cheering in the conscious-ness that by one's own exertions, and at one's own gait and time, one is leaving the toil and moil and torment of the town farther and farther in the distance." Without the thunder of the railroads and the crowds of pub-lic transportation, bicycles served as the only way to lose oneself in the splendor of nature, or so the most devoted riders reported. On a whim a cyclist could ride to the neighboring suburbs or countryside on the week-end or after work. "A little oil in the bearings, perhaps a few strokes of the inflator, a turn of the screw of the gear-case, stride over the saddle, and off you go!" Another avid cyclist described it: "You have no time-tables to conform to, and, with your baggage all on your wheel, you can change plans at a moment's notice. You can go where the tourists seldom go and stop where they never stop." There was something more personal about touring via the bicycle. Riders could enjoy a closeness with the places they visited that was simply inconceivable from looking out the window of a moving train. Cyclists valued that the bicycle afforded an unrivaled inti-macy with nature and an unrivaled mode of personal transport.[13]

This newfound independent mobility allowed city residents the possi-bilities of a segregated life: a workday in the chaotic, polluted city, and an evening or weekend of leisure spent in the unadulterated country air. For many, the latter made the former more bearable. Not long after returning from work, urban riders fled the city under dim-lit skies, looking for the fastest exit. One commentator astutely observed that it always seemed as though the "first aim" of urban cyclists was to "escape from the crowded part of the city," presumably in search of a contrary, nonurban landscape.[14] To aid these explorers, an entire industry developed, offering cycling maps, guidebooks, suggested routes, coveted tips, and almost always suggestions for how cyclists could most quickly exit the city.[15]

The phenomenon was widespread across America's largest cities. In no small part because of the bicycle path leading to its shores, Coney Is-land regularly welcomed throngs of city cyclists (fig. 6.1). There, dozens of shops offered to repair, clean, and check visitors' wheels, as riders from Manhattan and throughout Brooklyn waded into the ocean or napped

Fig. 6.1. A group of cyclists gathered on the beach at Coney Island, New York, in 1897. Reproduced with permission from the Museum of the City of New York.

along the oversized beach. Day-tripping (or often evening-tripping) cyclists in Coney Island became so numerous that the business of valeting bicycles turned into heated competition. The proprietors of the Albert & Rawlins shop promised to outdo their rivals by offering cycling customers a free cleaning and a guarantee (up to $100) that their bicycles would remain safe under their watch. Other businesses, including taverns, restaurants, and repair shops, soon began wooing, and catering to, the growing group of recreational riders. Eager to attract customers, one hotel proudly advertised that it paid special attention to "cyclists cuisine."[16]

In San Francisco as well, newspapers published bicycle routes that highlighted the most direct pathways to escape urban life. While railway cars offered San Franciscans a chance to espy the magnificence of Marin or the placid waters of nearby Lake Chabot, a reporter from the *San Francisco Call* advised his readers in 1897 that only the bicycle ensured a truly intimate experience, that "You must get close to nature's heart if you would feel it beat." Likewise, in Philadelphia, thousands rode each weekend to neighboring "country places" and in Chicago to nearby lakes and vistas, which transformed into backdrops for cycling parties and even cycling picnics.[17]

Fig. 6.2. "A Bicycle Picnic Party." Reprinted from *Munsey's Magazine*, May 1896.

Perhaps no activity is more emblematic of the kind of pastoral oasis that urban cyclists sought than the bicycle picnic (fig. 6.2). When the sun shone and the winds eased, groups of cyclists fled the chaos of Chicago on trips that could measure fifty miles. Riding across flat country roads, cyclists could pause and slake their thirst at one of the quaint farmhouses that ringed the city. As a veteran wheelwoman from Chicago explained: "A bicycle picnic is almost as good as a vacation. It gives you exercise and gets you out in the country, and gives you a great deal more fun than you can have just riding around the boulevards." Although picnic sites and other places of recreation could be accessed via train, the exact locations of such spaces were predetermined by where tracks had been laid, and the timing of such events was restricted by railroad management and the whims of the conductor. But on a bicycle, as the same Chicago wheelwoman pointed out, "you can go where you like" and when you like. Whether it was outside Chicago, Kansas City, or elsewhere, the practice of picnicking via bicycle had become so popular that cyclists could purchase a special bicycle attachment designed to tote a picnic basket.[18]

Everyday Americans extolled the bicycle as a means to break away from the normal course of metropolitan pandemonium. Being able to escape the city, move so freely around it, and with such swiftness were some of the most beloved characteristics of the machine. It is not surprising then that in the 1890s cyclists often zoomorphized their bicycles, analogizing their machines to birds, making it possible to fly in and out of the city. In the days before mechanized aviation, it was the bicycle that enchanted Americans. "I tell you, it's a bird!" a businessman boasted about his bicycle in 1896. Not alone, an envious mother from Illinois remarked, "I see my young daughters fly like an angel, and I hope some day to gather the impetus to fly." Referring to the 1895 Spalding Model D bicycle he had just bought, an instructor at Barnard College cheerfully declared that "my new wheel is a bird." For the many obsessed with speed, and before automobiles could satisfy their impulses, the bicycle provided an exhilaration of movement coupled with the possibility of transporting its driver into a different world. The ability to escape and "fly" away from the perils of city life was equally recognized by bicycle manufacturers. Some adopted avian inspired titles like "Falcon" and "Eagle," and many featured references to birds, wings, and angels in their marketing campaigns (fig. 6.3). Even advertisements for bicycle lubricants pledged to their customers that their well-oiled wheels would fly "like a bird."[19]

For those looking to "fly" even farther from the urban nucleus, touring groups and individual cyclists ventured deep into the hinterland on lengthy excursions. Vacationing and sightseeing journeys had been out of the realm of possibility for a majority of Americans. Even for those who owned a horse and carriage, traveling significant distances often proved too cumbersome for leisure. But by the end of the nineteenth century, with increased leisure time, an ever-expanding middle class, improved roads, and swifter and cheaper means of transportation, more and more city dwellers traveled farther and farther away from home. Although it would not be until the democratization of the automobile that vacationing and tourism became a mainstay of American culture, in the 1890s tens of thousands of cyclists pedaled their way on long-distance adventures. In the process, bicycles served as one of many modern inventions that complicated the meanings of spatial categories—urban, rural, and suburban.

More than a few cyclists spent months traveling across the continent, and even the globe, in feats of strength and endurance that captured the

Fig. 6.3. Advertisements from the 1890s, including this one from a French manufacturer, regularly featured women "flying" on their bicycles. Jean de Paleologue, Déesse, ca. 1895. Reprinted from the Library of Congress Prints and Photographs Division.

public's imagination. But more commonly, small groups of urban cyclists packed their bags for a weekend or even a week-long trip. Some set a course for a far-away metropolis, others for the hinterland. Joseph Bliss, a regular rider from the San Francisco area, took trips to Petaluma, Santa Rosa, Sausalito, Napa, and San Jose. Along the way, he stopped every fifteen miles or so for some rest, supper, cigars, or beer. Still others toured historical sites, soaking up historical remnants atop their futuristic machines. Civil War sites, one buff recounted, could easily be toured and experienced via the wheel. Sightseeing and long-distance travel via bicycle became popular enough that a crop of cycling clubs emerged, catering to those very activities, while guidebooks designed for urban riders gave tips on how to prepare for a multiday journey out of the city. The manuals included information about selecting luggage and packing efficiently, inspecting bicycles, finding a good companion, and choosing what to wear, where to ride, and even "how to breathe." Much like the ones popularized in later years for automobile drivers, roadside rest stops, often called a "Wheelmen's Rest," "Cycler's Rest," or a "Wheeler's Retreat" (fig. 6.4), provided food, drink, and respite for traveling cyclists.[20]

Although these tourists romanticized nature and the wilderness, their expeditions were not without modern comforts. Cyclists demanded paved roads on which to explore the "natural" countryside, amenities, restaurants, and hotels (those that offered reduced rates for cyclists were especially appreciated). Of course, they also rode on their bicycles—machines produced in a factory and representative of technological might.[21]

The practice of bicycle touring increased in popularity so rapidly throughout the 1890s that by 1897 Kodak developed a new device aimed at this segment of riders. Marketers pitched the "Bicycle Kodak" as a lightweight camera designed for bicycle tours in the country and as a tool for those urban dwellers who longed to remember the "quaint inn" in which they stayed and the "green fields" and "quiet cattle" by which they rode. Combining the popular hobbies of photography and cycling, tourists—

Fig. 6.4. This "Wheelmen's Rest" catered to San Francisco cyclists taking excursions outside the city. Reproduced with permission from the Bancroft Library, University of California Berkeley.

sometimes members of camera clubs, sometimes members of bicycle clubs, sometimes members of cycling camera clubs, and sometimes not affiliated with any organization—escaped the city in pursuit of snapping a portrait of nature. Cyclists brought back to the city images of an anti-urban landscape or historical site, providing a permanent reminder of a simpler place or a simpler time.[22]

Aside from trips to the countryside, cycling tourists visited other urban centers. Long-distance riders traveled between Boston, New York, Washington, DC, and Chicago, but more often cyclists from smaller cities would ride into their nearest, large metropolis for a day tour. Local papers printed suggested routes for cycling tourists and a list of the major attractions and sights, while bicycle shops invited visitors to have their wheels valeted, cleaned, or repaired.[23] Tourists on urban sightseeing trips and cyclists engaged in super-distance rides represented a select minority, however. The vast majority of cyclists already lived within cities and had neither the time, nor the resources, nor the desire to cycle around the world. Instead, most recreational cycling trips emanated from the urban core, with riders taking a short ride after work, in the morning, or on the weekend. Of course, many of the rides did not even penetrate the city limits. Short spins around the neighborhood were commonplace. But transporting oneself to some different, even if not so far away, setting was one of the bicycle's most valuable functions. The reward of these trips was celebrated not just by the individual riders but also by doctors, journalists, artists, and cycling advocates (of course, in this period, many doctors, journalists, and artists were themselves cyclists) who recognized the health benefits of such a journey. The value of these trips ran two ways: access to the open air and scenery absent in the city, and also the exercise itself.

HEALTHY CYCLISTS

Exercising for the sake of exercising was a relatively new phenomenon in the late nineteenth century. As part of what the historian John Higham has termed "The Reorientation of American Culture in the 1890s," Americans grew weary of the "dullness of urban-industrial culture" by zealously seeking adventure, refuge in nature, and a sporting life. As a result, not only did parks and wildlife sanctuaries attract crowds of visitors, but participation in college athletics soared. Gymnasiums peppered the urban landscape. So did YMCAs. Emblematic of the new doctrine of "muscular Christianity," YMCAs preached that athletics, recreation, and competition could instill character. Healthy people were good people; strength equaled morality. Americans quickly embraced "out-of-door" physical activities, imbibing the tenets of "the strenuous life." Some advocates of cycling even argued that through physical activity urban vices would decline. In an article entitled "The Bicycle and Crime," Cesare Lombroso, the well-known criminologist, reasoned that "the healthier men are, the better they are; and in so far as the bicycle makes for health it indirectly diminishes the cause of crime."[24]

Still, many fretted over the dangers of cycling for men and women who exercised too strenuously. The supposed consequences varied from an array of long-lasting ailments to the development of poor posture. Back and neck injuries were the most common concern. Explaining the dangers, one doctor alleged that a great many riders "contorted and distorted into hideous caricature of the shape of man—a creature doubled upon itself, crouching as if in fear, its face peering intently and anxiously, with contracted brows, compressed lips, pallid cheeks, and restless eyes." The many other supposed bicycle-related maladies included "bicycle hump, pop eye, bicycle neck, bicycle foot, and bicycle face."[25]

Overall, though, bicycles helped to usher in, and benefitted from, the new doctrine of physical exercise. At a sanitary convention held in Detroit in 1897, one member regretted that "within the last score of years a regular systematic physical exercise was practiced but slightly by our men and women." Because of the bicycle, described as the greatest device "conducive to physical development," all that was changing. A pair of doctors in 1896 declared, respectively, that "the evolution of the bicycle is probably the greatest factor which has influenced the spread of the doctrine of physical culture in this century" and that "thousands upon thousands of men and women who previous to a year or so ago never got any out-door exercise to speak of are now devoting half of their leisure time to healthy recreation." While their claims may have exaggerated the facts, these three physicians represent but a small sampling of the sizable group who came to thank the bicycle for sparking an exercise revolution.[26]

The benefits to newly active city dwellers were allegedly too many to count. Cycling exercised the rider's heart, lungs, back, chest, abdomen, and legs while providing, as one physician described, "mental refreshment" in a unique combination benefiting both "the mind and the body." This double dose of mental and physical well-being was widely described as cycling's greatest gift. The combination, a bicycle cheerleader noted, was the perfect remedy for three of the most significant causes of poor health among city workers: too little fresh air, too little physical activity, and excessive mental fatigue.[27] Of course, these workers were middle-class men working inside offices, sitting in chairs all day, not dockworkers or bricklayers.

As a prescription for mental and physical health, the bicycle was conceived of as more than an ordinary vehicle. In fact, the bicycle could allegedly cure almost any disorder. "It will soon be difficult to mention an ailment whose victims, provided they are not bedridden, may not, in somebody's opinion, derive benefit from the use of the bicycle," the *New York Medical Journal* noted in 1899.[28] In aggregate, physicians and the converted credited the machine with improving digestion; strengthening the heart and the liver; reducing or eliminating melancholia, rheumatism, gout, anemia, hernia, exhaustion, nervousness, aches, pains, and even homosexual desires; reducing fat; and developing courage, independence, intellect, and muscles.[29] These curative powers were just some of the many reasons the bicycle was regarded as an almost perfect instrument that could, if applied broadly, yield a utopian city.

Even for those wealthier residents who could often secure a more spacious and airy environment, a frenetic pace of life and living in such dense cities were the prime suspects in a number of urban maladies. Nervousness, fatigue, and depression were common symptoms of "neurasthenia," a widespread nineteenth-century diagnosis that characterized the ill effects of urbanization and the increased rapidity of daily life. City life and the overstimulation that came with it—the feverish pace, the ringing noise, office work, and so forth—overtaxed urbanites' nerves, leading to neurological disorder, or so the theory went.[30] The drudgery of modern life and work afflicted these largely middle-class professionals. In New York particularly, doctors diagnosed a series of diseases wrought by overexposure to the urban environment. One doctor even defined a new condition, "Newyorkitis." Supposedly it afflicted countless Manhattanites, especially those who had recently moved from the country to the city. As Dr. John Girdner wrote: "Newyorkitis is a disease in which the mind, soul, and body have departed more or less from the normal . . . the mental appetite of a Newyorkitic is morbid and perverted."[31]

In one respect, riders and doctors endorsed cycling to increase vigor, steady nerves, and, in many cases, cure neurasthenia and other maladies. One of many converts said: "I felt that the bicycle had saved my life. Certainly it did save me from a complete breakdown . . ." Doctors agreed. Lombroso, the criminologist who was also a physician, found that cycling could aid neurasthenia, chronic headaches, and an assortment of other ailments. He described the bicycle as "not a luxury, but a necessity" for anyone subject to "mental tension and nervous irritability," meaning, perhaps, anyone living in the modern American city. Other physicians documented their success in using the bicycle to treat neurasthenics. In an 1892 article, a well-known physician revealed that for each of his six patients the bicycle proved to be the long-awaited remedy.[32]

Yet speeding bicycles also played a part in the quickening of urban life and the accompanying mental fatigue. As an innovation in technology and speed, the bicycle emblematized the larger processes of urbanization and industrialization that stood at the heart of the newfound nervousness. Thus it was conceived of as both a cause of, and solution for, the chaotic nature of urbanity.[33] Some riders took the exhilaration too far. Scorchers sped around the city. Drag racers turned ordinary roads into makeshift velodromes. And speed limits and traffic laws did little to slow the rising number of traffic accidents. In this sense, bicycles added to the industrial roar of the American city—the clanging of pipes and the thunderous movements of the elevateds, the chaos on the streets and the medium-speed collisions, the obsession with speed and time saved. In fact, vehicles that supplied their users with superior speeds only created more demand for even greater speeds.[34]

The bicycle, then, was no simple "machine in the garden," teasing out tension between technological progress and the pastoral ideal.[35] By offering urbanites a physical and mental escape from the city, the bicycle served as more than a tool promoting the rise of the industrial city. The bicycle was less a *machine in the garden* and more of a *machine to get to the garden*. And it was the garden that provided the healthful tonics for the urban cyclists. In other words, the cleaner and healthier cities were the ones with the easiest exits.

Supporters also argued that the bicycle would lay the foundation for healthier people in generations to come. With more cyclists, one advocate promised, "we would have a stronger race." Not alone, others proposed that cycling "adds joy and vigor to the dowry of the race" and that "the bicycle promises substantial improvement to our race." In almost Darwinian language, promoters of cycling imagined that the physical strength and mental fortitude endowed by the great machine would have long-lasting, perhaps even evolutionary, consequences. As one author foresaw: "For my part, I venture to predict that the real *cyclo-anthropos* of the twentieth century will suffer less from his nerves and will be more muscular than the man of the nineteenth century." Supporters believed that the decisions they made now—exercising brain and body—would have repercussions on future generations. Strong mothers, fit fathers, and a resolute race awaited a future generation, bred, in part, by the bicycle. The bicycle was not the only technology that produced this kind of evolutionary thinking. Less than two decades later, at least one writer hypothesized that air travel could produce a superhuman (the "alti-man"), god-like, omniscient being who could fly through the air.[36]

In an era when health consciousness deepened and bicycles were widely accepted as a tool to relieve the stress of urban life and improve the health of its riders, bicycle manufacturers marketed their wares as not only practical vehicles and a means of recreation but also as health products.[37] Cycling advertisements and catalogs frequently referred to the advantages of exercise via the wheel and its medicinal effects. A 1901 advertisement for Monarch Bicycles promised that "An hour awheel with nature is the best tonic for the busy business man." Not only did bicycles provide physical health; the ad also claimed that cycling "broadens the mind and kills the worry." An 1891 advertisement for Columbia Bicycles published in *Cosmopolitan* emphasized cycling's health benefits specifically for women, as two images display the intended benefits of riding. The first woman is ailing, relegated to a chair, and glancing over at a vase holding a flower. The second woman is shown on her bicycle, stopped on the side of the road, merrily picking wild flowers. In a different manner altogether, the ad also speaks to a male audience. A portion of the text reads: "Is your wife an invalid? Are you constantly paying doctor's bills?" If so, the solution is a Columbia.[38]

A single 1893 catalog from the Pope Manufacturing Company advertising its Columbia bicycles included paragraphs of endorsements attesting to the healthy lifestyles led by its devotees. Not surprisingly, all of the endorsements came from members of the professional class. After all, they were the ones most likely to be buying bicycles in 1893 and the ones doctors worried about the most. A lawyer suggested that the bicycle was the perfect solution to remedy "the brain and nerve tissue destroyed in exacting professional work, performed in ill-ventilated offices, or worse ventilated court rooms . . ." H. W. Smith, a city businessman, concurred, suggesting that cycling did more for health than other sports. Not to be outdone, a clergyman joined the choir of bicycle-endorsers when he described the calming effects of riding: "I have found it beneficial to my health in lifting off that burden of weariness that comes after brain effort, or nervous strain, or tiresome tramping in parochial work."[39] While these endorsements could easily be written off as marketing hogwash, ordinary cyclists and doctors in the 1890s regularly reported the same effects. Not unlike his competitors, Pope realized that much of his customer base was comprised of men and women who fretted about the debilitating effects of urban life. As the catalogs and advertisements tried to make clear, the bicycle was more than a vehicle. It was a prescription for better health.

Cycling manufacturers and marketers were not the only ones looking to cash in on the conviction that bicycles could remedy urbanity's insalubriousness. Accordingly, health companies regularly sponsored cycling guidebooks, which offered suggested routes, maps, road conditions, and lists of cyclist-friendly hotels and restaurants. In just one example, the Pond's Extract Co. published a thirty-two-page pamphlet in 1897 of "Twenty-Five Charming Trips" to deliver New Yorkers out of the city. Sprinkled throughout the suggested routes were testimonials of Pond's Extract's curative properties. While the extract could treat bloody noses and a host of other ills, the pastoral scenery of the countryside would provide a therapeutic release for city dwellers—a truly holistic combination.[40]

HEALTHY CITIES

Many late-nineteenth-century Americans came to realize that clear skies, pure water, and proper sewerage could promote a healthier and more sanitary city—and a healthier and more sanitary population.[41] But so too could bicycles. Even though no one in the nineteenth century would have understood the significance of a carbon footprint or CO_2 emissions, a growing group of urban Americans became increasingly aware of the dangers of pollution.

Aside from preventing what had become semiregular epidemics, clearing smoke-filled skies, and providing clean water to the masses, reformers put cleaning streets at the top of their list of environmental causes. Under the umbrella of municipal and progressive reform, street improvement and its relationship to sanitation became a chief concern in the 1890s. With the great wave of industrialism came a great wave of pollution. Adulterated water fed, and thick air stagnated within, industrial cities. City streets too bore the evidence of pollution. Millions of horses meant millions of pounds of manure that found its way onto shoes and pants, or decayed and flew around the city air as toxic dust. (In Milwaukee, 133 tons of horse manure fell each day; in New York, roughly one million pounds.[42]) Horse carcasses lay sprawled across the cobblestones. Dirty steam engines pulled cars of people, emitting smoke all the way. Litter abounded. Wretched wastewater stood still in pools.

The increase in urban pollution prompted an increase in municipal reform efforts. The acceptance of germ theory, which placed a new emphasis on purifying America's soot-filled cities, played an important role. As an environmental historian described: "By the late nineteenth century, the saturation of cities and suburbs with air, water, refuse, and noise pollution finally produced an environmental consciousness among the complacent citizenry. Until this time, almost everyone had ignored questions of environmental quality . . . [and] had resigned themselves to pollution as an inconvenience to be endured." As a result, municipal engineers and reformers developed a fresh interest in purifying the urban environment. Some, many of whom saw the bicycle as a logical replacement, called for the elimination of horses. Partly because most urbanites used the streets and witnessed their foulness every day, it was the effort to clean the streets that emerged as a central plank in the larger campaign for environmental reform.[43]

Once the duty of abutting property owners, cleaning streets became a government responsibility, necessitating armies of sweepers, brooms in hand. But even with a large labor force, city streets proved difficult to clean. Unpaved and uneven surfaces were particularly ideal spaces for rotting rubbish to linger. With smooth, asphalted streets, however, decaying trash had nowhere to hide. Without paving streets it would be nearly impossible to "conquer" and "slay" the pollutants, the superintendent of Washington, DC's Street-Cleaning Department contended.[44] To ensure civic pride and an environment that promoted morality, the superintendent pleaded for more resources to pave and clean streets.

The chief advocate of the smooth-streets-equals-clean-streets campaign was the well-known street-cleaning commissioner for New York City. George E. Waring, Jr., who like his fellow Civil War veteran Albert Pope retained the honorific title of colonel, had been a noted agriculturist and drainage engineer. The Republican with an egg-shaped head and wispy moustache launched a frenzied campaign to clean the city's streets. He employed a large corps of street sweepers, known affectionately as the "White Wings," for the sterile uniforms they donned. To aid his effort, Waring enlisted the bicycle. Foremen wheeled across the city inspecting the roads and reporting on their cleanliness. He also set out on a three-month tour of Europe, a month of which he spent atop a bicycle, exploring what he conceived of as urban laboratories in Germany, France, and Switzerland.[45]

Waring recognized the value of bicycles, not only as practical vehicles for travel but also for their effect on city streets. Because of the bicycle's relatively light weight, cyclists riding along asphalt surfaces hardly wore down the pavement, thereby reducing the need for repaving. Moreover, cyclists helped advocate for smooth surfaces, and smooth surfaces ameliorated street pollution. So Waring joined forces with local cyclists to improve city streets. The Department of Street Cleaning and the local cycling organizations enjoyed such a cozy relationship that Waring was the invited guest of the cycling arm of the New York Athletic Club in 1897. The department even made a public announcement to all of its street cleaners, asking them to take extra care in searching for and removing any objects "apt to throw a bicycle rider" from his machine.[46]

Realizing the newly broad appeal of environmental reform, cyclists and cycling organizations like the LAW incorporated the reduction of pollution and disease as a component of the "good roads" campaign. According to the LAW's publication *Good Roads*, the new paving techniques had been designed to prevent pollution and "render the city sanitary." Theoretically, replacing horses with bicycles could root out much of the filth that dirtied the streets, soured the air, and was believed to be the cause of much disease. "Any observer can see that the filth incessantly deposited in the city streets is almost wholly due to animals," a prominent journalist reported in 1892. "With the disappearance of this, a vast amount of disease produced by the microbes thus continually sent broadcast into the air will be prevented" and a terrific "benefit to health" imparted. The notion that attractive, neatly organized space could mollify the hazards of urban life and uplift the crudest variety of urban residents gained significant acceptance by the 1890s. Clean streets fit within the larger project of civic improvement, rendering the urban population more morally fit. Cyclists joined an array of urban reform agencies, including Chicago's Hull House and New York's Women's Municipal League, both of which suggested that a clean city bred clean people by increasing personal hygiene and spreading the gospel of pride in oneself, character development, and proper decorum.[47]

Bicycles tiptoeing around the city also offered antinoise advocates the promise of a quieter world. Noise pollution became more than a nuisance by the end of the nineteenth century. The clip-clop of horses' hooves, the mechanical racket of engines, and the "shrill grinding" (as Stephen Crane wrote) of turning or breaking wheels could all be quieted. As a writer noted in 1892, urban transportation was the cause of excessive noise but could also be the solution: "All but an insignificant percentage of the exasperating noise and confusion of city life proceeds from the harsh rattle and clatter of vehicles in the streets." But with the popularity of cycling, "this will be entirely abated, and the main source of the nervousness that so universally afflicts city dwellers, will disappear." Another journalist likewise predicted that in the future, utopian version of the cycling city "there will be a delicious silence to begin with. No lumbering vans, no banging omnibuses, no clattering of iron hoofs upon asphalt." As a LAW official bragged, the bicycle was "noiseless, clean and a non-consumer;" everything that the stinking, loud, and polluting horse was not. Bicycles did not "consume" electricity or require horsepower, nor did they "consume" valuable urban space like elevateds and streetcar tracks, nor did they require any corporate investment. Bicycles required almost no special infrastructure, emitted no pollutants or odors, and quietly rolled through the raucous city—attributes well appreciated by late-nineteenth-century Americans.[48]

PARKS

Parks figured prominently in the cyclists' campaigns to improve their own health and that of the city itself. The broader urban parks movement derived from the increasing popularity of the doctrine of moral environmentalism and the back-to-nature movement. Together they suggested that better living conditions spawned better people and that the natural world was particularly well suited for developing a moral and healthy citizenry. As an urge for recreation and nature swept the urban populace in the 1890s, the increase in cycling grew in tandem with the expansion of park space. Although municipal parks might have been relegated to a square, constrained by existing urban development, and contained only manmade imitations of nature, parks offered a quick change of scenery. For those who could not fully escape the city's bounds, park designers sought to place "rural recreation," as Frederick Law Olmsted explained, squarely within the urban realm. Replicating a country environment within the city was exactly the point of most urban parks. Doing so, a park advocate argued in 1897, was to counterbalance all of the evils associated with city living: "The use of public parks is to promote the well-being and happiness of the people, to alleviate the hard conditions of crowded humanity, to encourage out-door recreations and intimacy with nature, to fill the lungs of tired workers from city factories and shops with pure and wholesome air." Although the benefits of city parks were becoming well known and small parks had become an important feature of city design for several decades, it was in the waning years of the nineteenth century that urban parks expanded mightily in scope. Advocates hoped that these parks could alleviate the escalating problem of urban life—that cities were filled with artificiality and had become too separated from nature and the therapy it offered. The nostalgic and/or bucolic names of some city streets and urban restaurants were the only reminders of the natural wonders that had once sat in areas now filled with tall buildings, crowded streets, steel, iron, and asphalt.[49]

In stark contrast to many of the formal gardens in Europe, the new American parks featured nature at its finest. Rolling hills, open spaces, and zigzagging paths served as a counterpoise to the gridiron layout of city streets. The increasing amount of space dedicated to parks reflected a heightened awareness of the need to bring nature within the city's fold. The municipal park system in Cleveland, Ohio, for example, increased its total park acreage from ninety-three to 1,500 acres from 1890 to 1905. Los Angeles, which could claim a mere half-dozen acres in 1880, possessed 3,700 acres of public park space by 1905. For decades European cities had boasted the largest and most appealing parks. With the United States urban park movement in full swing, American urban parks quickly outshined their European rivals.[50]

The acres of sprawling fields of green and miles of winding paths that emerged in American cities in the 1890s represented something quite different than the older city parks that had been woven into the urban fabric. Cyclists helped cement the park as an integral piece of the cityscape, while contributing to a new park aesthetic and environment—one that continued to appreciate the value of natural splendor, but that also recognized the place for active recreation and exercise. Once the quiet refuge for the well-to-do, early city parks gradually evolved into popular spots for recreation and sports. Although the commissioners of some notable parks, including New York's Central and Prospect Parks, begrudgingly afforded access to cyclists in the 1880s, only a select group of riders—uniform-wearing, badge-donning, cycling club members—were allowed to use the parks. Even by 1891, the lawmakers for Fairmount Park in Philadelphia regulated exactly how cyclists could ride. In order to ensure proper (well-mannered) riding, they restricted how high cyclists' legs could rise above the wheels. But as cycling exploded in popularity throughout the 1890s, armies of cyclists overwhelmed city parks. Middle-class cyclists were eager to ride through the parks, an activity once reserved only for those wealthy enough to own a carriage. On a pleasant spring Sunday in Cleveland in 1896, for example, nearly 15,000 bicycle riders rode through Cleveland Park, outnumbering pedestrians and easily outnumbering, by a three-to-one margin, the number of carriages that wheeled down the park's main drive. In Brooklyn several thousand cyclists rode across the rolling hills of Prospect Park each day; in Philadelphia 136,813 bicycles enjoyed the sprawling Fairmount Park in a single month in 1897 (it was not un-

Fig. 6.5. A Sunday in Prospect Park, Brooklyn, 1896.
Reprinted from *Munsey's Magazine*, May 1896.

Fig. 6.6. Riverside Park, New York, 1895. Note (in the lower right corner) an
example of the notorious scorcher. "Bicycling on Riverside Drive," *Harper's
Weekly*, June 15, 1895. Reproduced with permission from Albert and Shirley
Small Special Collections, University of Virginia, Charlottesville, VA.

usual to see twenty-five bicycles for every one carriage); and cyclists dominated Chicago's park drives as well. Because of the bicycle, "Never before
in the history of man have the public parks of cities been so truly breathing places of the people as they are now," a writer for *Forum* reasoned.[51]

Not everyone welcomed the whizzing bicycles. Since Central Park's
creators had imagined their park as a quiet refuge, providing "a relief and
counterpoise to the urban conditions" and offering an ideal setting for the
"quiet contemplation of natural scenery," park policies continued to favor "mental relaxation over physical exertion."[52] None other than Fredrick
Law Olmsted's design firm pled to the Boston park commissioners to keep
bicycle paths out of that city's parks, worrying that the "preserve of scenery" would be turned into a "bicycler's scorching track."[53]

Even though nineteenth-century city parks allowed certain forms of
exercise, officials circumscribed those areas of activity. Ice-skating was often promoted as a park activity, but the skaters were spatially restricted
to a single, confined lake. Croquet and boating were encouraged because
they maintained the tranquility of the parks. Horseback riding and carriage driving were a regular sight, but the horses usually trotted at a pace
not much faster than walking. By the 1890s, thousands of bicycles zoomed
around city parks.

Even though many parks contained winding, hilly drives meant not
only to mimic the curves of nature but also to discourage carriage drivers
from speeding through the park, there was little the park commissioners
could do to slow the cyclists who quickly overwhelmed these once tran-
quil spaces.[54] In Chicago, the Lincoln Park Commissioners resorted to Jef-
fersonian terms in declaring that the bicycle posed a threat "to the peace
of mind and safety of body" and jeopardized the park-goers' "pursuit of
happiness."[55] Indeed, park commissioners across the country cited an increase in the number of traffic accidents and speeding bicycles. Nevertheless, bicycle use continued to increase and, as a result, urban parks continued to evolve as sites for exercise and sporting recreation as much as for
simple relaxation.

Not long before, in the 1880s, Boston had opened the country's first
"recreation ground," inviting locals to run or play sports. But with the
enormous popularity of the bicycle, park commissioners could hardly ignore their new constituents and begrudgingly accepted a change in the
"nature" of urban parks, accommodating physical exercise and athletics.
Several cities even went so far as to erect bicycle tracks inside their public parks for racers to speed around or for everyday park-goers to use for
exercise.[56]

In the mid-1890s, Hartford welcomed five new parks. Although park officials sought to "exclude the sights and sounds of the street" in order to provide solace and promote relaxation, they relented by permitting vehicular travel (including bicycles) and active forms of recreation.[57] Perhaps they had no choice. The benefactor of the eponymous and cycling-friendly Pope Park was none other than the Colonel himself. The bicycle tycoon who donated the ninety-plus acres of parkland and who had, many years earlier, personally financed the legal campaigns to permit cycling in urban parks would surely not have had it any other way.

NIGHTTIME

Cycling in the parks was not just a daytime activity. Cyclists found that the parks offered unrivaled serenity at night and awoke those spaces that had traditionally quieted at twilight. In 1896, a parks commissioner in New York reported that the popularity of night cycling necessitated that city parks be outfitted with lights. Before cycling had become a force, "the parks were not thought a proper place to go at night. Of course, the cycle has changed this condition, and the parks are patronized by greater numbers after nightfall than in the daytime." Likewise, Chicago's Washington Park and Jackson Park welcomed thousands of cyclists "on pleasant nights [to] enjoy a good rest before speeding back to town." There, wheelmen and wheelwomen sat "together, to look out over the lake and wonder what the wild waves are saying. If the moon happens to be rising out of the lake it adds a new charm and makes the place especially attractive to bicycling lovers." Occasionally, people on horses and pedestrians could be seen, but as the *Chicago Times-Herald* reported, they appeared "strange and lonely and sadly out of place." At night, even more so than during the day, the parks were the dens of cyclists.[58]

Outside of the parks and on main streets around the country, cyclists also gathered at night. "The great avenues of our larger cities were made extremely picturesque in the dusk of evening by the endless line of bicyclists whose lanterns in the darkness produced the vivid effect of a river of colored fire," a journalist reckoned. While the mornings featured cyclists commuting to work and the daytime a mix of women, children, and casual riders, the scene changed dramatically after sunset, a Charleston observer reported in 1896. At night, they rode purely for pleasure. Their brilliant lanterns and moonlit wheels created a genuine attraction. In New York, newspapers confirmed that "thousands of the light wheels are spinning" each night, taking advantage of the relatively quiet roads and lamp-lit ambience. The Common Council in Philadelphia claimed that nearly twice as many cyclists rode at night compared to the day. And in Chicago, one wheelwoman recalled how her Astor Street neighbors wolfed down their dinners "for it was just a foregone conclusion that every one took a ride after dinner in the cool of the evening."[59]

That so many cyclists relished the evening air is well evidenced by the many cyclists charged with violating ordinances that required cyclists to carry lighted lamps after sunset. As part of the comprehensive traffic codes that cycling necessitated, most municipalities incorporated some kind of lighting provision. The extent to which cyclists failed to obey the law was borne out in police reports, news stories, and even song lyrics, including a very popular ditty "Get Your Lamps Lit!"[60] In Chicago, so many riders ignored the ordinance that lampless cyclists and their wheels filled jailhouses. From the mayor's perspective, jail time seemed an unfair penalty. City council agreed and enacted a new ordinance, which mandated that the arresting officer release the violators so long as "such person shall consent that the bicycle . . . without a lighted lamp, may be taken in custody."[61] In other words, the bicycle would be jailed instead of the cyclist. Perhaps the many lawbreaking, night-riding cyclists opposed the artificial light given off by cycle lamps or maybe they were just lazy, careless, or watching their pennies. Regardless, there is no doubt that a growing group of urban riders took to the streets at night.

No matter the city, nighttime offered a special attraction: a new environment in which to ride. The terrain and topography may have been no different, but cyclists relished the urban atmosphere at night. For some cyclists the attraction of riding at night was decidedly antiurban. Just as they fled the city for the romanticized natural landscape of the country, so too did overtaxed city dwellers find a romanticized cityscape after dark. With the moon came an idealized version of city life. As one recent scholar noted, "The night provided a special access to nature and made the blessings of the country available even in city streets." Quiet streets and darkened buildings hid the fixtures of urbanity. Accidents were far fewer and the pace of motion slowed to match the city's resting pulse. As one cyclist expressed: "If there is anything more charming in bicycling than a morning run it is a quiet evening spin by moonlight. The stillness unbroken by the soundless wheels, the absence of dust and wind, and the coolness of the air, the wired and shadowy charms of the landscape and street vistas, make it delightful to the imagination as well as to the senses."[62]

While the night offered a romanticized vision of the city, darkness could also signify the dangers and vices of the modern metropolis. Nighttime was long associated with crime and immorality, as shadowy streets seemed to invite the most unsavory activities. As the historian Peter Baldwin writes, "Modern urban night was not an extension of day; it was a liminal new world in which conflicting moral values mingled uneasily." Anxious city dwellers worried about what all those cyclists did at night, particularly women. To be sure, the cover of night offered an opportunity for unsanctioned activities, but also the chance to enjoy a new, albeit temporary, version of the city.[63]

At night, the spectacles of performance and promenade on main streets and boulevards took on a different meaning. Each night on the Boulevard a segment of the cycling community appeared (fig. 6.7). Glittering lamps and crescent moons only added drama to such performances. The cyclists who gathered there fortified Broadway's already growing reputation as the Great White Way and as a primary scene for spectacle. The northern section of the road and theater that was only years earlier described as a "howling wilderness" rapidly evolved into a "great bicycle thoroughfare" where the urban beat rang loudest at night.[64]

Fig. 6.7. On any given night on the "Boulevard," the modern city came alive. Cyclists transformed the asphalt path into a massive theater filled with lights and merriment. As a columnist for *Harper's Weekly* described in 1897, "Every night the lanterns of thousands of bicycles make of the Boulevard a marvellous spectacle." ("A Night Scene on the Boulevard," *Harper's Weekly*, August 28, 1897, 864) Reproduced with permission from Albert and Shirley Small Special Collections, University of Virginia, Charlottesville, VA.

This nightly parade became a fixture for those wanting to see and be seen—so much so that when a New York alderman proposed to divide traffic on the congested Boulevard, he insisted that the cyclists be kept on the inside portion of the road so that they could be "reviewed by pedestrians." Likewise, local press outlets from other cities noted how certain cyclists enjoyed the bicycle for its exhibitory nature, as they wheeled down the main thoroughfares "decked out in fantastic costumes," inviting spectators. Women especially attracted the male gaze and were accordingly warned about how to perform. "The ordinary wheelwoman would regard it as exceedingly bad form to race through the streets for the diversion and derision of irreverent male spectators," the *Rochester Herald* cautioned in 1896, before admitting that "a pretty young woman riding for recreation is indeed an engaging spectacle . . ." As cyclists wheeled around the city, their machines served double duty, playing the part of mobile stage and serving as minor characters in the everyday theater of the streets.[65]

That city living wreaked havoc on its peoples' health was a widespread belief. Bicycle manufacturers, doctors, reformers, public health advocates, and cycling promoters uniformly came to realize that late-nineteenth-century Americans held deep reservations about living in large cities. For many justifiable reasons, cities became labeled not only as breeding grounds for disease and pollution—air, noise, and water—but also as breeding grounds for a diseased people. The twin forces of industrialization and urbanization yielded a sedentary, exercise-starved, and nature-deprived race of urban dwellers. Perhaps, then, it is not so surprising that bicycles attracted so many and earned the praises of doctors who lauded the machines as the "great callisthenic of the world." Even *Scribner's Magazine* in 1896 suggested that "there is a psychic and moral void in city life which the 'bike' goes farther toward filling than any other institution." With great ease and speed, urban riders exercised their muscles, calmed their nerves, and found themselves amid a quieter setting. Thus the once both physically and mentally distant state of "the countryside" was now within practical reach. As a consequence, the boundaries between the urban and the suburban blurred, with cyclists able to experience both environments in the very same day. For at least a moment, the city became far less suffocating. As one author aptly summed up in 1897, "the bicycle seems destined to be an important factor in setting people to thinking about great problems of modern life." And for at least some city dwellers it was the bicycle that seemed capable of fixing those problems, making the modern city, in short, more livable.[66]

CHAPTER SEVEN

Riding for Utility: The Commuters

All spaces change over time. Even those spaces that experience few natural changes are imbued with different meanings in different contexts. For example, from the day fireworks announced the opening of the Brooklyn Bridge, New York's East River changed forever. Although the water was no cleaner or deeper than it was the day before, the Gothic towers that anchored the then-longest suspension bridge miraculously turned an obstacle into a doorway. Indeed, all spaces become defined not strictly by their absolute geometry but rather by the "gestures and actions of those who inhabit" them.[1] One of the most significant reconceptualizations of space emerged as a consequence of shifting spatial-temporal dynamics. Leading philosophers, physicists, and geographers have long grappled with theories that aim to characterize the relationship between time and space. The results are as varied as they are complex. But one useful tenet of relative spatial-temporal dynamics is quite simple: the annihilation of space through time. The size of a space functions inversely to the speed with which that space can be traversed.[2]

Over the course of history, new modes of transportation have contracted the distance between cities, subsequently revolutionizing culture and commerce. On a much smaller scale, bicycles altered the space within the city, affording greater mobility and a refashioned sense of the urban world. Bicycles enabled city dwellers to traverse the city like walkers, but with exceptional speed, something with which Americans were quickly becoming obsessed. The telegraph and telephone quickened communication, as the railroads destroyed distance. Newspapers reported about nautical speed records and sports columnists kept their devoted readers entranced with tales of galloping horses. Ragtime musicians pounded piano keys faster than the eye could see. On city streets, men glanced down at their pocket watches in frighteningly short intervals. Perceptions about time and space were in the midst of a great transformation. Life moved quicker. Speed was exalted. Distances asked to be overcome.[3]

A cause and consequence of the changing sensibilities, bicycles epitomized a "cult of speed" for those who sought "to conquer time and space." Noting that bicycles easily outpaced trotting horses, *Harper's Weekly* reported in 1895 that the "regular bicycle-rider's area is extended amazingly." Others cheered that the bicycle was rapidly "multiplying the reach of man's footsteps as the power-loom has multiplied the productivity of man's hands." A *Scribner's* columnist may have described the phenomenon best in 1894, defining the bicycle as "an annihilator of space." Urban mobility would never be the same.[4]

Cyclists discovered new parts of the city and indulged in the delights of the previously inaccessible hills, lakes, vistas, clean air, and fragrances that could only be found outside the city center. But they also found that within the city, people on wheels moved faster than almost anything else and that the bicycle offered among the most efficient door-to-door connection for practical travel. Plus, they fell in love with the bicycle's individualistic nature—the ability to go wherever and whenever one wished. While the majority of riders cycled for recreation, commuting cyclists rode in historically impressive numbers and represented an important segment of the cycling city. In fact, never again would the percentage of bicycle commuters be so high.

Out of the realm of mere pastime, cycling emerged as a convenient method of transportation in the 1890s. A report in 1896 described its evolution: "the bicycle, at first regarded more as a plaything, or as part of the machinery of a circus, to be used only by experts to amuse a crowd, as the trapeze, or the balloon, gradually worked its way and from a toy has come at length to be as practical for everyday use as the old fashioned horse and buggy." The bicycle had become a "necessity of civilization."[5] As practical cyclists joined those who rode for recreation, the total number of urban riders multiplied and city institutions commenced a campaign to accommodate them. Churches placed bicycle racks outside their halls of worship and offered attendants to watch over congregants' wheels. Some even held special bicycle-friendly services and featured cycling-related sermons (e.g., "The Bicycle as a Means of Grace").[6]

Local businesses also found themselves competing for cyclists. Both leisure riders and commuters required special amenities like racks, sheds, or valets to secure their vehicles. In the earliest years of the 1890s few restaurants, hotels, or other pleasure destinations offered secure storage, but by mid-decade it was a different story. Writing from Buffalo, a journalist indicated that "few stores or business houses are without a bicycle rack in front for their customers and a bicycle storeroom in the building for employees." "Bicycles are checked at the theatres and at the churches," he observed. The Minneapolis government also thought it wise to erect an 800-bicycle-rack shelter near a popular cycling destination. Bicycle accommodations had become so prevalent, in fact, that some city governments sought to slow the growing number of bicycle racks swallowing city sidewalks. In San Jose, California, a city councilman launched a campaign to limit the quantity and size of the bicycle racks that seemed to be overtaking his city. Even the most august urban institutions appreciated that their visitors often came by bicycle. Around the turn of the century, New York's Metropolitan Museum of Art built a bicycle room for its patrons. Whether it was the wealthy, the art-loving, or just those seeking efficiency, the prevalence of cyclists riding to businesses, schools, and places of public accommodation marked a decided shift in urban dynamics. Cyclists sped by on their way to work or to run an errand, casting a wider net on the city and enabling city institutions to vie for patrons across an increasingly expanding territory. In this sense bicycles made the city seem smaller.[7]

With bicycles able to traverse the city in such little time, commercial interests quickly adopted the new vehicle. Urban businesses exploited the "shrinking city" to save time and to narrow the perceived gap between customer and client. Boys on bicycles delivered almost anything. In Buffalo, oysters came by wheel. In Denver, bicycles towed ambulances and mobile bakeries. In Alabama, as a judge noted in an official court opinion, it had become a "matter of common knowledge" that cyclists regularly toted their goods and wares across the city. Doctors used bicycles "practically and profitably" to make house calls. And in 1896 the American District Telegraph began what would become an established industry practice of equipping its messenger boys with bicycles. By the turn of the century, teenage bicycle messengers dashing through the city had become a fixture of the urban environment. On a much smaller scale than the telegraph and the railroad that preceded it, bicycles contributed to the late nineteenth century's communications revolution.[8]

Aside from enabling a quickened communication network, bicycles also offered a unique method of patrolling the city. With the ability to maneuver as if on foot and with speeds in excess of fifteen miles per hour easily attainable, bicycles were employed to survey larger chunks of the city. Not to mention the ability to hunt down criminals. In 1895, the New York

Fig. 7.1. A group of cyclists is seen patronizing an ice cream stand, likely on 110th Street in New York in 1896. The photograph reveals two sets of bicycle racks, one built around a tree and the other attached to the building itself. Hortons Ice Cream shop was one of the many businesses that began to cater to its cycling customers. Reproduced with permission from the Museum of the City of New York.

Fig. 7.2. A series of bicycle racks outside retail shops in Rochester, New York, ca. 1896. Reproduced with permission from the Collection of the Rochester Municipal Archives.

police launched the first of what would become several mounted units. Ironically, the first cycling cops were charged with regulating bicycle traffic and ticketing their reckless brethren. Bicycle policemen continued to patrol New York's streets for decades to come and became an important feature in metropolitan police departments around the country. To similarly exploit the bicycle's prowess for eyeing the city, the Salvation Army launched its own bicycling unit. Members anticipated that a mounted corps could easily "chase a flying sinner" with a "squadron of mounted Salvationists dashing through the street . . . firing volleys of song and sermon without ever slackening their pace."[9]

But the most profound and practical function of the machine was to commute. Bicycles expanded the range of the city's reach, as workers from one part of the city rode to another and residents from outside the city cycled their way into town. In the 1890s in general, the pace of suburbanization quickened, when the impersonal forces of the industrial city led to an elevated appreciation for privacy, space, and the natural landscape. Electric streetcars and newly affordable homes also encouraged a move to the suburbs. Living outside the city and just a short commute from urban amenities was an attractive proposition, and having a bicycle unlocked the best of both worlds. As one editorialist described, a bicycle can "carry those who work in the city out to the suburbs, where they own or rent detached houses amid pleasant scenes and pure air, enjoying thus the beauty and quiet of the country together with the advantages of the city." Even as early as the late 1860s, *Scientific American* cited "one gentleman in the country who does business in the city" who had replaced his horse and wagon with a bicycle. Certainly, this had been an oddity at the time, but by the mid-1890s bicycle commuting was far from uncommon. In 1895, a reporter observed that "Already in every village and town the mechanic and factory hand goes to his work on his wheel. Thanks to this modern wonder," he added, "they can live several miles away from their work, thus getting cheaper rents and better surroundings for their children; they can save car-fares and get healthful exercise." And while *Arena* magazine and the *Philadelphia Record* may have exaggerated when they claimed that "around our great cities, the bicycle has been a leading factor in the building up of attractive suburbs" and that the bicycle enabled an unprecedented "demand for suburban or country homes for persons of small or moderate means," there actually were small towns outside of Philadelphia and Boston that became home to bicycle commuters.[10]

Unlike other forms of transportation, bicycles gave workers a practical door-to-door vehicle. Only horses shared that trait, but even those wealthy enough to purchase, house, and feed a horse could never reasonably expect to ride to work. On the other hand, bicycles could be stored inside or out, in one's home and at one's place of work. Special racks and bicycle holders welcomed wheels; riders could be seen carrying their folding bicycles up a flight of stairs before storing them in a corner, on the back of a door, or in a neatly designed piece of furniture. Dressed more like businessmen than typical cyclists, commuters toted their briefcases via any number of bicycle attachments, sported cycling accessories like "trouser guards" to protect their work clothes, and kept repair kits should tires flatten or mechanics falter. They rode at a comfortable pace (likely anywhere between five to fifteen miles per hour)—still fast enough to beat public transportation options—and regularly traversed distances more than ten miles.[11]

While the number of commuters never approached the number of those who rode for recreation, commuters represented an important segment of the cycling population and one that grew in tandem with the cycling city. Exactly how many cyclists commuted and how far they traveled is difficult to ascertain from extant sources. Yet contemporaries recognized that the bicycle's range radically altered cyclists' daily routine. One observer performed some simple calculations: "A man who lives in a suburban district . . . will go two and a half miles out and the same distance back, making his walk five miles." Based on the assumption that cyclists can travel about six times as far as walkers with the same exertion, the fledgling mathematician reasoned that the same man could travel fifteen miles out and back in any direction. Thus, he could enjoy commuting from anywhere within a 15-mile radius of his work—an area measuring more than 700 square miles. This was at a time when cities were still relatively compact and when many of the commuters who came by railway traveled less than twenty miles. Of course, it was not that simple. Although one of the greatest features of the bicycle was how little infrastructural support it demanded, cyclists still needed roads or paths. Commuters' routes and the decision to bicycle to work depended on the nature of a city's streets, their placement, and their quality, in addition to other more permanent factors, like topography and weather. Indeed, anyone standing in a major American city during "rush hour" would have observed that cyclists moved over well-worn paths. Each rider performed his or her own calculus, weighing distance and speed against a myriad of other factors. Many arrived at the same solution: avoiding hills, poor road surfaces, and streets clogged by streetcars and their slippery tracks.[12]

While it may be impossible to determine exactly where commuters rode to and from, traffic surveys, accident reports, and troves of anecdotal evidence confirm that commuting cyclists regularly rode through the city. Speaking in 1897 at an annual conference devoted to municipal improvements, one city engineer from St. Paul, Minnesota, warned that city designs must adapt to the new mode of commuting. An argument emerged about how best to accommodate cyclists, reorganize traffic, and lay bicycle paths. But there was no debate that "the use of the bicycle is now extended to almost every profession and occupation in life. Professional men in general and an army of clerks go to and from their houses and places of business, and the artisan to his work, on bicycles." The bicycle had earned its place as a legitimate and "proper vehicle for travel."[13] That the bicycle was used considerably for practical purposes was a matter of fact, expressed in court opinions and on city streets.[14]

At universities in Chicago, New York, Boston, and elsewhere, faculty members joined their students pedaling to class.[15] The habit of commuting to and around campuses became so popular that a professor at Princeton University advised that for the typical student, "the bicycle is a necessity of his life, and on it he rides to recitations and lectures, to his meal and to the athletic field." Likewise, high school students and teachers increasingly cycled to schools where basements often doubled as bicycle garages. Clerks, too, treasured "pedaling homeward after a tedious turn at the desk or sales counter." One architect went so far as to claim in court that his bicycle was an essential tool for his business. Government employees cycled to work with regularity as well. In Washington, DC, a group of over one thousand employees wheeled their way to the State, War, and Navy Departments, joining thousands of others who rode to work in the nation's capital. The Treasury Department even constructed a "bicycle stable" for its 1,900 employees. Located inside the Treasury Building, the stable sat above swimming pool-sized vaults filled with silver and bullion and housed some 500 bicycles. Each one had a special number and a corresponding parking spot. A similar, albeit less grand, "bicycle lodge" serviced Boston's cycling commuters, who could drop off their bicycles in the downtown district and conduct their day's business before riding home on their freshly detailed machines. In Chicago bicycle storage buildings, like modern day parking garages, offered urbanites a place to park their wheels for the night or by the hour. In Kansas City, a local reporter observed in 1896 that "anyone who will stand at a street corner or visit an industrial center at 6 o'clock any evening and count the bicycles that are used as conveyances for carrying workingmen and women home from their toil . . . will soon discover that the wheel is more an instrument of utility than of pleasure." While his conclusion that more cyclists used their wheels for transportation than for pleasure was likely erroneous, his observation about the number of commuters was not. Finally, as one Michigan judge cited as fact when deciding a case involving a cycling accident: "The bicycle has become almost a necessity for the use of workmen, clerks, and others in going to and from their places of work."[16]

That factory workers and wage laborers also regularly cycled to work is made clear by the many manufacturing centers, built in the late 1890s and early 1900s, with sizable bicycle rooms for commuting employees. The Gorham Manufacturing Company, for example, opened its new factory and casino (essentially an employee clubhouse) on May Day 1899. A producer of silver based in Providence, Rhode Island, the company boasted about providing its workers a number of amenities. Most notably, the new Gorham facilities included a bicycle room that stored 400 bicycles. Upon arrival, employees left their vehicles with an attendant, who kept the bicycles in a basement equipped with a numbered storage system and constant surveillance. Gorham's cycle valet was an expanded version of a previous program, which, despite its ten-cents-a-week fee, had proven quite popular. Even more telling is the fact that the company provided storage for 400 bicycles. The firm employed only 1,100 workers. The Gorham Manufacturing Company was not alone. In Dayton, Ohio, the National Cash Register Company built a "bicycle stable" with space for 800 commuting cyclists to store their bicycles (fig. 7.3). While the employees labored, boys tended to the wheels, washing bicycles and inflating tires. Countless other industrial and agricultural plants, in and around America's cities, accommodated the great number of cycling commuters.[17]

The bicycle accommodations did not go unnoticed. As one city engineer acknowledged, "provisions for the care of bicycles are now made in all large office buildings, manufacturing buildings, wholesale houses, and stores, where a large number of men and women are employed, and it is considered as essential to provide a place for the wheel." Photographs and blueprints reveal that the exuberant engineer spoke more wishfully than realistically. Indeed, the persistent demand for more cycling amenities reveals that not everyone felt well served by the existing infrastructure. In New York, cycling commuters demanded that city buildings increase their bicycle storage facilities (they claimed New York lagged behind Chicago, Boston, and Washington, DC) to accommodate their growing numbers. Certainly, such parking spaces could be found, but apparently there were not enough.[18]

Records from traffic accidents also reveal the popularity of bicycle

Fig. 7.3. The bicycle shelter at the National Cash Register Company in Dayton,
Ohio. Reprinted from the Library of Congress, Prints and Photographs Division.

commuting. Newspapers and municipal records not only confirm that cycling accidents were all too common, but oftentimes the reports included
valuable information about who cycled. One account of an 1896 accident
revealed that when Joseph B. Abecasis was struck by a wagon in New
York's midtown, he was in the midst of his daily commute via bicycle. As
usual, he had been zigzagging his way down New York's grid en route to
his office at the stock exchange.[19]

   Similarly, several traffic surveys confirm the prevalence of bicycles in
late-nineteenth-century American cities. Unfortunately, most surveys did
not include bicycles since engineers often used traffic counts as a way to
manage and plan for road paving. Consequently, they were mostly interested in the aggregate weight of traveling vehicles; since bicycles weighed
so little (relatively at least), counters usually did not bother to include

them. However, the few surveys that included bicycles are illuminating, particularly a series of counts conducted by the city engineer of Minneapolis. Those counts illuminate that urban cyclists constituted an important segment of the population that rode for utility and pleasure all year long. To be sure, more cyclists took to the streets on dry days in the warmer months. Nonetheless, the data also reveal that some persistent cyclists, almost certainly commuters, cycled regardless of the weather.[20]

It was a cold day, even by Minneapolis standards. The temperature on that December day in 1895 ranged from 15 degrees to 36 degrees Fahrenheit. Despite the winter chill, 1,475 bicycles sailed down a single thoroughfare in the heart of the city. For the entire week, cyclists accounted for an average of nearly 23 percent of all vehicular traffic on Nicollett Avenue. Sunday had the fewest cyclists, likely because of the lack of commuters. Monday was the least popular weekday and, not coincidentally, the only day with measurable rain. While there was no traffic count conducted in the spring or summer, the number of cyclists in those months would surely have been significantly higher. Based on the ratio of warm weather cyclists to cold weather cyclists gleaned from later traffic counts, the most popular cycling days in the summer of 1895 would have likely seen more than 6,200 cyclists riding by a single Minneapolis intersection. Although the number of horse-driven vehicles increased in warmer weather as well, bicycles probably constituted about 45 percent of total vehicle traffic on the best cycling days of 1895. Moreover, cycling in 1895 had not yet reached its peak in popularity. Over the course of the next two to three years, cycling in Minneapolis increased sharply, as it did in most American cities. Almost certainly, on some of the warm, sunny days in 1897 cyclists totaled more than 50 percent of all vehicular traffic passing between Fourth and Fifth Streets on Nicollet Avenue.[21]

The numbers are especially impressive. None of the counts included traffic after 7:00 p.m., at which point recreational riders often rode. The survey was taken in the winter in one of the country's coldest cities. And they recorded bicycle traffic at a point in time when cycling had not yet reached its peak in popularity and when the city was only beginning to asphalt large sections of its roads and lay bicycle paths. In 1900, Minneapolis was the nineteenth-largest city in the United States, with a population measuring 202,718 and a total workforce population numbering 85,889. During the peak of the season the year before, the city engineer of Minneapolis (not some wildly optimistic cycling club spokesman or sensationalist journalist) estimated that some 25,000 residents used bicycles on a daily basis, meaning that over twelve percent of Minneapolis's men and women, children and aged, cycled daily in the 1890s. On one winter workday, at just one intersection, 0.73 percent of the city's total population wheeled by via bicycle. (In 2013, about 0.62 percent of all Americans commuted by bicycle; Minneapolis in 2013 had the fourth highest percentage of commuting cyclists in the U.S. at 3.7 percent.) The total number of cyclists at the time, including recreational riders and those who only occasionally took their wheels out for a spin was likely around 90,000, meaning that around 44 percent of all those who lived in Minneapolis owned a wheel.[22]

Admittedly, Nicollet Avenue was home to more bicycle traffic than most other Minneapolis streets. Following protests from cyclists, engineers authorized the paving of a portion of Nicollet Avenue with asphalt in 1895. As the 1897 map from the city engineer's office reveals, asphalt topped relatively few of the city's downtown streets. Instead cyclists would have found most streets paved with less desirable cedar blocks. In fact, engineers conducted a separate traffic count in December of 1895 at a different (and less cycling-friendly) intersection in the city. Paved with brick, the intersection also had two fifteen-foot-wide streetcar tracks that could trip cyclists. Still, during the chilly workweek, counters recorded, on average, just over 500 cyclists passing by. The office of the City Engineer reported similar numbers at a third intersection, also clogged by streetcar tracks.[23]

Traffic surveys in other cities reveal similar trends. In September of 1898 in Chicago, counters stationed on the fringe of the downtown business district watched as sunlight and cyclists filled the city in tandem. They documented that thousands of cyclists rode their bicycle to work each morning. During the peak rush, from 7:30 to 8:00 a.m., the numbers grew more intense. In one five minute span, 900 riders hurried by. On the ever-popular Jackson Boulevard, counters noted that an astonishing 211 cyclists passed by in a single minute. (In modern day Copenhagen, busy paths during peak hours experience a rate of around 38 riders per minute.) The total number of riders counted in the three hour span, 10,522, is certainly much smaller than the actual number of cycling commuters. There were only three checkpoints covering only three hours of time. Even the counters acknowledged that "many an uncounted rider slipped through in the scrimmage." Chicago was, however, the nation's second largest city and home to more than a million and a half people. So while historically impressive, the number of cyclists paled in comparison to the many millions of five-cent fares collected by the city's El.[24]

In smaller cities as well, commuting cyclists steadily poured in throughout the morning. By the evening, a mass exodus ensued. An 1897 survey from Springfield, Massachusetts, conducted at 6:00 p.m., reported a "stampede" of riders emanating from the city's offices, shops, and factories. In just twenty minutes, a handful of traffic counters calculated 913 cyclists, overwhelmingly described as "business-like," who exited the downtown district, pedaling toward home. Alone, those 913 cyclists amounted to nearly 1.5 percent of the entire population of Springfield. On Philadelphia's Broad Street, counters tallied some 22,831 cyclists across three checkpoints on a pleasant spring Wednesday in 1896. Over a century later, Philadelphia could claim only 10,503 cycling commuters across the entire city. And that is despite the fact that Philadelphia in 2010 had a population that was about 18 percent larger than in the 1890s.[25]

Finally, a bicycle count from St. Louis in 1897 elucidates not only the relatively high percentage of people commuting to work via the wheel but also the character of the commuting class in general. At the corner of Fourth and Walnut Streets, reporters noted that 2,836 riders passed by between 5:30 a.m. and 8:30 a.m. on a scorching hot weekday in July. That an average of 945 cyclists rode by this single corner each hour was a remarkable enough statistic, but the commentary also revealed that the commuters represented a wide cross section of the city. The earliest cyclists represented the "janitor class," comprising black and white, old and young, some toting work supplies, others riding atop visibly dated machines, and almost none sporting sporty bicycle suits. Shortly thereafter, those who paid just a "little more attention to dress" whooshed by before the "schools" of clerks. Some of them had a full complement of bicycle clothes, many donned "golf caps," and most rode quality bicycles. Eventually, women came too, as did the slow-moving, well-groomed "office men."[26]

In St. Louis, Philadelphia, Harrisburg, Springfield, Chicago, Minneapolis, and elsewhere, not only was the total number of riders historically impressive, but so was the growth. The recognizable cycling population in the 1890s had grown from a group of just a handful of riders in the decade before. The rapid growth only made their presence more noticeable and impressive than it might have been otherwise and also suggested a future in which cycling might dominate urban travel. As these numerous traffic counts, reports from city councils across the country, and pieces of anecdotal evidence suggest, cyclists rode not just for recreation and not just under the moonlit skies or on weekends, but also for moving throughout the city during the week, to and from places of work.

In addition to those cyclists commuting into the city strictly via bicycles, many combined multiple forms of transportation. As the railroads transported crowds into cities each morning, riders from suburban homes too far from their place of work even for bike travel could ride to the rail station. That the railroads failed to provide secure storage for bicycles (a rival mode of transportation) was often a subject of complaint among suburban commuters. But with the "privilege" of "decreased rent," as a San Francisco newspaper described, and of enabling commuters to live not only farther from the city but also farther from the railroad station, many riders toted their wheels on the train and stored their bicycles at the urban terminus.[27]

Of course, bicycles merely joined and did not replace other forms of transportation. In the late nineteenth century, streetcars grew enormously in scope and in popularity. Nationally, between 1890 and 1902, the total mileage of streetcar tracks (most of which were electrified) nearly tripled and the number of cars in use doubled. Large cities saw the greatest expansion. In Philadelphia, the total number of streetcar passengers rose from about 99 million in 1880 to just over 292 million in 1900, as total track mileage increased from 298 miles to 470 miles. Even cyclists rode the cars when the weather turned bad or distances proved too great. While 292 million passengers and 470 miles of track may seem like spectacularly high numbers, many urban residents never rode the streetcars and much of the city remained inaccessible or poorly accessible by rail. The 292 million passengers represented about 128 rides per capita, or just below 2.5 rides per week per person. Most streetcar trips were used to access recreation and shopping or to connect to another form of transportation—riding to a local ferry or railway station; the majority of streetcar use was not for commuting.[28]

One reason may have been that certain sections of major cities often remained unserviced or poorly serviced by streetcars. Streetcars often moved only one way down a street and sometimes the inbound and outbound directions were several blocks apart. Moreover, many American cities, like Philadelphia and New York, adopted a grid system, which prevented streetcar tracks from running diagonally. Consequently city residents often found it more efficient to walk, or cycle, around the city. Because private companies operated urban streetcar lines, there was no unified system of tracks. Indeed, the absence of any long-term, formalized, city-wide planning crippled urban transit, which was not successfully conceived as a whole until many years later. The result was that riders were often forced to take multiple lines operated by different companies and thus required to pay more than the usual five-cent fare. Certain parts of the city, particularly those away from the downtown core, usually had very limited, if any, service. Even for those who found the destinations suitable, they would have to wait up to twenty minutes for the streetcars to arrive; remain patient as the car, which topped out between nine and twelve miles per hour, stopped all along the way; hope that they did not need service before or after the cars' operating hours; and expect to stand, since the average car had fewer than half the number of seats as its total capacity. It should not be a surprise then that Joseph Matod, a millwright from Buffalo, grew tired of his thirty-five minute, but only 2.5-mile, commute via a combination of the streetcars and walking. His solution was simple: the bicycle. If he rode at a very comfortable pace of ten miles per hour, the trip to work would have only taken him fifteen minutes. That streetcar accidents were far from uncommon (although neither were cycling-related crashes) and that streetcar operators became viewed as representative of all that was wrong with corporate America—corruption and emphasis of profit over safety—also discouraged others from riding the cars. Cycling had its advantages.[29]

In fact, the Pennsylvania Bureau of Railways concluded that cycling took away significant business from the streetcars. As the chief of the bureau hypothesized in early 1898, "the use of the bicycle by business people and pleasure seekers is the prolific source of the reduction in the receipts of many street railways." That assumption was based on a traffic survey conducted in Harrisburg in the fall of 1897. City officials tracked the number of cyclists vis-à-vis the number of streetcar passengers who passed a given point from 7:00 a.m. until 6:00 p.m. The data were clear: 1,962 people rode by on the cars, 4,116 (or 67.7 percent) on bicycles. Like much of urban America, cycling in Harrisburg was becoming a primary way to move about and "shrink" the city. In large part because of the bicycle, total streetcar usage across American cities had declined over the previous year, the *Street Railway Journal* reported in 1897.[30]

That same year, when the president of the New York State Street Railway Association delivered his presidential address, he waited but two paragraphs to mention one of the group's most pressing concerns: "The bicycle is now our too successful competitor." A national convention of railroad commissioners acknowledged the same thing. Streetcar operators around the country could no longer brush off the pesky bicycle as a nuisance. To patch their bleeding coffers, companies began to invite cyclists rather than shun them. Street railways offered to tow cyclists and their wheels to destinations in and outside of the city. Recognizing that "the furore for bicycling is very pronounced" in its city, the Pittsburgh Second Avenue Traction Company decided to "cater to the wheelmen" in order to recover the income lost due to cycling. Seats were removed and bicycle racks placed in their stead. Shuttling urbanites within the city and to the country roads beyond Pittsburgh's hills, these bicycle cars offered a fifteen-cent fare for both the bicycle and its owner. Even in San Francisco, where protesting cyclists and streetcar operators had violently clashed a year earlier, the Market Street Railway debuted its "bicycle hangers" in the summer of 1897. The devices, one attached to each end of the streetcar, could hold two bicycles. Charging five cents for the service, the Railway found that the racks quickly paid for themselves. The Railway Company in Rochester, New York, had a slightly less inviting offer for cyclists: a bicycle and its rider could be carried in the front of the car so long as either the rider or his vehicle was injured . . . and for double fare. And when streetcar operators opened recreation/amusement grounds on the urban fringe, in order to encourage, and profit from, such excursions outside of the city, the play spaces often included bicycle tracks (for recreational cyclists to circle). It was not just newspapers that thought the bicycle was a disruptive force. Streetcar operators did so too.[31]

In aggregate, the combination of streetcars, railroads, and bicycles enlarged the range of travel and expanded the bounds of commuting. Even though most workers continued to live (by today's standards) extremely close to their places of work, it was in the midst of the bicycle era that suburbanization began in earnest.[32] While streetcars have appropriately garnered more attention as a trigger in early suburbanization, bicycles should not be completely discounted as a serious tool for workers commuting into and around American cities. Bicycles promised (and automobiles gave) commuters the choice to live anywhere on the city's periphery and not just along a linear path of streetcar tracks. Bicycles provided door-to-door service, shortened commutes, reduced costs, and turned the commute into recreation instead of a chore. To be sure, the bicycle was often seen as a complement to and not a replacement for other forms of transportation; when the weather was bad or the legs tired, cycling no longer seemed the best option. Even though bicycles soon disappeared as popular vehicles for commuting, in the 1890s bicycles joined a combination of forces—other transportation technologies, innovations in home construction, and a deepening appreciation for the suburban aesthetic—that led people to rethink where they lived in relation to where they worked.[33]

Throughout the 1890s, bicycles evolved into practical vehicles used for an array of practical purposes. No longer simply the domain of a select class of men taking short leisure rides through the city, bicycles were put to use in almost every conceivable manner. As the *Philadelphia Record* reported in 1896, finally "the bicycle has been recognized as a machine so distinctly practical in its purpose and intended for real use, and, moreover, hard use" that bicycles no longer warranted special decorations or ostentatious displays.[34] Bicycles had become a completely normal fixture of urban life, as cycling commuters, delivery boys, and policemen blended into the urban landscape.

Historically, though, the number of those who commuted on wheels was anything but ordinary. Even if it is difficult to neatly piece together the relatively few traffic counts (many of which lack either specificity or context, or did not trace ridership over long periods of time), the data show in very clear terms that in the 1890s, American cities were, more than ever, cycling cities. As a percentage, more shops sold bicycles, more people wrote about bicycles, probably more people thought about bicycles, and, most importantly, more people regularly rode their bicycles than ever before or since. Although Chicago of 1896 or Washington, DC, of 1897 might not have seen the same kind of dependency on, or accommodation of, bicycles as contemporary cycling cities like Amsterdam and Copenhagen, they stand as a marker of how relevant cycling once was in American cities.

Just years before the invention of the safety bicycle, commuting via the bicycle had been an anomaly. For a brief period in the 1890s, it was anything but. And it would continue to become ever more popular . . . or so everyone thought.

CHAPTER EIGHT

Riding for Reform: Wheelwomen

When people think of cycling in the 1890s, they often think about women—for good reason. People talked about what bicycles meant to women as much as any other subgroup of the cycling city. Some were exuberant about the prospect of women riders. Others cringed. Either way they agreed that women on wheels threatened to challenge many of the unspoken rules that governed the urban world, particularly those related to gender and space. Public debate about the nature of cycling, and the nature of the city, quickly ensued. "Who can ride?" "How should they ride?" "What should they wear?" And, at least implicitly, "Who does the city belong to?" The answers and the questions themselves reveal not only the ever-changing dynamics of gender within American cities but also the powerful way in which a single invention can threaten to disrupt urban culture.[1]

Women cyclists also played a role in creating a general understanding of how people should cycle and how bicycles should function. Women, like men, cycled for recreation and to commute, but they embraced other uses as well. Bicycles served a larger political purpose for women, one that was more than occasionally at odds with other segments of the population, even within the population of cyclists. It should be of no surprise that these women understood the bicycle in unique ways, oftentimes complicated by class-based perspectives. How they came to understand the bicycle adds another important dimension to the cycling city, since they helped shape broader perceptions about the practice of cycling. On the one hand, they represented the democratic nature of the bicycle and fulfilled the promise of mobility. On the other hand, their stories expose the very real constraints of the urban world. Thus female riders symbolized the oft-cited supposition that bicycles would become available for everyone for every purpose, while also revealing how wrongheaded that theory was.

When bicycles first crossed the Atlantic, men rolled precariously atop the high-wheel machines. Women sat on the sidelines or comfortably on their tricycles. For some, the obvious dichotomy was welcome. Any woman who dared to master the bicycle was deemed a "circus lady" or a "semi-monster." But in the early 1890s, as manufacturers built, marketers pitched, and dealers sold specially designed ladies' safety bicycles, women began to embrace "the wheel."[2]

As quickly as women adopted the bicycle so too did their detractors find cause for concern. Defined as machines and often used for sport, bicycles posed a challenge for women who wanted to partake in what was perceived to be a masculine activity. To make matters more difficult, women had almost always been passengers, not drivers. Horses pulled and men steered the carriages that bobbed along the nineteenth-century city's crooked streets. Even when women did mount horses by themselves, they were encouraged to ride in the more ladylike sidesaddle position. Bicycles offered no such option. Instead, bicycles required women to mount and operate the machine in exactly the same way as men. There was plenty of suspicion about women's ability to steer and operate such a vehicle. More broadly, serious physical activity had long been viewed as acceptable only for men and for women on the margins. The expectation for "respectable" middle- and upper-class white women was quite different. Running was simply "unladylike." Even when walking, women were reminded to "walk with modest step and even pace."[3]

The debates about female cyclists spiraled into a national discussion, encompassing a range of issues such as femininity, Victorian respectability, and physical health. Opponents warned of muscular fatigue, poor posture, and a myriad of other ailments that the "fairer" sex inevitably succumbed to after prolonged bicycle trips. Some doctors fretted over the "unavoidable stimulation" resultant from the friction between the lady rider and the saddle. One doctor even went so far as to suggest that cycling weakened a woman's "power of resistance" and led to nymphomania, prostitution, and bastards. Other medical professionals cautioned that cycling could permanently damage female reproductive organs. But as more women began to ride and did so safely, more doctors challenged these suppositions, arguing that "the young woman with a pure mind . . . can come to no harm from bicycle riding." More than being innocuous, the bicycle could actually do women much good. These views represented two ends of the spectrum, as most medical authorities came to recommend cycling for women, but in modest doses. Female cyclists (some of whom were doctors themselves) helped doctors arrive at that conclusion. But the most powerful voices came from ordinary women who helped shape the medical discourse by writing opinion pieces in popular magazines. Through personal anecdotes and reflection, women riders challenged both the medical community and the prevailing notion concerning women's unsuitability for active recreation.[4]

Riding modestly meant not riding for too long, while also riding at acceptable speeds. The thrill of riding could be too great for someone to curb, however. "You might as well tell a girl to go to a ball room, and not dance," Dr. Gihon advised, "as to tell her to ride a bicycle and not ride fast." Nevertheless, a plethora of doctors came to prescribe the bicycle for urban women, as many of the universal health benefits of cycling and exercise in general (e.g., counteracting a sedentary lifestyle, reconvening with nature) applied doubly for women. Other doctors elucidated that the advantages were more than merely physical. When a woman rode a bicycle, "her mind [was] taken off of those things which have a tendency to perplex and madden." The result, one physician pointed out, was "an uncommonly happy, bright, and exhilarated set of faces which we see spinning down our streets."[5]

Perhaps the most prominent concern was that female bicycle riding endangered conventional beliefs and practices regarding public space. Although the notion of complete "separate spheres," where women lived in isolation from the public, male-dominated world, has long been discredited, urban geography certainly has an important gendered context. Public spaces are governed by a set of codes, formal and informal. Notions of domesticity and expectations of "ladylike" behavior pervaded not just the home, but the public sphere as well. Certain areas of the city were deemed "off limits" for respectable women. Traveling alone was discouraged. While loitering men might be flâneurs, such women were tagged as streetwalkers. Proper etiquette dictated that women should cut inconspicuous figures, avoid wearing bright colors, and do their best to move through the city unnoticed. "The quieter and less conspicuous her costume the better," the *Bicycling World* advice columnist moralized in 1895. Mobility itself had always been linked to freedom, so almost by definition women on the move "entered a zone of moral danger." Female cyclists moving through the city alone tested countless assumptions about proper behavior.[6]

By the turn of the century, women began to display a new ability "to negotiate the urban terrain on their own terms," by assuming a more public presence on the streets and in the workplace. This newfound independence was not the product of simple modernization and does not fall neatly into the Whiggish historical narrative; rather, progress was a result of "the determination of individuals and organized groups to redesign the city for their own purposes." Many of these individuals recognized the bicycle's role in their newfound mobility. For them, the bicycle held a unique meaning and promise. For men, the bicycle offered a faster commute, a new means of recreation, and a bridge on which to pedal away from the city; for women it offered something more: "it was a steed upon which they rode into a new world."[7]

By the last decade of the nineteenth century, a dramatic reconstitution of public space and social relations was already well underway. The increasing number of women who entered the workplace, politics, reform movements, and institutes of higher education helped challenge older notions of domesticity and women's place (or lack thereof) in the public sphere. In more places and in more ways, women took on public roles and occupied a public presence in the urban network. On railroad trains, women found cars just for them. They could now travel alone, albeit in a sheltered environment. Previously, crowded business and downtown districts had been largely occupied by men, but by the end of the nineteenth century, the composition and character of these areas had changed, as the popularization of the department store reordered the downtown aesthetic. The women who worked there, the women who shopped there, and the women who simply went downtown "to see and to be seen" transformed once male-dominated spaces into sites of commerce and culture for both women and men. Barred from the perceived dirty business that sullied city halls, women managed to take a more active role in the city. They sought to reorder and redefine urban spaces. Municipal housekeepers—so the theory went—could leverage their feminine morals and motherly instincts to clean and beautify the downtown districts they sought to call home. Not only did they lobby to scrub the street, wash down the sidewalks, take down obnoxious billboards, and erect decorative lampposts and ornamental trashcans, but the very act of doing so brought them— quite literally—to the streets of downtown.[8]

Beyond the well-maintained sidewalks and beyond the Ladies' Mile— the name given to a stretch of New York streets dominated by department stores—and even beyond the restaurants and opera houses that began to attract wealthier (although generally not unaccompanied) women, bicycles transported women around the entire city. As one woman wrote in 1895,

"Now and again a complaint arises of the narrowness of woman's sphere. For such disorder of the soul the sufferer can do no better than to flatten her sphere to a circle, mount it, and take to the road." As another columnist in the same year editorialized, "The greatest effect of the bicycle upon woman will be, we believe, the breaking down for all time of the numerous barriers created by the prejudice and irrational thought of the centuries in regard to her 'lot,' 'sphere,' 'place,' etc." Contemporaries argued that by allowing women to widen their "sphere," bicycles fostered not only increased mobility to travel in, around, and out of the city but also engendered feelings of freedom and independence.[9]

City newspapers acknowledged the phenomenon as well. "The fact remains, and cannot be disputed," the *Cleveland Critic* reported in 1896, that the woman "has advanced in her sphere since she took to the wheel." The *Baltimore American* noted, "This is probably the first athletic sport that has put women on equal terms with men . . . [and it] is also having a good influence in making the young wheelwoman self-reliant, inspiring her with confidence in her own ability and giving her a freedom and an independence that is born of her ability to take care of herself." "The independence of womankind has never had so great a champion as the bicycle," yet another paper declared. Thousands of similar remarks echoed among media outlets in the final years of the nineteenth century. But it was not just the journalists who helped to reflect, create, and distort reality in late-nineteenth-century America. Nor were they the only ones who had come to believe that bicycles could reconfigure the relationship between women and the city.[10]

A group of women riders described the bicycle as an almost utopian instrument. One female cyclist reported to the *New York Times* that the benefits of cycling were too many to count: "The first is that it gives one the gratification of being one's own master or mistress; another is the simplicity of the exercise, while the third is the fact, to which all riders can testify, that it improves the physical health, thus benefiting us mentally and morally." That was just the beginning. "Then there is a feeling of gratification in being independent of coachmen or grooms," Cora Potter continued. And finally, the long list of the somewhat less obvious benefits of cycling: "Since I began riding I have been capable of much additional hard work, my appetite has been improved, and I sleep better . . ."[11] Although some of these effects might have been placebo, Potter joined a chorus of women who heralded the bicycle as a cure-all. Their enthusiasm for cycling's revolutionary powers perhaps speaks to how desperately city dwellers sought an antidote to industrial urban life.

Converted cyclists proselytized the dogma of cycling to fellow women. Women encouraged their mothers, daughters, and friends to ride. To ease the learning process, several female cyclists authored entire books touting the benefits of cycling to reluctant women. The manuals taught female novices how to ride a bicycle, how to care for and maintain their machine, and how to select appropriate attire. In addition to practical advice, these female-authored books also served as a means to "regender the bicycle." While men marketed, sold, and initially constructed—both literally and socially—bicycles, the meaning of women's wheels evolved thanks to the users themselves.[12]

Not surprisingly, both bicycle companies and the women rider-authors endorsed cycling, but their particular messages reflected a divergent gender ideology. To that end, manufacturers began building machines designed to embody the varying gender roles. Men could buy the "Napoleon" model, women the "Josephine." Men could ride the sportiest of wheels outfitted for racing and women could find an assortment of models promising lightness and grace. The ladies' machines might also be outfitted with practical devices designed to ensure that women would not have to abandon their feminine garb. As many women cyclists surely realized, so long as they maintained their femininity, there would be fewer detractors who questioned their newfound mobility. Eager to sell bicycles to women, marketers focused on how women could maintain their traditional femininity while riding. They argued that bicycles were easy to master and could be ridden gracefully without vigorous effort or expert knowledge about the machine.[13]

Female-authored manuals, like Maria Ward's *The Common Sense of Bicycling* from 1896, suggested something quite different. Instead of dismissing the challenges of cycling, she submitted that women were physically and mentally capable of overcoming the very real hurdles involved in becoming a cyclist. She acknowledged that bicycles were complex machines that needed continued maintenance and that an owner could undertake repairs herself (figs. 8.1 and 8.2). Ward suggested that in the process of becoming a wheelwoman and mastering the art of riding and maintenance, a woman's "own powers are revealed." By authoring instruction manuals, Ward and others helped to continue to define the social meaning of the bicycle. In their construction, the bicycle became less "feminized." It was not that lady's bicycles were naturally suited for women; it was that ladies could become suited for bicycles. The requisite skills and perseverance to master the bicycle could be learned by and from women.[14]

Still, female riders faced an array of uncertainty. How should women

TURNING THE BICYLCE OVER

THE BICYCLE TURNED OVER.

Figs. 8.1 and 8.2. The author demonstrates for her female readers how to position the bicycle in order to perform maintenance and repairs. Reprinted from Maria E. Ward, *The Common Sense of Bicycling: Bicycling for Ladies* (New York: Brentano's, 1896), 128, 131.

cycle about the city? What is an appropriate costume? Are the rules governing behavior between the sexes different atop of a bicycle? The discussions
that ensued revealed that bicycles did pose a potential threat to traditional
gender norms and social relations. Some called it progress, others inde-
cency. Sensing a potential sea change, journalists for cycling periodicals,
advice columnists, etiquette experts, and even bicycle merchants weighed
in on the ways in which urban women could and should ride bicycles.

Few etiquette books, which as a genre proliferated in the final decades
of the nineteenth century, failed to notice the rising popularity of cycling
and its effect on social relations. Books advised their readers about the
proper way to mount, ride, and cycle about the cityscape. Female etiquette
experts featured in popular advice columns also generally approved of lady
cyclists, under one condition: that they remained "ladylike." Guides included a detailed set of rules designed to guarantee that women maintain
their femininity and virtuousness while riding. Most importantly, female
cyclists needed to distinguish themselves from the most masculine of
riders—those riding for sport or thrill of speed. Etiquette authorities advised that women cycle in an erect position, never ride a bicycle with racing (curved-down) handlebars, and never ride at a "race pace." Moreover, to
ensure that women on wheels preserved their integrity, guides often suggested that single women going out for a spin always be accompanied by a
chaperone. Since "every one rides nowadays," the author of one such book
from 1896 noted, this task was "an affair easily managed."[15]

Men, too, needed to understand the implications of women joining the
ranks of urban cyclists. Those who bought their bicycles inside Chicago's
Siegel, Cooper & Company's eight-story department store received a free
copy of a *Cycling Record Book*. The notebook gave purchasers space to
record their rides and distances, introduced neophyte wheelmen to the local traffic laws, and lectured men on how to behave around their female
companions on wheels. Proper road etiquette dictated, so the pocket-
sized guide explained, that a true gentleman holds a lady's wheel as she
mounted it and that a man always ride on a woman's left so he can "have
his right arm ready to give assistance." There was a long list of other rules,
some rational, others far from it.[16]

Most of the voices sounding off about female cyclists directed their
instruction to women. Major cycling periodicals, like *Bicycling World*,
featured regular advice columns for women riders. Others, including
American Wheelmen, published entire issues devoted to female cyclists,
while whole magazines, like the *Wheelwoman*, catered exclusively to an
all-female cyclist readership. Together they provided practical informa-

tion about cycling, bicycle-related news, and a host of advice (and debate) about the ways in which women should adopt the bicycle. These issues of how cyclists should "behave" became such an important feature of late-nineteenth-century American life that the relevant debates echoed in channels far removed from just the cycling press. In fact, advice for women riders came from media outlets of every kind and from every region. In New Orleans, the local paper gave some simple advice to the southern belles of the Crescent City who hoped to remain the darlings of that city: "sit straight, ride slowly, have the saddle high enough, use short cranks, never, never chew gum, conduct yourself altogether in a ladylike manner and sensible people will not shake their heads in disapproval when you ride." The suggestion to use short cranks was of particular importance, as those women who favored long cranks were "positively wrong," as one writer in 1897 declared. Longer cranks required an increased range of motion, which resulted in an "ungraceful" and "hygienically wrong" elevation of the knee. Even *Good Housekeeping* magazine weighed in on how bicycles transformed traditional etiquette and proper comportment outside the home. The magazine's writers endorsed cycling, but they stressed that women must work hard to maintain their respectability as they rode about the city. Refinement, the magazine implored, should not be "throw[n] to the winds." *Good Housekeeping* cautioned its readership about riding too fast or on the sidewalks, wearing an "immodest costume," and, most certainly, from making "new acquaintances while on her wheel." The final point was underscored by an admission that coed bicycling and mingling had led to rather "objectionable intimacies." Ultimately, and perhaps most importantly, advice experts argued, women cyclists were just that— women. And maintaining their femininity while engaged in an activity that appeared to some as anything but feminine was essential.[17]

Outside of the press, the debates over female cycling and the insistence that women riders retain their femininity carried over into the streets. One cycling parade in particular illustrates how bicycles complicated traditional masculine and feminine constructs and the enduring constraints regarding female behavior in public. On the last day of spring, 1891, more than a thousand cyclists took to Brooklyn's winding roads for a grand parade. Throngs of spectators walled the streets and fought for seats on a grandstand perched above Flatbush Avenue. At the head of the parade fifty-eight female cyclists rode, all led by Miss Paige, a noted member of a popular bicycle club, the Prospect Lady Cyclers. The women riding alongside (or, to be exact, leading) men received applause from onlookers all along the course. At first glance, the parade looms as a remarkable example of the social fluidity engendered by the bicycle. Sweaty women and men cruised through Brooklyn together, led by a female cyclist. That women had a central role in the exhibition at all was somewhat of a rarity for nineteenth-century parades. Yet the confines of this gender fluidity were equally clear.[18]

Watching the festivities, a group of notable Brooklynites sat amidst the crowd waiting to dole out several prizes to the most distinguished paraders. The criteria for the women's awards did not include speed or efficiency, and certainly not anything to do with the "military precision" (a rather masculine distinction) of the all-male Harlem Wheelmen, which had earned that group thunderous applause. Indeed, many of the wheelmen marched uniformly in clubs, following orders from club officers, including positions like "commander," which came with a military-like badge. The cyclists responded to coded messages sent via bugle or whistle that indicated to the trained listener when to "mount" or "fall in" and the speed at which to ride. As one cycling parade marshal remembered, each cycling "officer" was to salute with his right hand, keep his men six feet apart, and lead his white-gloved, sword-carrying, uniformed battalion through the city.[19]

The female cyclists marched to different expectations. The parade judges ranked the women solely on their personal appearance and the ways in which they had decorated their bicycles. Ultimately the judges awarded the grand prize to two young women on a tandem tricycle, decorated with roses and red, white, and blue streamers. The prize was a "tortoise-shell and gold hairpin." Clearly, existing gender norms mitigated some of the gains in women's mobility. As historian Mary Ryan has shown, parades can reveal ". . . in a particularly powerful, publicly sanctioned way, how contemporaries construed, displayed, and saw the urban social order." In this case, the organizers of the parade clearly delineated what constituted proper order and behavior: women could ride bicycles, but only in a gender-appropriate context. While women could parade through the streets, participating in what had been seen as an overtly masculine activity, they were expected to do so with grace, beauty, and, above all, femininity.[20]

Cycling was one of the rare pursuits that when done right could secure either one's masculinity or one's femininity. Perhaps distressed by the loss of independence, cultural paradigm shifts, and changing gender relations that came with the rise of industrialization and urbanization, some men became "unusually obsessed with manhood."[21] Since the fiery battles of the Civil War had been extinguished so long before, some men in this era of "overcivilization" displayed a heightened need to display their manliness. Some took up boxing or football, others lifted weights, and some raced bicycles. While men marched on wheels to military orders and sped around city corners, women utilized the bicycle to fashionably promenade through the city. These competing masculine and feminine identities managed to coexist briefly, but for certain men, women's adoption of the wheel robbed the bicycle of its value.

DRESS REFORM

The imperative that women riding through the city maintain their femininity was at the core of the hubbub circling the issue of women's dress. As a fashion historian recently wrote, when women began to take up the bicycle they "had nothing to wear." At least, they had no practical options. But as cycling entered the mainstream, women riders began experimenting with clothes more conducive to athletics. Some women used cycling as an opportunity to test the boundaries of conventional fashion. Others tried to adapt traditional dress, and some noncyclists wrote off the idea of "sporting women" entirely. Sports and sportswear had long been associated with masculinity. But that was changing. Earlier in the century, select women had ventured out-of-doors to play croquet, tennis, and to swim and skate. As cycling peaked, so did golf, which attracted men and women (though usually in segregated groups), and by the close of the nineteenth century, women's athletics, including gymnastics, rowing, and basketball, had become a regular experience for those attending women's colleges.[22]

To varying degrees, these pursuits challenged existing norms concerning female athleticism and appropriate dress. Although women began to take up sporting activities in greater numbers, few activities were as public as cycling. For instance, female tennis players served and volleyed within the confines of a small (and often private) court. The ladies playing basketball at any of the handful of all-girls colleges (some of which hosted bicycling clubs and courses) did so indoors and away from any male onlookers. Female cyclists, however, drove through crowded downtown districts, inside city parks, and around the city, all the while subject to public scrutiny. There was even a growing contingent of professional female bicycle racers. Admittedly, the clothes designed for indoor physical activities (e.g., basketball) could change more quickly, more drastically, and with less controversy because they were played in private and without men. By their very nature, certain outdoor sports also necessitated significant changes in sportswear. By the 1890s, for example, women could acceptably be found in bloomers and short sleeves . . . so long as they were in the water. Cycling garb presented its own unique set of demands. The clothes needed to be practical, but also fashionable and deemed appropriate for mixed-gender spaces. Cycling was much more than a form of recreation; it was also a means of travel. And so if swimwear became acceptable on the beaches, but only the beaches, the stakes for cycling dress were much steeper because women traveled throughout the city. Also, women eventually got off their wheels. And when they did, cycling clothes became just clothes. In the end, it was a combination of reforms in those newly popular outdoor and indoor activities that merged to create modern sportswear for women.[23]

Nevertheless, considering that cycling was one of the most popular forms of active recreation, it is not surprising that the debates over cycling dress became the focus of the much larger (and older) discussion about women, sports, and dress. And even though the dress reforms that accompanied the bicycle were just one part of the larger narrative, they have become the central story told generations later. This is in no small part due to the fact that the contemporary media exaggerated the number of those willing to don bloomers and the supposed ill effects of doing so. In a rare 1896 traffic survey that recorded such data, counters in New York observed that only 63 out of 2501 female riders (2.5 percent) sported bloomers.[24] Bloomers were real but not common. The debates about bloomers were real and common.

Like most issues of fashion, Americans adopted cycling dress unevenly from city to city and according to socioeconomic status. No matter the city, the heart of the debate was exactly the same: femininity and modesty. Those concerned about women donning masculine clothing waged a war against the improper outfits. In some cities local officials and community organizations even tried to make wearing bloomers in public illegal. The Detroit City Council voted down (twenty to ten) one such measure, which would have defined wearing bloomers as a misdemeanor and subject to a ten dollar fine. While some women did continue to wear traditional clothing, few could ignore the difficulty those clothes presented on a bicycle. Tight corsets and heavy fabrics made it hard to breathe, stay cool, and maneuver on wheels. Long skirts flared, swept up city dirt, and could easily snag in the moving parts of the bicycle. Dress guards and elastic at the bottom of skirts could mitigate the dangers of fabric catching and skirts blowing, but riding was still an uncomfortable experience. So wheelwomen adopted a range of dress that threatened to disrupt traditional views of fashion, including divided skirts (often matched with boots); shortened skirts that sat well above the ankle, where they likely met a pair

Fig. 8.3. The Pope Manufacturing Company issued a series of dolls in 1895. The dresses of the dolls were chosen from a national contest in which women across the country designed the clothing themselves. In the process (at least according to the information on the back of the doll) participants helped determine what constituted "appropriate dress." Pope's office sent the set of six dolls to anyone willing to send in five two-cent stamps. Reprinted from the Library of Congress, Prints and Photographs Division.

of leggings; knee-length bloomers that were often worn with an overskirt; female versions of knickerbockers or trousers that looked a whole lot like the men's versions; flexible corsets; and an endless range of hats and sleeve styles. Overall, while women's fashion on the wheel pushed the boundaries of propriety, few women were willing to bare their ankles or adopt the most risqué costumes. Many found a balance—a new style of clothes that felt emancipatory and progressive and that appeared to only modify, rather than replace, traditional clothing.[25]

Nevertheless, and despite the fact that the relatively short cuts and more masculine qualities of bicycle clothes (whether it be bloomers, a divided skirt, or even leggings) might have been cause for insults or a soured reputation, some women embraced the new clothing (on and off the bicycle) as much as they embraced the machine that required the wardrobe change. In fact, the clothes and the bicycles together became associated with "modernity and independence." Even if most women stopped short of wearing bloomers, the visibility of their bicycle costumes played a minor role in making such clothes acceptable. As one reporter recalled in the summer of 1896: "Three years ago a modest American woman would hardly have ventured out on the street in New York with a skirt that stopped above her ankles, and leggings that reached obviously to her knees. To-day she can do it without exciting attention. She simply has on her bicycle clothes. . . ." Indeed, bicycle clothes contributed to the long and drawn-out process of female dress reform thanks to activists who came to promote bicycle clothes for more than just their practicality. Bicycling had a greater impact on dress reform than many other sporting activities (e.g., skating, croquet, and golf) because of its popularity, but it fell far short of single-handedly ushering in transformative change. In truth, the relative acceptance of bicycle clothes cannot be separated from the fact that other forms of physical activity, which also demanded dress reform, became popular at roughly the same time as the bicycle. And so while a small percentage of women did wear bloomers, and a lot of people fretted about the possibility that bloomers would become ubiquitous, the debate was mostly just another Gilded Age media sensation.[26]

NEW WOMEN

The women who challenged Victorian-era norms concerning dress, domesticity, and "proper" behavior became known as "New Women." A fixture of urban society by the 1890s, the "New Woman" epitomized those who grew tired of longstanding social norms and who sought a new era of female independence. Many remained unmarried and pursued college educations and professional careers. They were, in the words of another historian, "independent, athletic, sexual, and modern," attributes often bestowed to female cyclists at the time. Explicitly linking the two groups, *Godey's Magazine* wrote about the bicycle: "It is the actual medium through which the 'new' woman has evolved herself." Cycling and "New Womanhood" reinforced one another, as women looking to assert their independence utilized bicycles, while advocates believed that cycling fostered mobility and confident women. As a member of the Ladies' Cycling League of Minneapolis toasted in 1895, "The girls of today who hold prominent places are the strong, healthy girls who do not scream when they see a mouse, nor get frightened when a snake crosses their path—the girls who

ride on cycles." Indeed, women weaved through traffic and down busy urban corridors, enjoying the sense of power that came with it.[27]

"New Women" also "questioned the 'natural' division of women and
men's lives into separate spheres of social activity." As part of a sweeping
change in American urban culture toward the end of the nineteenth century, leisure activities increasingly moved from homosocial to heterosocial
in nature. Bicycles played a role too as they provided more opportunities for
women and men to engage in leisure and recreation together. As one educator argued in 1896, the bicycle "has encouraged to a degree never before
imagined to be possible the comradeship of the sexes" and, as a result, "is
probably the greatest agent in breaking down barriers strengthened by centuries of tradition. Give to a woman a right to participate in the pleasures,
exercise, and pastimes of men, and the absolute equality of sexes is not far
away." While that expectation was surely overly optimistic, some of the
rigidities governing how to approach a member of the opposite sex, how
to introduce oneself, and, ultimately, the character of dating did indeed

Figs. 8.4 and 8.5. Advertisers regularly depicted the "New Woman" in their
marketing campaigns. This cover of *Bearings* magazine (*facing page*) dramatizes
and exaggerates the idea of these new wheelwomen, donning bright colors,
revealing a generous portion of their legs, and riding at a good clip and in a
carefree manner—so much so that they are even able to read (*Bearings* magazine,
presumably) while riding! *Above* is an ad from Stearns Bicycles, which features
a woman with short hair and a short skirt who is "coasting." Reprinted from
Charles A. Cox, *Bearings*, undated, American Art Posters, Print Department,
Boston Public Library; J. Ottmann Lithograph Co., Stearns Bicycles, 1896.

seem to have eased atop bicycles. Mixed groups on bicycles regularly rode
through the city and participated in the same bicycle-centered social activities. A group of female and male clerical workers in Philadelphia, for example, fraternized outside of the workplace by going for a long ride, broken
up by a picnic and watermelon fight. Outside of the office and on bicycles,
these kinds of interactions became more common and acceptable.[28]

As more women cycled through the city unescorted, a few dressed in bloomers and many more in other bicycle costumes, the "New Woman" became less of a fringe element and more mainstream. "It has been woman's success in attaining almost inaccessible places, without appearing bold or unladylike," one writer chronicled, "that has caused a revolution in the feeling against the 'new' woman." Still, there was a limit. A "New Woman" cyclist who in 1896 sported "blue golf stockings, with red diamonds at the top, tight brown knickerbockers, a man's coat and rakish jockey cap" had, apparently, overdone it. One female onlooker teased ". . . well, I don't blame men for making fun of some people! Just look at her! Low handle bars, too!" The racing-style handlebars and clothing designed for a man represented too much of a violation of gender norms, at least for this one spectator. Nevertheless, shrewd bicycle manufacturers realized that these "New Women" represented a growing portion of their customer base. For "New Women" riders and, perhaps more importantly, the not-so-"New Woman" who wanted to be a "New Woman," advertisers painted an idealized picture of post-Victorian femininity. Before any other industry did so, bicycle companies featured women outside of the home in their advertisements.[29]

As the "New Women" on wheels carried hopes of progress, certain elements of society grew even more cautious about female cyclists. While the medical community originally had a mixed reaction to women cycling, the most outspoken opponents to female cyclists had only minor concerns about the potential for physical harm. The real danger was moral hazard. The exact nature of those hazards depended on the type of woman.

CLASS AND GENDER

Cycling increased mobility for all, but it did so in radically different ways. Society women, eager to flaunt their status and wealth outside of the home, generally shunned bloomers and joined elite clubs or patronized exclusive cycling academies, often riding indoors or at least at a safe distance from unsavory onlookers. Middle-class women rode mostly for leisure as well, touring through city parks, neighboring sites, city streets, and, mirroring the activity of society women, for making their "calls" (delivering their personalized cards via bicycle). Lower-level, white collar, working women rode some for recreation and in imitation of the middle-class that they so anxiously hoped to join. They also rode for practical travel, particularly for commuting. Clerks, office girls, stenographers, and others swirled around the city en route to or returning from their places of business.[30]

One schoolteacher's diary from 1899 gives a glimpse of the many ways women used their wheels. The forty-four-year-old from Olympia, Washington, described her daily bicycle commutes and how cycling made running errands, visiting friends, and taking trips to "pick wild strawberries on the prairie" a delight. She reminisced about how she "wheeled" to the Woman's Christian Temperance Union convention and how she fancied day trips to Tacoma and "wheeling around the city." Just like men, women used the bicycle for an array of purposes.[31]

All commuters had to deal with a range of issues, from fighting traffic to finding parking and negotiating inclement weather. But women on wheels faced difficulties all their own. They faced the potential for moral condemnation by challenging the traditional urban boundaries that defined where proper women belonged. For society women on wheels, respectability and status could be wagered and lost by the "improper" use of the bicycle. Tradition and status anxieties especially pressured society women to conduct themselves in a dignified manner, which often meant moving invisibly through the city. Some thought that society women belonged only inside homes, at club functions, and in select private spaces. Certainly they had no business publicly, and therefore brazenly, wheeling through the streets. A manners expert described the ideal of such a woman: "She dresses daintily and inconspicuously—effaces herself, in fact, as much in this exercise as she does in all public places." Experts agreed that for the surrounding suburbs and country that ringed American cities the rules were "not as rigid," but urban spaces, filled with watchful eyes, demanded certain protocols. Yet women on wheels tested the definitions of "appropriate" behavior and, in some ways, altered those very conditions that had for so long governed public space. No longer confined to elegant city parks during the "fashionable hour," society women regularly cruised down Boston's Commonwealth Avenue and New York's Boulevard. As Maureen Montgomery has written, "Leisure activities enabled women of the *haute bourgeoisie* to gain access to the city" and "helped to legitimize women's presence in public." And no leisure activity (cycling was almost purely recreational for most affluent urbanites) was more public than cycling.[32]

With public space came public examination. "The sight of women on bicycles suggested independence, mobility, and emancipation, which, taken together, threatened the traditional confinement of society women to domestic space and to those public places where social interaction was carefully regulated." The omnipresent public gaze invited scrutiny but also the opportunity to convey a carefully constructed image of oneself.

Through fashionable cycling suits and luxurious bicycles, wealthy women promenaded through the streets, advertising their access to wealth, and, in the process, implicitly differentiated themselves from the rest of the ever-expanding base of cyclists. Women's magazines that gossiped about female celebrity cyclists—famed actresses, royalty abroad, and wives of wealthy industrialists—conveyed the idea that cycling, done in the proper manner of course (meaning cycling in select groups, donning appropriate clothes, and riding atop the most extravagant machines), could connote aristocracy, prestige, and wealth. Readers surely welcomed this assurance, considering that the democratization of once-luxury goods only hardened class anxieties. These anxieties manifested themselves with wealthy women practicing "conspicuous leisure" and "conspicuous consumption," as Thorstein Veblen described in his penetrating 1899 study *The Theory of the Leisure Class*. These women joined a larger class of late-nineteenth-century affluent urban women who consciously displayed their status in public.[33]

Working women, who depended on bicycles for practical transportation as well as for recreation, rode through the city in quite a different manner. In certain ways they were more mobile. If "respectable" women risked their reputation by traveling to certain parts of the city, those without a reputation had less to lose. And the urban map—in terms of both mobility and gendered and moral geography—was in the midst of great revision. Nevertheless, reformers worried that certain city spaces remained dangerous for working women who might fall victim to various temptations.[34] Female cyclists could also be the subject of direct control.

In 1895, three female schoolteachers from New York discovered that the bicycle provided the best way to traverse their roughly two-mile commute. The school's Board of Trustees saw it differently. The Board castigated the teachers for setting a wholly improper example for students. One trustee thought it wrong for any "young lady" to take to the wheel, but that it was especially dangerous for a caretaker of children to adopt such a devilish mode of transportation. A second trustee expressed his concern about the indecent clothes necessitated by their bicycles. Today, "they wear skirts, of course, but if we do not stop them now," the board member lamented, bloomers, trousers, and other objectionable outfits would be sure to follow.[35] This kind of control over schoolteachers was evident more broadly in the way that school boards hired, paid, and influenced female educators across the country. Unlike other municipal workers, city teachers were expected to be virtuous and to embody the feminine ideal.[36] For some, these expectations applied to all women on bicycles.

THE ANTICYCLING CRUSADE

In 1896, the debates over the appropriateness of women cyclists bubbled over during a feisty campaign that captured national attention. President Charlotte Smith of the Woman's National Rescue League launched an assault that would garner her fame, hatred, and the undisputed title of the most outspoken protester against female cyclists. Mrs. Charlotte Smith denounced cycling as part of a larger, lifelong campaign to improve the lives of working women. Over the course of her career, the reformer had worked to create lodging houses, job training programs, and a national union of female clerks; to ensure that women received equal pay for equal work; and to provide moral support for the growing numbers of "unfortunate women" living inside America's cities. She was also a noted supporter of women inventors. In these efforts, Smith embodied the progressive woman, exerting political influence, taking to the streets, and working to uplift the urban populace. But it was the issue of cycling that elicited Smith's most zealous crusade (she did once lead a similar campaign against the "wicked bachelor politician").[37]

According to Mrs. Smith, cycling was universally destructive: "The bicycle is the devil's advance agent, morally and physically." Allegedly, it was supremely dangerous for women. She believed that cycling promoted immorality, immodesty, and unwomanly behavior, and fostered "evil associations," as the activity itself tempted "young girls into paths that lead directly to sin." The basis of her oversimplified argument was that more young women seemed to embrace a new, and more lax, set of social values *and* that more young women seemed to be riding bicycles. With both claims containing some elements of truth, no amount of logic could convince the stern-eyed crusader otherwise. Smith tapped into the conservative predilections of Victorian-era Americans and successfully garnered a legion of followers who joined her at mass protests and shared her vision of inaugurating a widespread "anti-bicycle movement."[38]

With national headquarters in Washington, DC, and branch offices in Boston, New York, and other cycling cities, the National Woman's Rescue League provided the muscle for Smith's assault. While Smith gave speeches and published editorials on the subject, she enlisted her fellow "rescuers" in an army of bicycle eradicators known as the "bicycle brigade." Formed to "smite" the "hellish thing" from city streets, the "bicycle brigade" wasted no time. The troop employed an array of strategies to expose the immorality of female cyclists. In one such scheme, Smith conscripted several of her loyal followers for undercover work. Posing as ordinary cyclists, the bicycle soldiers rode through town recording statistical and anecdotal evidence about the women riders they passed. "How many girls have a chaperon; how many girls start alone and come home accompanied by men . . . ; how many go to roadhouses; what do they drink, how late do . . . girls remain out on their wheels at night?" were just some of the questions they hoped to answer. Women shadowed women as cyclists spied on cyclists.[39]

Although Smith found a band of devoted followers, in general Americans denounced her. Old and young, women and men, joined in criticism of Smith that often matched the vitriol with which she condemned cycling. Although a select group of male doctors, ministers, and critics continued to warn against female cycling, Smith and her all-female brigade found few men willing to support them. While some males sought to circumscribe how women should cycle and, more generally, control female behavior, very few men (or women, for that matter) opposed cycling so adamantly and vocally. Nonetheless, Smith's list of enemies quickly outpaced her allied brigade. Indeed, probably the most striking effect of Smith's efforts was the number of people she angered who, in the process of lambasting Smith, articulated their own support for female bicycle riding.[40]

Scores of editorials were written in direct response to Smith's actions. In 1896, the words of Mrs. Eliza Archard filled newspaper columns: "I regard the bicycle as the greatest one means of emancipating women that has come in the last fifty years" and as a "great moral engine."[41] Others attacked each of Smith's well-known claims one by one. When Mrs. Smith declared that bicycles inflicted "a great curse" on America, ultimately resulting in an "army of invalids," an impassioned reader and woman cyclist countered that "bicycling is a curse" if "giving woman advantages and broader fields in the walks of life, which make her superior to her less ambitious sister of the past . . . is a curse. If breathing God's pure air, lingering among the flowers, birds and green fields, in preference to stifling in the town's narrow limits during the few hours snatched for recreation, cause one to become the invalid of the future, then we shall return to our old haunts."[42]

Undaunted, Smith marched on. "All this 'pure of heaven' racket," she responded, "makes me weary of life." Physically and morally the bicycle was crippling, she insisted. However outrageous some of her points may have seemed, other claims may not have been completely off base. Substantiating one of Mrs. Smith's central concerns, a New York police captain witnessed that bicycles fostered some less than savory activities. Captain McNamara reported in 1896 that "great numbers of women have taken to the wheel because it helps them in their business." Prostitutes on wheels could exploit the benefits of cycling as much as anyone, the captain explained: "They can dress to show off the form, they can make acquaintances easily, they can reach resorts and mingle with pleasure-seekers on an equal footing. We had to stop one woman a little while ago. She was young, good looking and very well dressed. She made a fine show on the wheel. She used to ride to the Shelter, at Coney Island, and make that place her headquarters for getting acquainted with men." While cycling prostitutes were surely uncommon, some critics joined Mrs. Smith in condemning everyday women cyclists who they believed behaved in a manner not altogether different from prostitutes. In literary sources from the 1890s, writers linked the brazen female cyclists who dressed inappropriately, exposed too much of their bodies, sought public attention, and pushed the boundaries of social convention to prostitutes.[43]

Meanwhile, reports indicated that women on wheels cycled their way to the city's nooks and crannies most suitable for trysts. Hundreds of "bicycle maidens" congregated in one such spot hidden near a city landmark, extinguished their bicycle lamps, and shared benches with their male companions "in attitudes not at all suggestive of modesty or prudence." An 1896 guidebook for the "complete bachelor" also suggested that the age-old rules governing relations between single men and women were falling by the wayside. The how-to manual reminded its male readers that the "idea that a man has the privilege of addressing any woman on a bicycle is most erroneous." Apparently that rule was oft forgotten. Others reported that the bicycle gave women a "general license" to ignore common decency: "To go out afoot and make new acquaintances haphazard on the street would be accounted a dreadful breach of propriety. To go out and make them on a wheel is quite another matter. For a girl to exhibit her leg to the knee in promenading would be immodest. To exhibit it on a wheel is regular." Bicycles had changed the social calculus governing women's behavior in public. Women of all classes rode through cities without escorts or chaperones. The very same women "who would not dream of walking alone in Central Park or of going unattended to the matinee" gleefully pedaled atop New York's streets alone. Maybe Smith had reason to worry after all?[44]

Maybe not. Smith surely exaggerated the moral dangers of cycling. And as time went on, and as her platform grew, so too did her hyperbole. In fact, the more outrageous Smith's attacks, the louder she shouted them. She soon launched an attack on religious leaders who doubled as cycling advocates. The conspiracy theorist alleged that ministers promoted the bicycle to their congregants, not because they saw the value in cycling but because they were in the bicycle dealers' pocket. Supposedly, bicycle salesmen gave ministers a free set of wheels in exchange for their influence. The allegations went nowhere. Neither did her attempts to secure legislation that would have banned bicycles. Neither did Smith's campaign.[45] Her efforts were perhaps best summed up by a tongue-in-cheek poem. Published in a humorous dictionary under the entry "Smithareen," the poem underscores not only the attention Smith's antibicycle crusade garnered, but also its fate:

> The wheels go round without a sound–
>   The maidens hold high revel;
> In sinful mood, insanely gay,
> True spinsters spin adown the way
>   From duty to the devil!
> They laugh, they sing, and–ting-a-ling!
>   Their bells go all the morning;
> Their lanterns bright bestar the night
>   Pedestrians a-warning.
> When lifted hands Miss Charlotte Stands,
>   Good-Lording and O-mying
> Her rheumatism forgotten quite,
>   Her fat with anger frying.
> She blocks the path that leads to wrath,
>   Jack Satan's power defying.
> The wheels go round without a sound
>   The lights burn red and blue and green.
> What's this that's found upon that ground?
>   Poor Charlotte Smith's a smithareen![46]

Despite the institutional support of the National Woman's Rescue League and Smith's volunteer multicity bicycle brigade, the mounting popularity of cycling could not be stopped—at least for now.

REFORMERS

While Charlotte Smith gained national prominence by protesting against cycling, various reformers saw the bicycle as a new tool to advance women's rights. That bicycles served as an agent of reform was a theme embraced by many in the 1890s. Women credited it with bringing some semblance of equality between the sexes. "The magic carpet," as one writer in the popular women's monthly *Godey's Magazine* remarked, put the female cyclists on "absolute equality with any man." The author further explained: ". . . there is something women of every class have learned to prize as a shorter road to freedom than wide, welcoming college doors, or open gateways to the polls. In possession of her bicycle, the daughter of the nineteenth century feels that the declaration of her independence has been proclaimed."[47] Although leading reformers would have had grounds to charge *Godey's Magazine* with exaggeration for putting the bicycle in the same category as women's suffrage or access to higher education as methods to garner equality with men, three of the late nineteenth century's most important activists welcomed the bicycle as an integral tool in the larger campaign for women's rights.

Frances Willard, Susan B. Anthony, and Elizabeth Cady Stanton all became advocates of female cycling in the 1890s. Known for devoting their lives to empowering women, each of these leaders saw the bicycle as doing exactly that. Willard, a suffragist, educator, and temperance advocate, had long been a proponent of cycling, believing that the bicycle offered would-be drinkers a pleasurable alternative to an afternoon in the saloon. (Although it is impossible to tell if cycling actually aided in the temperance movement, many individual cyclists recorded stopping for alcohol on their trips and tippling at wheelmen's rests.[48]) But Willard came to believe that the bicycle's strength lay in its power to transform women's lives. Not only could cycling improve women's health, but the "illimitably capable machine," as she believed it to be, would also provide new momentum in the campaign to settle the "woman question." If more women rode, then more women would adopt rational dress, then more people would accept such clothing, then more people would think about women differently. Willard became such a devotee and advocate of cycling that in 1895 she published a widely read memoir entitled *A Wheel Within a Wheel: How I Learned to Ride the Bicycle with Some Reflections by the Way*. The book recounted the elder stateswoman's struggles and ultimate satisfaction in conquering "the wheel" (she lovingly nicknamed her bicycle "Gladys"). It served as a lengthy paean, describing how the bicycle could promote equality and health and endow women with access to a "wider world."[49]

Fellow reformers Susan B. Anthony and Elizabeth Cady Stanton concurred. Anthony declared that the bicycle "has done more to emancipate women than anything else in the world. I stand and rejoice every time I see a woman ride by on a wheel. It gives women a feeling of freedom and self-reliance. It makes her feel as if she were independent." Stanton too saw the bicycle as a potential tool for reform. From issues ranging from religion to dress, she hoped that the bicycle would provoke debate and help foster women's independence. As Stanton wrote in an article about cycling, bicycle riding was an all-around boon for modern women. Not only would cycling improve women's health and "steady their nerves," but it would also render women more "self-reliant" and erode the old restrictions limiting women's participation in the public sphere. The result, Stanton believed, was that the bicycle deserved to be classed as "one of the greatest blessing[s] in the 19th Century." Susan B. Anthony, Elizabeth Cady Stanton, and Frances Willard were three of the most influential women reformers of the nineteenth century. That this same triumvirate uniformly and heartily endorsed cycling for women highlighted the bicycle's potential power to reframe women's place in the city and, ultimately, women's place in politics, government, economy, and the world. Therefore suffragists naturally endorsed the bicycle as a tool (much like voting) to empower women.[50]

Stanton (born in 1815), Anthony (born in 1820), and Willard (born in 1839) not only endorsed the bicycle as three distinguished reformers but also as members of the elder generation. Age, a category often ignored by a generation of historians obsessed with race, class, and gender, played a crucial role in the democratization of bicycles and the subsequent effects on the urban population. "It used to be a dreary old world for the grandmothers," a West Virginian recorded in 1897. But now "gray hairs are as common upon a bicycle as ebon locks." "Youths and maidens, gray-bearded gentlemen, and fat ladies in bloomers may to-day be seen toiling through our park roads on the 'steed of steel,'" reported a local paper in San Francisco. No matter the age, all riders reckoned with learning how to ride a bicycle and enjoyed the childlike splendor of "flying" through the air. Of course, not everyone found the device so easy to master. The then fifty-plus-year-old professional historian and amateur curmudgeon Henry Adams recalled having "solemnly and painfully learned to ride the bicycle."[51]

But many older men and women joined their younger counterparts with avidity. Like Frances Willard, it was their age that made mastering the art of the bicycle a distinctive pleasure. As Willard wrote:

> Besides there was a special value to women in the conquest of the bicycle by a woman in her fifty-third year, and one who had so many comrades in the white-ribbon army that her action would be widely influential. Then there were minor reasons:
>   I did it from pure natural love of adventure . . .

Second, from a love of acquiring this new implement of power and literally putting it underfoot.

Last, but not least, because a good many people thought I could not do it at my age.[52]

Like so many others her age, Willard proved them wrong.

Older women, younger women, society women, working-class women, middle-class women, women leisure-seekers, women paraders, women commuters, and women from various corners of the urban world found something attractive about the bicycle. "New Women" on wheels expressed their desires for independence and equality via the bicycle. Reformers viewed the bicycle as representative of emancipation and power; others saw it as representative of all that had gone wrong with young city women. Supporters credited the machine with opening up the city, enlarging the urban map, and allowing for greater visibility of women. Protestors fretted about the overt public nature of women cycling and, particularly, about the accompanying clothes they wore. Exactly how much women's lives changed, exactly how emancipating and exulting the bicycle made women feel, and exactly how much the bicycle promised women a newfound mobility and threatened to usurp traditional gender norms is impossible to quantify. But there is no doubt that to those living in the 1890s cycling city, the bicycle appeared to provide women with a revolutionary tool, even if the changes it helped usher in were something less than revolutionary.

CHAPTER NINE

The Crash

How could society ever spurn the bicycle, a writer for *Forum* magazine asked in 1896. His answer was simple: they won't. Cyclists had, he explained, discovered a "new power,—the most valuable he has acquired since he learned to walk,—and it is henceforth a part of his equipment for his struggle with life. Is it probable that having once become the possessor of a power like this the human race is going to abandon it? As well might we expect it to abandon railways, and gas, and electricity!"[1] The soothsayer never imagined what was coming. Neither did anyone else.

Several years earlier, bicycles began to colonize American cities. What had been only a few hundred riders slowly grew to a few thousand, before exploding into an army of millions. In 1896, American cities looked quite different than they had in 1886. Bicycle paths, lanes, and cyclists no longer seemed out of place. City streets were not only filled with bicycles but also owed at least some of their shape to the very wheels that spun across them. By the early twentieth century, however, the formerly ubiquitous bicycle had faded away. Sales plummeted. People stopped riding. And the once powerful voices clamoring for better roads, bicycle paths, and laws favorable to cyclists hushed. The cycling city was no more . . . at least in the United States.

The few authors who have examined the sudden decline in cycling offer various theories, most notably the development of the automobile. The automobile was an important factor, but not in the way most people think. Other writers unconvincingly attribute the fall to the massive commercialization of bicycles, which reduced prices and quality. Several historians have even hypothesized that "in the Spanish-American War those seeking an emotional release from contemporary pressures came upon a more exciting outlet than cycling."[2] Other critics have looked at contemporary cycling cities around the world and attributed their success to flat terrain, moderate weather, high population densities, and a dearth of cars relative to American cities. But the question should not be: Why don't Americans ride bicycles? The real question is: Why did they ever stop?

SIGNS OF DECLINE

When the twentieth century approached, evidence that the popularity of cycling was diminishing was hard to miss. Newspaper columns, once filled with regular accounts of rising bicycle sales, bicycle races, advances in bicycle technology, bicycle club news, and bicycle advertisements, began to feature just the occasional story (fig. 9.1). The once thundering herd of commuters shrank to a pitter-patter of a select few. By 1904, the City Engineer of Minneapolis reported that the once well-trafficked bicycle paths of the Twin Cities had "grown up with weeds."[3] In the final years of the nineteenth century, the dozens of bicycle journals catering to industry insiders and bicycle enthusiasts suddenly folded. Some adopted broader titles, others shifted their focus to the automobile, and still others disappeared entirely. *Good Roads* magazine, a periodical that once combined the interests of the cyclists with the good roads movement, became almost entirely devoid of references to bicycles. Even more noteworthy, member-

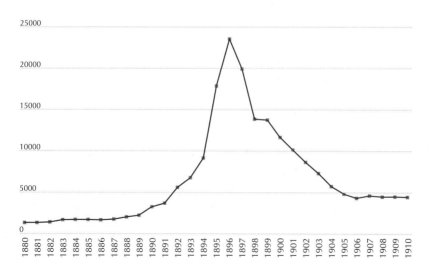

Fig. 9.1. Articles related to bicycling. The graph illustrates the number of articles and advertisements printed in the *Atlanta Constitution, Chicago Tribune, Los Angeles Times, New York Times, New York Tribune, San Francisco Chronicle*, or the *Washington Post* containing any of the following words: bicycle, cycling, cyclist, wheelmen, or wheelman.

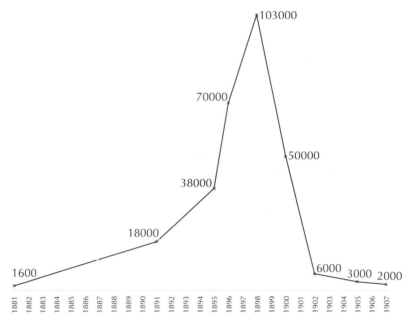

Fig. 9.2. Membership in the League of American Wheelmen. Estimates
from Phillip P. Mason, "The League of American Wheelmen and
the Good Roads Movement"; Burr, "Markets as Producers and
Consumers"; *LAW Bulletin and Goad Roads*, January 1, 1897.

ship numbers for the LAW declined precipitously around the turn of the
century (fig. 9.2). The previously robust and politically powerful organization, which at one point boasted over a hundred thousand members, lost
its base and political clout practically overnight.

Bicycle shops that had seemed to line every major city shut their doors.
Bicycle factories stood still.

In perhaps the clearest indication of the waning enthusiasm for cycling, bicycle sales slumped mightily. Topping out in 1899, the number of
machines produced domestically declined at an even faster rate than it had
climbed. As demand fell, prices dropped, margins were squeezed, and the
market became oversaturated. In a futile effort to fight off the plummet-
ing sales, several of the remaining bicycle manufacturers, including most
of the largest producers, merged to form the American Bicycle Company
(ABC) in 1899. By 1902 the company went into receivership.[4]

Of course, the exact timing of the collapse varied from city to city, but
the trends unfolded nationally. In 1896, newspapers published more about
cycling than they ever had or ever would. In 1898, membership in the LAW

reached its peak. And in 1899, domestic bicycle production soared for the final time before tumbling.

Anecdotal reports confirmed the quantitative data. *The World To-Day* recalled in 1902 that it was only a few years earlier that anyone "who did not ride a bicycle was looked upon as peculiar." By then, the opposite held true. In 1912, *Outing* magazine, a journal devoted to recreation and nature, and which itself had previously been filled with cycling-related articles, conceded that even in the largest cities only a few wheelmen could be counted. A far cry, one of its authors noted, from the 1890s "when the exodus by every highway leading out of the city rivaled on a Sunday morning in number at least, that historic departure from Egypt" and when cyclists "counted the time lost which took [them] from the saddle to pay tribute to the ordinary necessities of life."[5]

At the time, many Americans could not understand why the bicycle fell out of favor so quickly and sharply. As a writer for the *Cycle Age and Trade Review* asked in 1901:

> Do the men and women who rode cycles in the years gone by ever stop to think of the enjoyment they got out of them? Are the city parks and the country ride less inviting than they were then? . . . Do we never need to travel from place to place, without waiting for a train or a street car? . . . Is the price of a bicycle, formerly four times as great as now, too great a drain on our pocket-books? . . . Can anyone answer these questions satisfactorily? If not, why, in the name of goodness and common sense, do our bicycles lie rusting in the garret or the cellar?[6]

Accusing industry insiders was a common response. Trade magazines often blamed their own readers, the bicycle dealers, for no longer wearing bicycle clothes, organizing group rides, joining cycling clubs, advocating for good roads, and, most appallingly, for no longer riding a bicycle. As the defeated writer for the *Cycle Age and Trade Review* pointed out, the "lack of enthusiasm in cycling is due," ironically, "to the negligence of the men to whom cycling is of greatest interest." Dealers admitted as much. Few, though, offered an explanation for their newfound ambivalence toward cycling. There was no doubt, though, that the era of the cycling city was over.[7]

THE FALL OF THE AMERICAN CYCLING CITY

While the relationship between the bicycle and the automobile is oft misunderstood, there can be no doubt that bicycle sales and the number of those cycling through the city dropped steeply as the twentieth century beckoned—long before automobiles became popular. Sales figures, registration statistics, and traffic data all reveal that there was at least a decade gap between when bicycles began to disappear and when automobiles appeared in large numbers. In fact, the number of registered automobiles did not approach the several million bicycles in use by Americans during the 1890s until around 1920. Even by 1910, only a cumulative total of 458,377 automobiles had been registered (fig. 9.3). In the late 1890s, manufacturers churned out roughly one million bicycles each year. In 1904, several years into the bicycle slump, domestic production fell by nearly a million units from the previous high. That meant manufacturers produced a million fewer bicycles each year, a number that could not come close to being replaced by the measly 54,590 automobiles registered at the time. Automobile sales did not replace bicycle sales. The bicycle had already been left for dead.[8]

Traffic counts from American cities in the late nineteenth and early

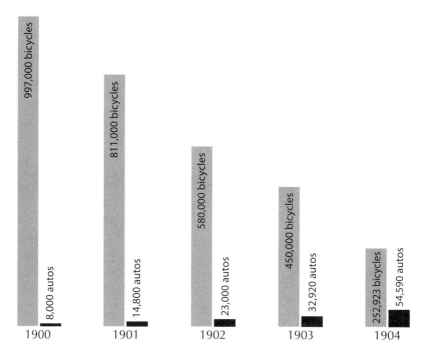

Fig. 9.3. Bicycle production vs. auto registrations in the United States.
Estimates from Bruce Epperson, "How Many Bikes?" in *Cycle History 11*,
with a minor revision provided to the author; *Highway Statistics: Summary
to 1945, Public Roads Administration*, Federal Works Agency (Washington,
DC: United States Government Printing Office, 1947), 16–27.

An addition to his sign.

Fig. 9.4. Bicycle and automobile rest, 1905. *Outing*, August 1905, 538.
Reproduced with permission from Albert and Shirley Small Special
Collections, University of Virginia, Charlottesville, VA.

twentieth century similarly reveal that even a decade after cycling began
to fall out of favor, the number of automobiles on streets lagged far behind
that of bicycles. Writing in 1905 for *Outing* magazine, H.P. Burchell provided the timeline: "The bicycle had its day as a popular means of travel
and touring. An interregnum followed. The ale-houses again sank into de-
suetude and scores of them were not aroused into wakefulness until a year
or two ago when the prolonged toot, toot of the automobile horn told them
that good times were coming around once more." Although the "interregnum" was considerably longer than the author suggested, old wheelmen's
rest stops, inns, and taverns, did begin to look for a new source of revenue
rather quickly (fig. 9.4).[9]

Yet it is clear that the introduction of the automobile was important.
Whether attending one of the many well-choreographed bicycle shows or
browsing the scores of bicycle advertisements in a local newspaper, pro-
spective cyclists were sold on the promise of technology. The bicycle was
a modern, luxury good; ball bearings, forks, tires, rims, handlebars, gear-

ing, and the like were all part of a package that entranced a growing group of buyers and sellers. What *new* features did a particular model offer? An emphasis on novelty and obsession with the latest technology resulted in enthusiasts trading in their wheels each season, but it also made it less surprising that the bicycle would lose its luster, as major improvements in bicycle design were infrequent. And although few could reasonably expect to purchase an automobile, the very existence of such vehicles altered the perception of bicycles as symbols of innovation, progress, and modernity. Some of the most devoted fanatics of cycling transferred their enthusiasm for two wheels to four. Bicycle club memberships sagged, as automobile clubs first started to appear in cities. Many of those forming and joining the automobile societies were the very defectors who had abandoned their cycling clubs. Emblematic of the transformation, the Century Wheelmen of Philadelphia in 1902 converted their empty bicycle room into a parking garage for automobiles. That same year, a group of motor clubs coalesced to form the American Automobile Association, an organization that would follow in the footsteps of the LAW. Many remembered and learned from the successes and ultimate failure of the bicycle.[10]

The shift of interest from bicycles to automobiles was most visible among those most invested in the bicycle industry. Bicycle mechanics became automobile mechanics. Bicycle manufacturers became automobile manufacturers. Schwinn designed and built an automobile as early as 1896 and Colonel Pope, the once-heralded father of the American bicycle industry, began producing automobiles as well. He enthusiastically reported that his 15,000-strong squad of bicycle agents were "fairly howling" for automobiles in order to meet the expected demand. That the man known as the "father" of the American bicycle industry began investing his time and money in promoting automobiles certainly did not help the flagging bicycle market. As the prices for bicycles marched steadily downward and as sales began to slow from peak levels near the turn of the century, other dealers and manufacturers jumped at the idea of a new product. Helping to legitimize and promote that market were automobile trade magazines, some of which debuted in the mid-1890s, despite the fact that there were hardly any automobile sales yet in the U.S. Even if Americans had not yet caught automobile fever, industry leaders in the bicycle trade had.[11]

Bicycle enthusiasts, industry insiders, and recreational riders became automobile enthusiasts for the very same reasons that they had been attracted to cycling. In its earliest years the automobile was essentially a sports car, a recreational toy for the wealthy, just as the bicycle had originally been. And it drew many of the same people who had been devotees of the bicycle, those who had helped make cycling a pastime, and those who had led the clubs and the lobbying efforts to improve road conditions and the cycling landscape in general. They tended to be more recreation minded, wealthier, and in a position to form a formidable lobby. Viewed by some as an expensive toy that frightened horses and threatened the serenity of urban parks (just as the bicycle had), the automobile ultimately came to represent the same things that made the bicycle so appealing: freedom, mobility, exclusiveness, independence, and health. Like their cycling ancestors, automobile clubs took group rides, lobbied for better roads, showed off their machines, and, more than anything, enjoyed the camaraderie. City dwellers relished the thought of escaping the city and tourists dreamed of the once far-away lands that now seemed within easy reach. Marketers pitched the automobile as freeing, health-inducing, and life-improving. Exhibitors wowed crowds with electrified displays of automobiles, selling fantasy via technological might. Sanitarians praised the machine for having the ability to replace horses and make the city cleaner. Doctors insisted that it could restore the nerves of, and bring the fresh rural air within easy reach of, urban dwellers. As two historians put it, "This device was merely two bicycles, attached to a platform and powered by a motor: the automobile." Likewise, when the historian Clay McShane writes "more than any other consumer good the motor car provided fantasies of status, freedom, and escape from the constraints of a highly disciplined urban, industrial order," he could easily be describing the bicycle in the 1890s. The bicycle gave Americans their first private vehicle. Bicycles first allowed riders to skirt the hassles and crowds of public transportation. It was atop bicycles that people commuted to work, promenaded down the boulevard, and fled the city for the tonics of the country. As a newer, more luxurious, faster, and motorized vehicle, the automobile appealed to an emerging majority—even if few could afford it at the time.[12]

Visionaries, engineers, and city builders also gravitated toward the possibilities of the automobile. The kinds of grand plans that involved crisscrossing, bicycle-only boulevards; elevated bicycle paths and bridges; massive bicycle parking garages; bicycle valets; interstate bicycle roads; and laws catering to cyclists were no more. The dreamlike images painted by literary and visual artists in which bicycles seemed to solve every problem known to mankind faded away. Instead, technologists, engineers, sanitarians, and the first cohort of professional city planners reimagined their cities revolving around automobiles. For those who saw in the bicycle a means to create a new type of city where people moved about freely, utopian cities became car cities rather than cycling cities. Even Colonel Albert Pope himself predicted that cities of the future would be transformed by the automobile. He once thought the same about bicycles. Edward Bennett and Daniel Burnham's *Plan of Chicago* (1909) included wide, attractive streets to circulate people and commerce and, of course, the automobile. They idealized the automobile, a tradition that master planners and visionaries like Le Corbusier and Robert Moses would carry forward well into the twentieth century. Though cars had not yet taken over the streets, they had already taken over the minds of a select group of important people.[13]

Others have assumed that if it was not the automobile, it must have been the streetcar that killed the bicycle. Indeed, the popularity of the streetcar continued as bicycle use declined. However, the rapid growth and electrification of streetcars occurred throughout the entire rise and fall of the bicycle era. The number of streetcar and bicycle trips both increased. Even as late as 1898, streetcar operators panicked about the popularity of cycling. Within a year or two, they had nothing to fear. Little evidence suggests that once-avid cyclists suddenly found that mass transit had improved so remarkably overnight.[14] By that time, bicycle prices had fallen even further, making the economics of commuting by bicycle compared to streetcars even more favorable.

In reality, cycling's demise had less to do with cyclists abandoning the bicycle for another form of transportation—streetcars or automobiles—and more to do with its loss of social and cultural appeal. In this respect, automobiles were significant. However few they were, the very existence of automobiles helped render bicycles less novel and fashionable.[15] Even more importantly, bicycle prices steadily declined and a secondhand market expanded. This occurred gradually throughout the 1890s and sharply toward the end of the decade with the overproduction of bicycles. But the overproduction did not cause the collapse; it was a symptom of the fact that people had already stopped riding.

To be sure, the accelerating price declines only exacerbated the actual cause of decline: competing social visions about cyclists and bicycles. With more classes of people riding and more people riding for practicality, cyclists lost their social standing. In 1901, an author said as much: cycling "has ceased to be fashionable simply because the possession of a wheel is now quite possible to everyone."[16] "Bicycling became unfashionable," another writer observed in 1905, as affordability increased.[17] Although journalists had praised the bicycle for its potential to level social classes, the reality is that the majority of socially conscious middle-class cyclists stopped cycling as the practice democratized. The evidence suggests that this was not a coincidence.

No longer a social tool or another mark of fashion, bicycles were abandoned by middle-class professionals and the urban elite in greater proportion than anyone else. The bicycle then became conceived of as a vehicle for the working class. Workers might have continued to cycle to the factory, but no one would seriously consider promenading on one's bicycle. Even some working-class riders, likely because of their own social aspirations, stopped cycling. In the longer term, the bicycle eventually became a child's plaything. But in the midst of the cycling city, the bicycle managed to be many things to many people. Groups of riders constructed this technological artifact in manners that suited their particular desires. Some wanted a faster way to travel around the city. Some saw it as a means to better health. Some saw it as an entry ticket to social clubs. Some saw it as a symbol of modernity, while others, a marker of equality. Some delighted in the thought of owning their very first vehicle. Some simply wanted to participate in a popular phenomenon. With unique motivations, cyclists endowed their bicycles with unique meanings.[18]

Ultimately, the contradictory notions became difficult to sustain. Class-conscious, middle-class cyclists rode for both practicality and fashion. In pursuit of the former, they now risked losing the latter. Women cyclists broadened the base of riders but turned off some who privileged the sportier and more masculine connotations of cycling. Older folks conquered the wheel, making it less attractive for the younger, smarter set. Scorchers scared off pedestrians, horses, and the kinds of cyclists who envisioned the bicycle as a means of Victorian respectability. Although there was a brief moment in which competing social groups adopted the bicycle, time wore on. As more and more varieties of people began to ride, others no longer found bicycles so appealing.

DIVERGENT FUTURES

Ironically, in terms of the number of cyclists, the breadth of cycling amenities, and the cultural devotion to cycling, American cities had trumped all others. Yet the bicycle died a quicker and more absolute death in the United States than almost anywhere else. Around the world, bicycles continued to serve as a viable tool. The benefits with respect to health and exercise, flexibility and mobility, and affordability did not suddenly expire at the turn of the century. Nor did its usefulness evaporate, even in the wake of automobiles, subways, public buses, and other forms of urban transportation.[19]

In the 1890s cycling became widespread in urban centers across the globe. The ways in which city governments, citizens, and the built environment adapted to cycling often followed a similar path. In Germany in the early 1890s, bicycle schools began to dot the largest cities, as men continued, and women began, to catch bicycle fever. Like their brethren across the Atlantic, German riders fought against restrictions and complained about the inconsistency of regulations. Berlin walled off a portion of its city to cyclists; Munich required cyclists to attain a driver's license; Neustadt's riders sported bicycles with mandatory license tags; most other municipalities required lamps and bells, while policymakers and riders continually debated how to classify and regulate bicycles. The mission of the League of American Wheelmen mirrored that of the *Ligue Nationale pour l'Amélioration des Routes* organized in Belgium. In the 1890s in the Netherlands, scores of bicycle clubs catered to elites and attracted newcomers looking to race, tour, socialize, or commiserate about the ubiquitous cobblestone. Vienna reported a problem with scorchers, while Austrians in other cities weighed the merits of a bicycle tax. A United States consul general stationed in Japan reported that the bicycle was "being used extensively as a cheap method of locomotion in the seaports and large cities." Mexico City was abuzz with spinning wheels. Torontonians reported that "the wheel today is king" and that the "enthusiasm for the wheel has pervaded all classes of the community." Dazzling bicycle shows drew thousands of visitors to Milan and Paris, just as they had in Chicago and Manhattan. Parliamentary debates in New Zealand in 1898 included not only matters of high politics and finance but also serious discussions about a Cycle Traffic Bill, sparking talk of bicycle taxes, the "new woman" on wheels, and the power of the cyclists' lobby. And cargo manifests from 1896 and 1897 revealed that American bicycles regularly floated their way to Denmark, Spain, the Netherlands, Italy, France, Germany, Switzerland, England, Russia, Australia, New Zealand, the British West Indies, Cuba, Mexico, Chile, Peru, and Africa.[20]

London and Paris, in particular, experienced a flurry of bicycle-induced transformations. Scores of bicycle clubs and several cycling publications catered to new cyclists in 1890s London. Arthur Conan Doyle and H. G. Wells introduced bicycles into their fiction, while cycling royalty cemented cycling's prestige. Like female cyclists in the United States, British women found the machine invigorating and emancipating. The hullabaloo about proper cycling attire spiked on both sides of the Atlantic. The medical community and church leaders in England, as they had in the United States, expressed an early concern about the physical and moral hazards of cycling. The warnings went largely unheeded.[21]

Across the Channel, Parisians flocked to the wheel, riding for pleasure and utility. Touring the summer countryside, commuting to work, and parading down the grand boulevards cut by Baron Georges-Eugène Haussmann, cyclists roamed in and about the capital city. The pace with which Parisians embraced the wheel was startling and drew the attention of American riders.[22] Magazines, both popular and cycling specific, regularly chronicled the cycling scene around the world and nowhere more so than trendsetting Paris.[23] Whether it was Paris or the soon-to-be-crowned cycling nation of the Netherlands, cycling witnessed an explosion of popularity in European cities in the 1890s, but it did not come near America's obsession with the wheel. America led the way in creating cycling-related infrastructure, developing new traffic regulations and roads, and manufacturing and marketing bicycles. There was no doubt that American cities led and others followed. Quickly, that trajectory began to change.

As bicycle markets slumped and as cycling paths stood barren in the United States, other cities across the Atlantic experienced no such slowdown. To be sure, in some cities, including London, the enthusiasm for cycling abated. Fewer advertisements ran. Fewer novels featured the bicycle as a protagonist. There were fewer bicycle clubs and fewer bicycle shows. But across much of Europe, bicycle sales and ridership experienced no such slack; in fact, cycling increased. In Denmark in 1907, reports from the United States Department of Commerce indicated that cycling in the Scandinavian country was only continuing to grow. In Copenhagen alone, some 50,000 of the 450,000 inhabitants rode bicycles. With cycling paths in the streets and an urban planning environment in which "everything is done to encourage the use of cycles," ridership grew at the same time that American interest diminished. In the Netherlands, whose cities eventually became the model for incorporating bicycles, cyclists continued to pedal through the city. By the 1930s, every other Dutchman owned a set of wheels. Germans increasingly took to the wheel, and in 1935 bicycles outnumbered automobiles by more than a seven-to-one margin.[24]

French cities did not witness a slowdown either. Across the country, the number of cyclists continued to grow at a rapid rate. In a ten-year span beginning in 1900, the number of registered bicycles grew nearly threefold. The pace of growth ultimately moderated, but, in general, the number of French cyclists continued to expand until the 1950s. In fact, by the time World War II broke out, bicycles represented a critical source of transportation in most sizable European cities. Americans' neighbors to the north also kept cycling long after Americans stopped. The number of licensed bicycles in Winnipeg nearly doubled between 1908 and 1913. In China, despite the generally poor road conditions, the number of riders adopting the bicycle crept higher, albeit slowly, in the earliest years of the twentieth century and began a slow march that would quicken to a feverish pace by midcentury. In many foreign cities the paths to the cycling city were just beginning to be laid.[25]

As was the case for the entire twentieth century, cities in Asia and Europe became the places where cyclists rode to work, for play, and for utility and where bicycles became an integral component of the transportation network. American cities—their planners and would-be cyclists—veered from the trajectory set in the 1890s. If anything, at the time it seemed that American cities would continue to be the most influenced by, and accommodative to, the bicycle. After all, even though many places experienced a cycling boom in the 1890s, American cities had more cyclists, more bicycle paths, and larger and more powerful bicycle lobbies than the places that would become known as cycling cities in the twentieth century. Only in the 1920s did the Netherlands become a "cycling nation." By then, Dutch tourists remarked that "in America, the bicycle [had] become a prehistoric means of transportation." A couple of decades earlier, the people of Amsterdam (often on American-made bicycles) got swept up by a bicycle fever that would have looked rather tame to an American tourist at the time.[26]

One of the distinguishing features of the American cycling boom was the bicycle itself. Compared to Europeans, Americans purchased bicycles designed more for recreation and less for utility. Although there were plenty of models (and accessories) for commuters and workers of all sorts, manufacturers usually marketed their products to middle-class riders seeking casual recreation. They and their users promoted the idea that bicycles should be attractive in their own right and especially lightweight. Often they had minimal brakes, sometimes none at all. Most rode without baskets or parcel holders and stands. The seats were rather uncomfortable. And most bicycles featured a pair of single-tube tires. These tires became commonplace on only American bicycles, not because they were superior but because when Colonel Pope first began manufacturing safety bicycles, he was looking to save money on production costs. They were perceived to be fast and sporty, but they were difficult to repair, especially compared to tires that featured a distinct inner tube that could be fixed or replaced separately. The lighter wood rims that Americans preferred were much less durable than the steel alternatives.[27] The sporty American bicycle suggests that Americans privileged aesthetics, not because of any predetermined technological path but rather because of the ways in which riders and manufacturers imagined their bicycles. Users and manufacturers helped to construct—literally and socially—a device that promoted middle-class leisure. As working-class riders began riding, they complicated this notion.

But it was not the limitations of the machine that caused the collapse; after all, millions of Americans happily bought and rode these bicycles throughout much of the decade. People did not suddenly grow weary of repairing or maintaining their wheels, nor did they begin clamoring for more practical accessories or more comfortable seats. Instead American bicycles signaled a decided emphasis on social and recreational cycling, which in turn speaks to cycling's demise. Social and recreational cycling was more easily subjected to the changing winds of the social climate and more likely to fall out of favor than practical cycling. In those cities around the world that would ultimately become cycling meccas, bicycles did not fall out of fashion so abruptly since there were more cyclists riding for practical purposes. They did not share Americans' preference for light and handsome bicycles (not so coincidentally, Americans have not always favored the most practical automobiles). In the United States there were, at least relatively, an impressive number of bicycle commuters, but surely even some of those commuting by bicycle did so because it was both convenient and signaled middle-class respectability.

Those that did keep cycling for efficiency and economy in the United States, the ones more likely to pedal to work, were the least affluent and the least influential inside city hall. The majority of those in the 1890s who pushed for friendlier laws, better roads, and new bicycle paths rode their recreational wheels for social reasons and soon disappeared. Indeed, the cycling lobby in the United States collapsed quickly and deeply, compared to several European cities in which major cycling organizations managed to persist. It was, after all, through politics that cyclists used their collective power to improve the urban landscape. In turn, the improved landscape invited more people to join the cycling phenomenon. When the elites in the United States abandoned the League of American Wheelmen and other associations and turned their attention to automobiles, they left their former organizations with far less support and fewer resources than their counterparts in Europe. For example, in the Netherlands, the major procycling group, the *Algemene Nederlandsche Wielrijders Bond* (ANWB), still exists. As European cycling clubs moved forward, they continued to demand additions and improvements to bicycle-related infrastructure, most notably cycling paths. Unlike in the United States, the desire to lay cycle paths in Germany and the Netherlands actually increased once cars started to appear on the roads. This was possible only because the organizations maintained their membership and leaders, something that could not be said for their American cousins. While cyclists may have benefitted from separate paths, some of the impetus for such projects in Europe came from automobilists who sought to make the roads easier and safer to traverse by moving pesky cyclists out of the way. In the United States this was hardly the case—there were too few cyclists to clog the road. Ultimately, the inability of American wheelmen to secure the enduring support of the state (unlike cyclists in Europe and unlike the automobile advocates who succeeded them) proved catastrophic in the long term and rendered the prospects of a return to the cycling city dim.[28]

Cyclists in the United States also could have pushed further to integrate cycling into the hands of municipal management rather than their own. Likewise, if cyclists had not (for the most part) successfully resisted municipal efforts to tax and register bicycles, there might have been a more permanent and continuing source of funds set aside for cycling-related infrastructure. And if cyclists had not successfully resisted efforts to regulate their machines (e.g., to require brakes), some of the resistance toward them might have subsided. Across Europe regulations unfolded unevenly, but on the whole, cyclists across the Atlantic were more likely to be subjected to stricter regulations and favorable public policy. French cyclists registered their wheels each year. German cyclists abided by a series of laws limiting how and where they rode. In the Netherlands, cyclists faced a series of regulations, including requiring brakes and, beginning in 1899, a bicycle tax. The funds went directly into improving bicycle-related infrastructure. And although leaders eventually lifted the initial tax, they reinstituted it decades later, which provided not only a fiscal boost to a struggling economy but also the monies to improve transportation infrastructure. The tax, just like those floated in the United States, had been opposed by the leading bicycle clubs in the Netherlands. Luckily for them they lost their case. When it came time to build roads and paths, the fact that the cyclists contributed financially (even if not quite happily) was not lost on either the riders, who demanded bicycle paths, or the planners, who created the blueprints for a city that welcomed cyclists. Indeed, throughout the first half of the twentieth century, municipal governments in cities across the Netherlands grappled with how to promote cycling and, in 1935, officials in Amsterdam designed a comprehensive plan for the city to ensure that it remained commutable for cyclists. The goal was to design a "bicycle city." In the Netherlands, and in certain other European centers, the state continued to play an important role in fostering urban cycling throughout the twentieth century. Whether purposefully or not, European cyclists managed to institutionalize cycling into the state much more successfully than did Americans. Promoting bicycle use through carefully designed and municipally managed infrastructure and law, and doing so on a continuous basis, may be the most important factor for the enduring success of urban cycling.[29]

Ironically, the American wheelmen's initial strengths worked against them. They won the right to cruise down boulevards on brakeless bicycles, to skirt license and registration requirements, and to largely avoid "wheel" taxes. When the city failed to provide the cycling infrastructure and amenities cyclists desired, they raised their own funds to build them. But the consequences were significant. Once the army of cyclists dwindled to a devoted few, as the LAW and organized cyclists saw their membership rolls thin, and as some of the industry leaders shifted their interest to automobiles, the chorus of lobbyists no longer stood strong. While this shift may not have had a great effect in the short run, since cyclists stopped riding not because of a lack of infrastructure but because cycling no longer held the cultural and social value it once had, it did create a long-lasting environment with little cycling infrastructure and organizational support—a world that would discourage cycling for many years to come.

Just like its birth, the American cycling city's death was both unexpected and the result of many things. Most importantly, the smart set and their followers no longer found that their machines served as a social marker. The bicycle could not sustain itself as a fashionable social tool and also as a utilitarian tool; every use undermined another.

More so than anywhere else, the American cycling city disappeared frighteningly fast, but there were some long-lasting effects. The municipal traffic laws that cyclists helped write and the roads that cyclists helped pave did not disappear; rather, they served as the pretext for thinking about and building the transportation network of the twentieth century. Bicycle paths endured long after the cycling city, as did debates about the bicycle's place on and off the road. Questions about women and mobility, the democratization of public spaces, the relationship between cities and their hinterlands, and the effects that modes of transportation have on the urban environment and the health of its people had only begun to be asked and answered. Perhaps most importantly, the experiences in the 1890s helped cement the notion of what a bicycle was in an American context. The popularity of the bicycle as a fashionable, sporting device, designed for middle-class recreation, would cast a long shadow. Although some devoted riders continued to use their wheels for utility, there was no doubt that the world in which both the school-aged and the old-aged worshipped their wheels, in which newspapers and debutantes gossiped about the wheel, and in which mayors and lawmakers fought to appease cyclists was no more. Looking backward, a writer for the *Baltimore American*, in an article entitled "The Passing of the Bicycle," described the long-gone bicycle era of the 1890s: "Men and women, old and young, adults and children—all rode the wheel. The parks, the streets and roadways were filled with riders of the steel steed, and whenever one passed a couple or a group in deep conversation the one subject of talk was sure to be the wheel . . ."[30] In 1903, the age of America's cycling cities already seemed like ancient history.

EPILOGUE

In the span of a single year, the *New York Times* ran hundreds of articles considering the bicycle's place in the city. Chronicling a range of subjects—bicycle commuting, bicycle lanes, bicycle safety, the wealthy on wheels, bicycle thieves, women and bicycles, bicycle technology, bicycle accidents, bicycle fashion—the newspaper coverage in New York revealed a deep interest in cycling. The same could be said for most American cities. The year was 2014, but it could just as easily have been 1897. Of course, times have changed dramatically. The article about bicycle safety was not about new traffic laws or whether or not bicycles should have brakes but rather a story about inflatable helmets—ordinary-looking scarves that function like air bags. The piece on women and bicycles was not, as it might have been in the 1890s, a discussion about whether women should ride and what they should wear but was instead about a new advertising campaign encouraging women to reclaim their youth by putting down their smartphones, neglecting the chores of adulthood, and getting back on a bicycle. And in a manner not all that dissimilar from that of the journalists in the 1890s who wrote about cycling royalty abroad and the smart set at home, recent articles highlighted fancy hotels that provide fancy bicycles for their fancy guests, swanky art galleries filled with cycling-related works, specially designed bicycles meant for touring vineyards, and tales of celebrities cycling recklessly. (In 2014 it was Alec Baldwin; in 1895 it was the Duke of Marlborough.) In the modern world, the bicycle again threatens to become an important part of the American urban landscape.[1]

The twentieth century was largely a lost century in terms of the American cycling city.[2] Only a few years after cyclists invaded American cities in the 1890s they began to disappear. Admittedly, as the Great Depression swept through the country in the 1930s, Americans looking for cheap transportation and those old enough to have fond memories of the "gay nineties" briefly revived the excitement. Newspaper columnists wondered if the bicycle was back to stay. It was not. Four decades later, Americans fell in love with the wheel again. From 1970 to 1973, bicycle sales more than doubled, as baby boomers took to ten-speeds in record numbers. Some cities launched invigorated campaigns to lay bicycle paths and install other cycling amenities. But within a few years domestic sales sagged again. To be sure, there have been some attempts to promote cycling in cities and a handful of bold (even some successful) experiments. Most famously, planners in Davis, California, in the 1960s began to design their city around the bicycle.[3] By and large, though, the rest of the country's cities made few such efforts.

Throughout much of the twentieth century, few Americans depended on bicycles for transportation. The vast majority who rode did so for recreation, and the machine became defined as a child's toy instead of a legitimate vehicle. Few commuted by bicycle and even fewer imagined a world in which our cities were suddenly filled with hundreds of thousands of cyclists pedaling to work, in parades, to protest, for health, to flaunt their status, or to play a part in the everyday street theater. That such a group could, and did, transform the city seems hard to imagine in a world in which the bicycle has lost its place.

Nevertheless, a full century after the demise of the American cycling city, a resurgent movement has begun. Across American cities, bike lanes are being striped, bicycle paths are being laid, and city planners are devising creative ways to incorporate bicycles into traffic. Protesters are again marching through the city on wheels. In the 1890s they demanded better roads, fairer traffic regulations, and for the streetcars to be put in their place; today they ride to secure their place in the city as they express their disgust for automobiles with histrionics. The current backlash printed regularly in the press and online again reveals a concern that unruly cyclists are beginning to take over cities. Today complaints about scorchers (no one uses this term anymore) who ride on sidewalks and salmon (ride against traffic) down city streets echo across the media spectrum. Culturally, bicycles and cycling have reentered the mainstream. Featured as objects of art and as icons printed on clothing and coffee mugs, bicycles are everywhere. Presidential candidates are seen atop their wheels, bicycle messenger bags hang over the shoulders of sport coats and tee shirts, and a professional cyclist, Lance Armstrong, is a national celebrity, albeit a disgraced one.

Most importantly, city planners are finally taking the bicycle seriously again. As gas prices have risen, as global warming has entered into the mainstream consciousness, as obesity has become a national pandemic, as sustainability has entered the lexicon of planning, and as cities become more congested, cycling has returned as a favored prescription among a broad group of advocates. Twenty-first-century planners are re-realizing that bicycles have the potential to pave healthier cities and breed healthier people. Looking across the Atlantic with envy, American city planners have visited the cycling meccas of Amsterdam and Copenhagen, studied the public bike programs in Paris, and weighed the benefits of London and Stockholm's antiautomobile congestion pricing schemes.

American cities have tried to launch similar programs. In 2007, New York City planners crafted a broad and bold proposal for "A Greener, Greater New York" by the year 2030. The blueprints reveal the myriad of ways in which the city plans to promote and accommodate cycling. Paved greenways offering cyclists car-free lanes, water views, and express travel will circumscribe the entire island of Manhattan. Connecting to the greenways, a network of off-road bicycle paths, painted bicycle lanes, and on-road, curbed bicycle lanes will serve the city's growing number of cyclists. In all, the city envisions laying a whopping 1,800 miles of bicycle lanes. Meanwhile, the city has been busy planting bicycle racks, distributing free bicycle maps, and experimenting with new ways of promoting bicycle traffic.[4] In 2013, Citi Bike began offering New Yorkers bicycles they could share, ride, and park at any of the many kiosks dotting the city. Within ten weeks of its debut, more than 40,000 bicycle trips were made in a single day. Indeed, anyone walking around Manhattan today cannot miss the bright blue bicycles, each of which features chain and splash guards, a roomy basket, blinking lights, three gears, and (quite conspicuously) its sponsor's logo. In just the first four months, users logged more than seven million total miles. Despite some financial difficulties, Citi Bike expects to expand with more bikes and more locations.[5]

Chicago, which boasts more than 160 miles of its own bike lanes, has set a goal of having at least 5 percent of all trips within a five-mile range be via a bicycle. The city plans to extend its bicycle network to some 500 miles and in 2013 introduced its own bike share system. Portland, Oregon, which typically earns top marks from cycling advocacy groups for its efforts to promote cycling, has found that smart planning can rapidly increase bicycle traffic. As of 2013, almost 6 percent of all commutes were taken by wheel. Washington, DC, and Pittsburgh have had similar success encouraging cycling, as has almost every major American city. The US

Census Bureau found that from 2000 to 2013 the number of cycling commuters, albeit still a tiny group, increased 62 percent.[6]

Even with the rapid decline in urban cycling that followed, one New Yorker's bold declaration in 1897 that "the bicycle is a permanent institution among the people of the earth" still rings true. There are more than a billion bicycles in the world today, and bicycles are being produced at a rate twice that of automobiles. The first private vehicle available to the masses, the bicycle remains the most popular vehicle in the world. Of course, many of these bicycles and the cyclists who use them as primary vehicles live outside of the United States, but even in American cities the bicycle has retained a small presence in the urban sphere. Over the last 120 years, a select group of messengers, police, children, speedsters, and commuters have continued to find pleasure and utility in the bicycle. Unlike most other inventions of its age, the bicycle has never completely disappeared. To a remarkable degree, the bicycle is the very same machine serving many of the same purposes it had over a century ago.[7]

As Americans are reacquiring an enthusiasm for "the wheel," some are predicting that the bicycle will again rise to prominence. Whether or not that is the case, the bicycle's role in urban development and city life should not be underestimated. We need only look around the world today to find examples of places in which bicycles shape the city and the lives of its residents. We can also look back in time to the 1890s. There we will find the lost city of cycling—a place that reveals that American cities were once infused with a robust bicycle culture, a place that can explain why that culture was absent for so long ever since, and a place that can help us understand the possibility of what might have been and what might come next.

NOTES

INTRODUCTION

1. Nathaniel Southgate Shaler, "The Betterment of our Highways," *Atlantic Monthly*, October 1892, 506.

2. "Bicycle Problems and Benefits," *Century Magazine*, July 1895, 474–75.

3. Sylvester Baxter, "Economic and Social Influences of the Bicycle," *Arena*, October 1892, 578–83.

4. Joseph B. Bishop, "Social and Economic Influence of the Bicycle," *Forum*, August 1896, 682. Yet another supporter claimed that the bicycle's benefits had become so universal that "it is impossible to conceive of anything to supplant or supersede the bicycle; not even a practical flying machine." "In the Cycling World," *New York Tribune*, March 29, 1897. A different author, wondering aloud about the future of urban transportation, wrote that "It is not to be supposed that mankind, having got possession of such a convenient, cheap, and effective instrument of locomotion as the bicycle, will consent to do without it." "The Future of the Horse," *New York Times*, December 24, 1899. Finally, one writer predicted that the bicycle's usefulness, in terms of practicality and recreation, would make it "as much a matter of course as a pair of boots in a civilized person's equipment." "Future of the Bicycle," *New York Daily Tribune*, December 18, 1898.

5. There are, of course, several historical studies about bicycles and cycling. Norman Dunham's dissertation from 1956 provides a terrific overview of the history of the bicycle in the United States, but his study focuses on the earliest era and before my study begins. In the early 1970s, Robert Smith published a "social history" of the bicycle that is filled with remarkable anecdotes covering a broad array of themes, even if few are investigated fully. The study, however, lacks scholarly rigor, is plagued with dubious claims, and is heavy on narrative and light on analysis. More recently, David V. Herlihy has produced a fine volume chronicling the entire history of the bicycle. That study, albeit quite useful for anyone interested in bicycle technology, devotes its pages mostly to the evolution of the machine and less to the bicycle's impact on the development of cities. Zack Furness focuses on the bicycle's cultural (and more modern) impact, while two recent books examine nineteenth-century cycling, but only in Wis-

consin and Boston, respectively. See Norman L. Dunham, "The Bicycle Era in American History" (PhD diss., Harvard University, 1956); Robert A. Smith, *A Social History
of the Bicycle, Its Early Life and Times in America* (New York: American Heritage
Press, 1972); David V. Herlihy, *Bicycle: The History* (New Haven: Yale University Press,
2004); Zack Furness, *One Less Car: Bicycling and the Politics of Automobility* (Philadelphia: Temple University Press, 2010); Jesse J. Gant and Nicholas J. Hoffman, *Wheel
Fever: How Wisconsin Became a Great Bicycling State* (Madison: Wisconsin Historical
Society Press, 2013); and Lorenz J. Finison, *Boston's Cycling Craze, 1880–1900: A Story
of Race, Sport, and Society* (Amherst: University of Massachusetts Press, 2014). See also
the proceedings of the annual International Cycling History conference.

6. "The Athletic Craze," *Nation*, December 7, 1893, 423; Frank W. Hoffmann and
William G. Bailey, *Sports & Recreation Fads* (New York: Haworth Press, 1991); Andrew
Marum and Frank Parise, *Follies and Foibles: A View of 20th Century Fads* (New York:
Facts on File, Inc., 1984).

7. While historian Sam Bass Warner, Jr.'s pioneering book *Streetcar Suburbs: The
Process of Growth in Boston, 1870–1900* (Cambridge: Harvard University Press, 1962)
may have overemphasized the process by which streetcar development shaped the
contours of residential neighborhoods on Boston's fringe, recent historians who have
eschewed such studies as too deterministic have often failed to provide better models
for urban historical development. For more on the transition within the field of urban
history from technological determinism toward a more cultural approach for understanding city development, see Timothy J. Gilfoyle, "White Cities, Linguistic Turns,
and Disneylands: The New Paradigms of Urban History," *Reviews in American History*,
26, no.1 (1998): 175–204. For examples of histories that employ alternative frameworks
to understand urban growth, see Elizabeth Blackmar, "Re-walking the 'Walking City':
Housing and Property Relations in New York City, 1780–1840," *Radical History Review*
21 (Fall 1979): 131–48; and Thomas W. Hanchett, *Sorting out the New South City: Race,
Class, and Urban Development in Charlotte, 1875–1975* (Chapel Hill: University of
North Carolina Press, 1998).

8. See Lewis Mumford, *The City in History* (New York: Harvest Books, 1961).

9. Arthur Meier Schlesinger, *The Rise of the City, 1878–1898* (New York: Macmil-
lan Company, 1933), 90–92; Clay McShane and Joel A. Tarr, *The Horse in the City:
Living Machines in the Nineteenth Century* (Baltimore: Johns Hopkins University
Press, 2007), 57–70; Robert C. Post, *Urban Mass Transit: The Life Story of a Technology*
(Westport, CT: Greenwood Press, 2007); Charles W. Cheape, *Moving the Masses: Urban
Public Transit in New York, Boston, and Philadelphia, 1880–1912* (Cambridge: Harvard
University Press, 1980).

10. J. & E. R. Pennell, "Twenty Years of Cycling," *Fortnightly Review*, August 1,
1897, 191.

11. Henry J. Garrigues, "Woman and the Bicycle," *Forum*, January 1896, 578.

12. Throughout this book I have tried to pay attention to regional differences
wherever possible. In some instances, however, certain themes played out so unevenly
across American cities that they defy general characterization. For instance, the debate
over Sunday cycling—the religious issue of whether cycling should be permitted on
Sundays—reflected a city's religious ethos more than anything to do with cycling per se.

13. Ted Curtis Smyth, *The Gilded Age Press, 1865–1900* (Westport, CT: Praeger, 2003), 154–55; Gerald J. Baldasty, *The Commercialization of News in the Nineteenth Century* (Madison: University of Wisconsin Press, 1992), 81–146; Michael Schudson, *Origins of the Ideal of Objectivity in the Professions: Studies in the History of American Journalism and American Law, 1830–1940* (New York: Garland Publishing, 1990), 161–85.

14. Phillip P. Mason, "The League of American Wheelmen and the Good Roads Movement: 1880–1905" (PhD diss., University of Michigan, 1957); Thomas Cameron Burr, "Markets as Producers and Consumers: The French and US National Bicycle Markets, 1875–1910" (PhD diss., University of California, Davis, 2005); *LAW Bulletin and Goad Roads Magazine*, January 1, 1897; Bruce Epperson, "How Many Bikes?" in *Cycle History 11: Proceedings of the 11th International Cycling History Conference, Osaka, Japan, 23–25 August 2000*, ed. Andrew Ritchie and Rob van der Plas (San Francisco: Van der Plas, 2001), with a minor revision provided to the author.

15. Although I am using the term "cycling city" in a historical and analytical sense, it was not entirely uncommon for writers in the 1890s to refer to various American cities as "cycling cities." For example, see "Washington Cyclists," *Washington Post*, June 6, 1897; "The Cyclist Reigns," *Atlanta Constitution*, July 5, 1896.

CHAPTER I

1. Axel Josephsson, "Bicycles and Tricycles," in US Census Bureau, *Twelfth Census of the United States* [1900], vol. X, pt. IV, *Manufactures* (Washington, DC, 1902), 324–29.

2. David V. Herlihy, *Bicycle: The History* (New Haven: Yale University Press, 2004), 15.

3. Norman L. Dunham, "The Bicycle Era in American History" (PhD diss., Harvard University, 1956), 7–8; Herlihy, *Bicycle*, 19, 75–76; Charles Eadward Pratt, *What & Why: Some Common Questions Answered* (Boston: Press of Rockwell and Churchill, 1884), 21. The terms "velocipede" and "bicycle" were often used to describe the same types of vehicle. For further clarification on the two terms, their meanings, and how nineteenth-century riders used them, see Herlihy, *Bicycle*, 23.

4. Stephen Goddard, *Colonel Albert Pope and His American Dream Machines: The Life and Times of a Bicycle Tycoon Turned Automotive Pioneer* (Jefferson, NC: McFarland & Company, 2000), 67–73.

5. For more on the production of the high-wheelers and the evolution of bicycle manufacturing, see David A. Hounshell, *From the American System to Mass Production, 1800–1932: The Development of Manufacturing Technology in the United States* (Baltimore: Johns Hopkins University Press, 1985), 189–217; Bruce D. Epperson, *Peddling Bicycles to America: The Rise of an Industry* (Jefferson, NC: McFarland & Company, 2010).

6. Mark Twain, *The Complete Essays of Mark Twain* (New York: Da Capo Press, 2000), 553. For more recollections from high-wheel cyclists, including one amusing description of how a rider learned to ride (and scraped his knuckles) by wheeling between a narrow space in between two brick buildings, see Clipping File, "Sports, Cycling," Chicago History Museum, Chicago.

7. Goddard, *Colonel Albert Pope and His American Dream Machines*, 9–10; Twain, *The Complete Essays of Mark Twain*, 555–57.

8. In today's dollars, a $120 bicycle would cost, using the Consumer Price Index, $2,900. If the price is calculated according to the rate of unskilled wages, it would equal $16,400. Measuring Worth, accessed February 27, 2014, http://www.measuringworth.com/uscompare/.

9. For more on the death of the high-wheeler and the evolution of the bicycle, see Wiebe E. Bijker, *Of Bicycles, Bakelites, and Bulbs* (Cambridge: MIT Press, 1995), 19–100.

10. Herlihy, *Bicycle*, 251. For a detailed look at the safety bicycle and its predecessors, see Tony Hadland and Hans-Erhard Lessing, *Bicycle Design: An Illustrated History* (Cambridge: MIT Press, 2014).

11. Martha Moore Trescott, "The Bicycle, a Technical Precursor to the Automobile," *Business and Economic History* 5 (1976): 55; Glen Norcliffe, *The Ride to Modernity: The Bicycle in Canada, 1869–1900* (Toronto: University of Toronto Press, 2001), 55; Herlihy, *Bicycle*, 261, 323; Paul Rubenson, "Patents, Profits & Perceptions: The Single-Tube Tire and the Failure of the American Bicycle, 1897–1933," in *Cycle History 15: Proceedings of the 15th International Cycle History Conference*, ed. Rob van der Plas, 87–97 (San Francisco: Van der Plas Publications, 2005).

12. "Bicycles in China," *World To-Day*, June 1903, 725. See also Frank Berto, "The Electric Streetcar and the End of the First American Bicycle Boom," in *Cycle History 17: Proceedings of the 17th International Cycling History Conference*, ed. Glen Norcliffe (San Francisco: Van der Plas/Cycle Publishing, 2007), 96; "Buying of Bicycles," *News* (Westchester, PA), July 17, 1896, in Newspaper Clippings Related to Cycling and Cycling Clubs, May 26, 1896–February 11, 1897, and undated collection, New-York Historical Society, New York; "General Notes," *Anglo-Japanese Gazette*, September 1902, 46.

13. "How the Finest Bicycles are Made," *Review of Reviews* (advertising supplement), April 1894, 19. See also Paul Rubenson, "Missing Link: The Case for Bicycle Transportation in the United States in the Early 20th Century," in *Cycle History 16: Proceedings of the 16th International Cycling History Conference, University of California, September 2005*, ed. Andrew Ritchie (San Francisco: Van Der Plas, 2006), 73–81. For more on how outside forces, including users, shape technological development, see Wiebe E. Bijker and John Law, *Shaping Technology/Building Society: Studies in Sociotechnical Change* (Cambridge: MIT Press, 1992); and Nelly Oudshoorn and Trevor Pinch, *How Users Matter: The Co-Construction of Users and Technologies* (Cambridge: MIT Press, 2003).

14. Herbert Alfred Garatt, *Modern Safety Bicycle* (New York: Whittaker & Co., 1899), 138–39, 182; Herlihy, *Bicycle*, 261–62. By the end of the decade a number of different types of brakes were made available and there was even an option for a multi-gear bicycle, though the majority of bicycles purchased during the boom years contained a single gear (Norcliffe, *The Ride to Modernity*, 63–65). For more on how technologies are shaped by society at large and on the wrongheaded perception that technologies "might have been otherwise," see Bijker and Law, *Shaping Technology/Building Society*.

15. Josephsson, "Bicycles and Tricycles," 335; Wiebe E. Bijker, Thomas P. Hughes, and Trevor Pinch, eds., *The Social Construction of Technological Systems: New Direc-*

tions in the Sociology and History of Technology (Cambridge: MIT Press, 1989); Luis A. Vivanco, Reconsidering the Bicycle: An Anthropological Perspective on a New (Old) Thing (New York: Routledge, 2013), 37–41. Of course, bicycle technology did evolve, and manufacturers flirted with many alternative forms, even if the basic shape remained the same. Moreover, it was not uncommon for some cyclists to purchase a bicycle every year or so as they traded in their older model. The manufacturers, likewise, advertised their new wheels as innovative, even if the improvements on a year-to-year basis were minor. This should not be confused with planned obsolescence, as there is no evidence that manufacturers deliberately designed their bicycles to become obsolete or less fashionable over time; rather, new models were simply advertised as being decidedly better than the last.

16. Professional copywriting was new in the 1890s as most advertisements before then had been crafted by the manufacturers themselves. Bicycle manufacturers were some of the earliest companies to employ such specialists. See Pamela Walker Laird, Advertising Progress: American Business and the Rise of Consumer Marketing (Baltimore: Johns Hopkins University Press, 1998), 176–82.

17. Damascus Bicycle Catalog (Terre Haute: Terre Haute Manufacturing Co., 1897).

18. Enquirer (Cincinnati), June 6, 1896, in Newspaper Clippings Related to Cycling and Cycling Clubs, New-York Historical Society, New York; Marmaduke Humphrey, "A Cycle Show in Little," Godey's Magazine, April 1896, 367–72; Lawrence Goldstone, Birdmen: The Wright Brothers, Glenn Curtiss, and the Battle to Control the Skies (New York: Ballantine Books, 2014), 38–40.

19. David E. Nye, Electrifying America: Social Meanings of a New Technology, 1880–1940 (Cambridge: MIT Press, 1990), 386. See also Howard P. Segal, Technological Utopianism in American Culture (Syracuse: Syracuse University Press, 2005).

20. Joseph J. Corn, The Winged Gospel: America's Romance with Aviation (Baltimore: Johns Hopkins University Press, 2001), 46–47.

21. Although it is not the focus of this study, bicycle racing in the late nineteenth century attracted an enormous and devoted following. Peter Nye, Hearts of Lions: The Story of American Bicycle Racing (New York: W. W. Norton & Co., 1989); Peter Nye, The Six-Day Bicycle Races: America's Jazz-Age Sport (San Francisco: Cycle Publishing, 2006); Andrew Ritchie, Major Taylor: The Extraordinary Career of a Champion Bicycle Racer (San Francisco: Bicycle Books, 1988); Major Taylor, The Fastest Bicycle Rider in the World (Worcester, MA: Wormley Pub. Co., 1928); Charles Meinert, "Singles Sixes in Madison Square Garden," in Cycle History 7: Proceedings of the 7th International Cycle History Conference (San Francisco: Rob van der Plas, 1997). For more on spectator sports and the emergence of the modern city, see Gunther Barth, City People: The Rise of Modern City Culture in Nineteenth-Century America (Oxford: Oxford University Press, 1980), 148–83.

22. Bishop, "Social and Economic Influence of the Bicycle," 680–91.

23. Races pitting cyclists against moving trains were not entirely uncommon. Most famously, Charles Murphy earned the nickname "Mile-a-Minute" after he successfully rode, for an entire minute, in the slipstream of a train moving at sixty miles per hour. As the New York Times article from 1899 reported about the stunt, the cyclist "proved that human muscle can, for a short distance at least, excel the best power of steam and

steel and iron." Advertisements for bicycles also emphasized this theme, including an ad from Remington Bicycles featuring a cyclist outpacing a speeding train. "Beat a Mile a Minute," *New York Times*, July 1, 1899; Remington Arms Co., "Remington to the Front," 1895.

24. As quoted in Christopher Thompson, *The Tour de France: A Cultural History* (University of California Press, 2006), 27. This particular rider was French.

25. Jean Porter Rudd, "My Wheel and I," *Outing*, May 1895, 124.

26. Frances E. Willard, *A Wheel Within a Wheel: How I Learned to Ride the Bicycle with Some Reflections by the Way* (Chicago: Woman's Temperance Publishing Association, 1895), 75

27. *Bicycling World*, May 15, 1880, 222, as quoted in Thomas Cameron Burr, "Markets as Producers and Consumers: The French and U.S. National Bicycle Markets, 1875–1910" (PhD diss., University of California, Davis, 2005), 83.

28. Glen Norcliffe, "Popeism and Fordism: Examining the Roots of Mass Production," *Regional Studies* 31, no.3 (1997): 269; Charles Eadward Pratt, *The American Bicycler: A Manual for the Observer, the Learner, and the Expert* (Boston: Houghton Osgood and Co., 1879).

29. *American Wheelman*, August 27, 1896, 18; *Harper's Bazaar*, March 1896; "Cycle News," *New York Recorder*, July 20, 1896, in Newspaper Clippings Related to Cycling and Cycling Clubs, New-York Historical Society, New York; *Chicago Bicycle Directory: A Reference Book of the Trade, 1898* (Chicago: Carr & Mensch, 1898); "For Women Cyclers," *Boston Post*, June 14, 1896, in Newspaper Clippings Related to Cycling and Cycling Clubs, New-York Historical Society, New York; Newspaper Clippings Related to Cycling and Cycling Clubs, New-York Historical Society, New York.

30. Roland Marchand, *Advertising the American Dream: Making Way for Modernity, 1920–1940* (Berkeley: University of California Press, 1985), 1.

31. In the 1880s, bicycle manufacturers represented three of only about seventy-four companies that advertised, on a regular basis, through national channels. James D. Norris, *Advertising and the Transformation of American Society, 1865–1920* (New York: Greenwood Press, 1990), 40–48. For an examination of how bicycle manufacturers advertised their products through illustrative artwork, see Jack Rennert, *100 Years of Bicycle Posters* (New York: Harper & Row, 1973). Until the 1900s most advertisements were product centered. Only around 1914 did a small group of advertisers begin "to appreciate the advantages of selling the benefit instead of the product—illumination instead of lighting fixtures, prestige instead of automobiles, sex appeal instead of mere soap." Marchand, *Advertising the American Dream*, xxi, 10.

32. Frank Presbrey, *The History and Development of Advertising* (New York: Greenwood Press, 1968), 363, 412–13; Ross D. Petty, "Peddling the Bicycle and the Development of Mass Marketing," in *Cycle History 5: Proceedings of the 5th International Cycle History Conference, Cambridge, England, September 2–4, 1994*, ed. Rob van der Plas (San Francisco: Bicycle Books, 1995), 108–9; "Bicycles," *New York Recorder*, February 6, 1895. For a broader perspective on the evolving field of marketing, particularly the beginning of national, brand-name advertising, see Richard S. Tedlow, *New and Improved: The Story of Mass Marketing in America* (New York: Basic Books, 1990).

33. "The Columbia Advertising," *Printer's Ink*, February 9, 1898, 58–60; Arnold,

Schwinn & Co., *Fifty Years of Schwinn-Built Bicycles: The Story of the Bicycle and its Contributions to Our Way of Life* (Chicago: Arnold, Schwinn & Co, 1945), 47.

34. "The Columbia Advertising," *Printer's Ink*, February 9, 1898, 58–60.

35. Norcliffe, "Popeism and Fordism," 276; *New York Bicycle Directory* (New York: New Bicycle Directory Publishing Co., 1896), 29; Stuart Charles Wade, *A Bird's-Eye View of Greater New York and its Most Magnificent Store* (New York, 1895), 61; Robert A. Smith, *A Social History of the Bicycle, Its Early Life and Times in America* (New York: American Heritage Press, 1972), 27–28; "Army of the Wheel," *Washington Post*, April 1, 1896. For one woman's account of her experience at a riding school, see Lillian Francia, "On a Wheel in the Metropolis," *Sportsman's Magazine*, October 1896, 45–50, in Newspaper Clippings Related to Cycling and Cycling Clubs, New-York Historical Society, New York; "Bowman Cycling Academy," *Sun* (New York), December 9, 1896; and "Society is on Wheels," *Morning Times* (Washington, DC), March 1, 1896.

36. Burr, "Markets as Producers and Consumers," 312–13.

37. For example, portions of West Madison Street and Wabash Avenue in Chicago were popularly referred to as a bicycle or cycle row. See George D. Bushnell, "When Chicago Was Wheel Crazy," in *The Chicago Sports Reader: 100 Years of Sports in the Windy City*, ed. Steven A. Riess and Gerald R. Gems, 84 (Urbana: University of Illinois Press, 2009); and "Cycling," *Outing*, July 1893, 78.

38. *Chicago Bicycle Directory*; City of Copenhagen, *Copenhagen City of Cyclists: Bicycle Account 2010*; Directory of Chicago Bicycle Shops, accessed June 7, 2013, http://www.chicagobikeshops.info/bikeShopList.php?sort=name&loc=city&keywords=; City of San Jose, accessed March 5, 2013, http://planning.sanjoseca.gov/planning/gp_update/documents/_2008-10-brochure-amsterdam-paves-the-way-for-cyclists_000.pdf; City of Philadelphia, *Journal of the Common Council of the City of Philadelphia, from April 6, 1896 to September 24, 1896, Vol 1* (Philadelphia: Dunlap Printing Company, 1896), 20–24; Jesse J. Gant and Nicholas J. Hoffman, *Wheel Fever: How Wisconsin Became a Great Bicycling State* (Madison: Wisconsin Historical Society Press, 2013), 147; *Pittsburgh and Allegheny Directory for 1898* (R. L. Polk & Co. and R. L. Dudley, 1899); *Business and Professional Directory of Detroit and Surrounding Towns* (Detroit: H. M. Snyder Co., 1899); *Geer's Hartford City Directory* (Hartford: Hartford Printing Company, 1897). The data from Philadelphia indicates that there were 271 shops that "either made or sold" bicycles but does not separate the two categories. The vast majority of these shops were certainly sellers, not producers, of bicycles, and even some of those who made bicycles also sold them directly. It should also be noted that in Pittsburgh bicycle shops outnumbered liveries, but only marginally.

39. Wade N. Praeger, "Fin de Cycle Seattle, the American Bicycle Craze of the 1890s" (master's thesis, Western Washington University, 1997), 95. See also "The Point of View," *Scribner's Magazine*, June 1896, 783.

40. Goddard, *Colonel Albert Pope and His American Dream Machines*, 97; *Damascus Bicycle Catalog*, 5; "How the Finest Bicycles are Made," *Review of Reviews* (advertising supplement), April 1894, 19.

41. H. A. Lozier & Co., *Cleveland Bicycles Catalog*, 1896, in National Museum of American History Library American Trade Literature Collection, Washington, DC; Pope Manufacturing Co., *Cycling for Ladies* (Boston: Pope Mfg. Co., 1892); Ross D.

Petty, "Women and the Wheel," *Cycle History: Proceedings of the 7th International Cycle History Conference, Buffalo, NY, USA, September 4–6, 1996*, ed. Rob van der Plas (San Francisco: Rob van der Plas, 1997), 118–24. At least one manufacturer reported that ladies' bicycles accounted for one third of all sales. Traffic data, explained more fully later in the book, reveal that women probably constituted closer to one quarter of the cycling population (Goddard, *Colonel Albert Pope and His American Dream Machines*, 97).

42. A. G. Spaulding & Bros., *1890 Cycling and Photographic Catalogue* (New York, 1890); Pope Manufacturing Co., *Columbia Bicycles Catalogue* (1893); Humber & Co. America, Ltd., *Humber and Co. America Ltd Catalogue* (Westboro, MA, 1896); *Wheel and Cycling Trade Review*, August 26, 1892, 34; Norcliffe, *The Ride to Modernity*, 121–23.

43. For an overview of the literature on consumer agency and how historians have understood the ways in which purchasers have personalized meanings of consumption, see David Steigerwald, "All Hail the Republic of Choice: Consumer History as Contemporary Thought," *Journal of American History*, 93, no. 2 (September 2006): 385–403.

44. Vivanco, *Reconsidering the Bicycle*, 43. Vivanco's anthropological perspective provides an excellent opportunity to consider the ways in which the meaning of the bicycle was contested and fluid.

45. Raymond H. Clarybooks, *The Making of Golden Gate Park: The Early Years, 1865–1906* (San Francisco: California Living, 1980), 75; Thompson, *The Tour de France*, 11. The prices for some of the custom bicycles surpassed $500, a sum easily ten times the price of a typical new bicycle.

46. "Proprietary Articles," *Century Magazine*, accessed April 23, 2013, http://collections.si.edu/search/tag/tagDoc.htm?thumb=true&recordID=siris_arc_244363&hlterm=record_ID%3Asiris_arc_244363; Joseph J. Corn, *User Unfriendly: Consumer Struggles with Personal Technologies, from Clock and Sewing Machines to Cars and Computers* (Baltimore: Johns Hopkins University Press, 2011), 49–50.

47. William Leach, *Land of Desire: Merchants, Power, and the Rise of a New American Culture* (New York: Pantheon Books, 1993), xiii. See also Ellen Gruber Garvey, *The Adman in the Parlor: Magazines and the Gendering of Consumer Culture, 1880s to 1910s* (New York: Oxford University Press, 1996). For more on the rise of the urban department store, see Barth, *City People*, 110–47. For an example of a Wanamaker advertisement for bicycles, see *Good Roads Book and the Rules of the Road Magazine, with Excellent Maps for Cyclists, Horsemen and Pedestrians* (New York: New York State Division, League of American Wheelmen, 1898), 26.

48. "Effective Window Dressing," *Cycle Age and Trade Review*, December 16, 1897, 162; *Cycle Age and Trade Review*, April 27, 1899, 790; Nicholas Oddy, "The Cycle on Display," in *Cycle History 16: Proceedings of the 16th International Cycling History Conference, University of California, September 2005*, ed. Andrew Ritchie (San Francisco, 2006), 143–46. For more on the staging of consumer goods, see Leach, *Land of Desire*, 39–70.

49. Dale A. Somers, "A City on Wheels: The Bicycle Era in New Orleans," *Louisiana History: The Journal of the Louisiana Historical Association* 8, no. 3 (Summer 1967): 234; *New York Bicycle Directory*, 3–9; "Bicycles of All Kinds; The Big Cycle

Exhibit in Madison Square Garden," *New York Times*, January 8, 1894; Smith, *A Social History of the Bicycle*, 33.

50. "Opening their Big Show," *New York Times*, January 5, 1896; Bushnell, "When Chicago was Wheel Crazy," 88.

51. "A Day with a Bicycle Model," *New York Journal*, September 27, 1896, in Newspaper Clippings Related to Cycling and Cycling Clubs, New-York Historical Society, New York.

52. "A Model in Bloomers," *Columbus State Journal*, September 27, 1896, in Newspaper Clippings Related to Cycling and Cycling Clubs, New-York Historical Society, New York.

53. For more on the number of bicycles produced, see Bruce Epperson, "How Many Bikes?" in *Cycle History 11: Proceedings of the 11th International Cycling History Conference, Osaka, Japan, 23–25 August 2000* (San Francisco: Van der Plas). Epperson claims that the traditional estimates of bicycle production, including the figure that more than eight million bicycles were produced from 1891–1900, are overblown. His own estimate for this period, which may be a bit conservative, puts the number of bicycles made in the United States closer to 5.5 million.

54. "Listen to His Tale of Woe," *Baltimore Sun*, June 15, 1896.

55. Josephsson, "Bicycles and Tricycles," 325.

56. "Mighty Army on Wheel," *Boston Globe*, July 5, 1896, in Newspaper Clippings Related to Cycling and Cycling Clubs, New-York Historical Society, New York.

CHAPTER 2

1. "The Point of View," *Scribner's Magazine*, February 1896, 256; "The World Awheel," *Munsey's Magazine*, May 1896, 131; "The Bicycle as a Social Factor," *Philadelphia Record*, September 16, 1896, in Newspaper Clippings Related to Cycling and Cycling Clubs, May 26, 1896–February 11, 1897, and undated collection, New-York Historical Society, New York; "A Democratic Vehicle," *Detroit Free Press*, as quoted in E. Nash, *Historic and Humorous Sketches of the Donkey, Horse and Bicycle* (Little Rock: Press of Tunnah and Pittard, 1896), 44.

2. "Tire Gossip," *Munsey's Magazine*, March 1897. Another estimated that there were four million cyclists in 1896. Alfred S. Johnson, ed., *The Cyclopedic Review of Current History, Vol. 6* (Buffalo: Garretson, Cox & Co., 1897), 970–71; US Census, accessed May 10, 2009, http://www.census.gov/population/censusdata/urpop0090.txt.

3. "The Wheel and the Canine," *Union and Advertiser* (Rochester), June 15, 1896, in Newspaper Clippings Related to Cycling and Cycling Clubs, New-York Historical Society, New York; Blake McKelvey, *Rochester on the Genesee: The Growth of a City* (Syracuse: Syracuse University Press, 1993), 140–41.

4. *Army and Naval Journal*, June 20, 1896, in Newspaper Clippings Related to Cycling and Cycling Clubs, New-York Historical Society, New York.

5. New York City Taxi and Limousine Commission, *2014 Taxicab Fact Book*, accessed March 26, 2014, http://www.nyc.gov/html/tlc/downloads/pdf/2014_taxicab_fact_book.pdf.

6. "Washington Cyclists," *Washington Post*, June 6, 1897; "The Mad Biking Days,"

San Francisco Examiner, February 5, 1925; *Densmore et al. v. City of Erie*, as cited in *Pennsylvania County Court Reports, Volume XX* (Philadelphia: T. & J. W. Johnson & Co., 1898), 519; Bruce Epperson, "How Many Bikes?" in *Cycle History 11: Proceedings of the 11th International Cycling History Conference, Osaka, Japan, 23–25 August 2000*, ed. Andrew Ritchie and Rob van der Plas (San Francisco: Van der Plas) with a minor revision provided by the author; *City of Emporia v. Wagoner*, as cited in *Pacific Reporter, Volume 49* (St. Paul: West Publishing Co., 1897), 701; Clay McShane and Joel A. Tarr, *The Horse in the City: Living Machines in the Nineteenth Century* (Baltimore: Johns Hopkins University Press, 2007), 16.

7. For example, see City of Minneapolis, *Annual Report of the City Engineer for the Year Ending Dec. 31, 1895*, 22–25; "Appendix No. 16," *Journal of the Common Council of the City of Philadelphia, From April 6, 1896 to September 24, 1896, Vol. I* (Philadelphia: Dunlap Printing Company, 1896), 20–24; "In and About Springfield. The 6 O'Clock Bicycle Crowd. Throngs Going Home from Work," *Republican* (Springfield, MA), October 17, 1897.

8. Epperson, "How Many Bikes?," 49, with a minor revision provided to the author.

9. *Wheel and Cycle Trade Review*, May 15, 1896, 74, provided via email from Thomas Cameron Burr (March 10, 2010).

10. "Is the Use of the Bicycle Decreasing?," *Philadelphia Inquirer*, December 1, 1898.

11. For example, see City of Minneapolis, *Annual Report of the City Engineer for the Year Ending Dec. 31, 1895*, 22–25; City of Minneapolis, *Annual Report of the City Engineer of the City of Minneapolis* (Minneapolis: City of Minneapolis, 1906), 16–17.

12. A survey from the morning commute in Chicago documented women riding at a very low rate, though the survey sought to capture commuters, a subgroup of which women comprised a disproportionately low percentage. A more representative sample taken throughout an entire day in New York recorded that women accounted for close to 20 percent of all traffic. *Wheel and Cycle Trade Review*, May 15, 1896, provided via email by Thomas Cameron Burr (March 10, 2010); "Figures on Wheels," *Chicago Daily Tribune*, September 18, 1898; "The Bicycle Industry," *Review of Reviews* (advertising supplement), June 1896, 17; Stephen Goddard, *Colonel Albert Pope and His American Dream Machines: The Life and Times of a Bicycle Tycoon Turned Automotive Pioneer* (Jefferson, N.C.: McFarland & Company, 2000), 97; Ross D. Petty, "Women and the Wheel," in Rob van der Plas, ed., *Cycle History: Proceedings of the 7th International Cycle History Conference, Buffalo, NY, U.S.A., September 4–6, 1996* (San Francisco: Rob van der Plas, 1997), 124; Thomas Cameron Burr, "Markets as Producers and Consumers: The French and U.S. National Bicycle Markets, 1875–1910" (PhD diss., University of California, Davis, 2005), 260–61; Serena Beeley, *A History of Bicycles* (Secaucus, NJ: Wellfleet Books, 1992).

13. *Wheel and Cycle Trade Review*, May 15, 1896; "Figures on Wheels," *Chicago Daily Tribune*, September 18, 1898; US Census Bureau, "Figure 2–4. Percent Distribution of the total Population by Age: 1900 to 2000," *Demographic Trends in the 20th Century* (November 2002), 56; Marble Cycle Manufacturing Company, *Smalley Bicycle Catalog*, 1894, accessed July 7, 2013, http://cdm16066.contentdm.oclc.org/cdm/compoundobject/collection/p16066coll6/id/58. For more on children and cycling, see

Margaret Guroff, "Kid Stuff: The Bicycle and American Youth," paper presented at the annual meeting for the International Cycle History Conference, Baltimore, Maryland, August 7–9, 2014; Robert J. Turpin, "'Our Best Bet is the Boy': A Cultural History of Bicycle Marketing and Consumption in the United States, 1880–1960" (PhD diss., University of Kentucky, 2013), 115–70.

14. Adna Ferrin Weber, *The Growth of Cities in the Nineteenth Century: A Study in Statistics* (New York: The Macmillan Company, 1899), 427.

15. McShane and Tarr, *The Horse in the City*, 79.

16. Ibid.; Barbara Young Welke, *Recasting American Liberty: Gender, Race, Law, and the Railroad Revolution, 1865–1920* (Cambridge: Cambridge University Press, 2001), 257.

17. Axel Josephsson, "Bicycles and Tricycles," in U.S. Census Bureau, *Twelfth Census of the United States* [1900], vol. X, pt. IV, *Manufactures* (Washington, DC, 1902), 328.

18. Jesse J. Gant and Nicholas J. Hoffman, *Wheel Fever: How Wisconsin Became a Great Bicycling State* (Madison: Wisconsin Historical Society Press, 2013), 147; Pope Manufacturing Company, *Columbia Bicycle Catalog for 1900*; Robert L. Steiner, "Learning from the Past—Brand Advertising and the Great Bicycle Craze of the 1890s," in *Proceedings of the Annual Conference of the American Academy of Advertising: Advances in Advertising Research and Marketing* (Knoxville: The Academy, 1978), 38. A $100 bicycle in the 1890s would equal about $2,760 in today's money using the Consumer Price Index (CPI) or a whopping $12,200 if the value is calculated using a labor value metric based on unskilled wages. A $10 bicycle equals about $276 today in terms of CPI or $1,220 in terms of unskilled wages. Measuring Worth, accessed October 16, 2012, http://www.measuringworth.com/calculators/uscompare/result.php.

19. "The World Awheel," *Munsey's Magazine*, May 1896, 155; James B. Townsend, "The Social Side of Bicycling," *Scribner's Magazine*, June 1895, 704–5; "The Wheel at Newport," *Bicycling World*, August 30, 1895, 581; Maureen E. Montgomery, *Displaying Women: Spectacles of Leisure in Edith Wharton's New York* (New York: Routledge, 1998).

20. Frank Presbrey, *The History and Development of Advertising* (New York: Greenwood Press, 1968), 412; Dora L. Costa, "The Wage and the Length of the Work Day: From the 1890s to 1991," *Journal of Labor Economics* 18, no. 1 (2000): 161–65; Jerome P. Bjelopera, *City of Clerks: Office and Sales Workers in Philadelphia, 1870–1920* (Urbana: University of Illinois Press, 2005), 2, 17; Sears, Roebuck & Co., *Models of 1898*, 9.

21. "The World and the Wheel," *Times* (Watertown) in *Boston Transcript*, June 13, 1896, in Newspaper Clippings Related to Cycling and Cycling Clubs, May 26, 1896–February 11, 1897, and undated collection, New-York Historical Society, New York; Robert A. Smith, *A Social History of the Bicycle: Its Early Life and Times in America* (New York: American Heritage Press, 1972), 29; W. W. Stall, *Bicycles, Tricycles, & Amateur Photographic Goods, Season of 1889* (Boston, 1889). At least one opponent of women cyclists cited a particular advertisement offering to exchange a "child's white crib" for a "lady's bicycle," as evidence that some mothers were more interested in joining the "charmed circle of cyclers" than being a good mother (Joseph B. Bishop, "Social and Economic Influence of the Bicycle," *Forum*, August 1896, 688). Within the coterie of

scholars studying bicycle use in the late nineteenth century, the question of whether a secondhand market for bicycles enabled a true democratization of the machine remains a favorite source of contention. My research indicates that there was indeed a robust secondhand bicycle market. For more on installment plans and consumer credit in this era, see Lendol Calder, *Financing the American Dream: A Cultural History of Consumer Credit* (Princeton: Princeton University Press, 1999).

22. A. G. Spaulding & Bros., *1890 Cycling and Photographic Catalogue* (New York, 2nd edition 1890), New-York Historical Society, New York; "What a Bicycle Costs," *Harrisburg Independent*, June 20, 1896, in Newspaper Clippings Related to Cycling and Cycling Clubs, New-York Historical Society, New York; "Information for Cyclists," *New York Evening Sun*, July 4, 1896, in Newspaper Clippings Related to Cycling and Cycling Clubs, New-York Historical Society, New York.

23. Arthur P. S. Hyde Diaries, 1892–1896, New-York Historical Society, New York; "Good Things to Let," *Chicago Daily Tribune*, May 6, 1895.

24. William Leach, *Land of Desire: Merchants, Power, and the Rise of a New American Culture* (New York: Pantheon Books, 1993), 3–5.

25. Charles Lanier, "The World's Sporting Impulse," *Review of Reviews*, July 1896, 58.

26. As quoted in James M. Mayo, *The American Country Club, Its Origins and Development* (New Brunswick: Rutgers University Press, 1998), 47–49.

27. Gary Allan Tobin, "The Bicycle Boom of the 1890s: The Development of Private Transportation and the Birth of the Modern Tourist," *Journal of Popular Culture* 7, no.4 (Spring 1974): 841; "Current Comment," *Godey's Magazine*, April 1896, 449; Phillip G. Hubert, Jr., "The Bicycle. The Wheel of To-day," *Scribner's Magazine*, June 1895, 692–93; Marguerite Merington, "Woman and the Bicycle," *Scribner's Magazine*, June 1895, 702; Mrs. John Sherwood, *Manners & Social Usages* (New York: Harper & Brothers, revised edition of 1901), 322. See also "The Wheel is King," *Jacksonville Times Union*, June 22, 1896, in Newspaper Clippings Related to Cycling and Cycling Clubs, New-York Historical Society, New York; "New York Herald; Chicago," *Inter Ocean* (Chicago), August 12, 1895. For more on the historical role of horses in urban transportation, see McShane and Tarr, *The Horse in the City*.

28. "What a Bicycle Saves," *New York City Leader*, August 5, 1896, in Newspaper Clippings Related to Cycling and Cycling Clubs, New-York Historical Society, New York; "The Secret of the Bike's Success," *New Orleans Picayune*, June 14, 1896; "In and About Springfield," *Republican* (Springfield, MA), October 17, 1897.

29. William A. Douglas and Williams Lansing, "Housing Conditions in Buffalo," in *The Tenement House Problem*, ed. Robert W. DeForest and Lawrence Veiller (New York: The MacMillan Company, 1903), 127.

30. For example, see "Dr. T. B. Kingsbury, Run over and Badly Hurt, last Night, by a Colored Bicyclist," *Semi-Weekly Messenger*, December 14, 1897; *St. Louis Courier-Journal*, July 11, 1897, as quoted in Joe Ward, "Bicycle Commuting in the Late 19th Century," accessed May 5, 2013, http://www.louisvillebicycleclub.org/Default.aspx?pageId= 917133; Anonymous Diaries, 1899–1946, Schlesinger Library, Radcliffe College, Boston; Bjelopera, *City of Clerks*, 93–101.

31. Hull House residents, however, frequently made use of bicycles. Shannon

Jackson, *Lines of Activity: Performance, Historiography, Hull-House Domesticity* (Ann Arbor: University of Michigan Press, 2000), 156

32. John F. Kasson, *Amusing the Million: Coney Island at the Turn of the Century* (New York: Hill and Wang, 1978), 29–37; Stuart M. Blumin, *The Emergence of the Middle Class: Social Experience in the American City, 1760–1900* (Cambridge: Cambridge University Press, 1989), 144–46; Steven A. Riess, *City Games: The Evolution of American Urban Society and the Rise of Sports* (Urbana: University of Illinois Press, 1989), 5.

33. *LAW Bulletin and Good Roads*, February 10, 1899; "The World Awheel," *Munsey's Magazine*, May 1896, 158.

34. *Physician and Surgeon*, September 1898, 411; "The Secret of the Bike's Success," *New Orleans Picayune*, June 14, 1896; "The Bicycle as a Social Factor," *Philadelphia Record*, September 16, 1896; Charles Zueblin, "Abolition of Grade Crossings," *Municipal Affairs*, December 1901, 826–27; Joseph B. Bishop, "Social and Economic Influence of the Bicycle," *Forum*, August, 1896, 683; "Influence of the Wheel," *Albany Press Knickerbockers*, June 29, 1896, in Newspaper Clippings Related to Cycling and Cycling Clubs, New-York Historical Society, New York. Some had hoped that mass-transit systems, with passengers of different backgrounds rubbing elbows and sharing an intimate space, would produce class "levelism." Riders, though, more often than not found the experience uncomfortable and antagonizing. Glen E. Holt, "The Changing Perception of Urban Pathology: An Essay on the Development of Mass Transit in the United States," in *Cities in American History*, ed. Kenneth T. Jackson and Stanley K. Schultz (New York: Alfred A. Knopf, 1972), 325–26.

35. Marmaduke Humphrey, "A Cycle Show in Little," *Godey's Magazine*, April 1896, 368.

36. For more on how certain cyclists, in this case middle-class and well-to-do urbanites, used bicycles as a means to connote status, see Daniel London, "Keeping a Respectable Distance: The Rise and Fall of the Bicycle as an instrument of Gentility," in *Cycle History 20: Proceedings of the 20th International Cycle History Conference, Freehold, New Jersey (USA), July 30–August 1, 2009*, ed. Gary W. Sanderson (Cheltenham, UK: John Pinkerton Memorial Publishing Fund, 2010).

37. Blumin, *The Emergence of the Middle Class*, 192.

38. Norman L. Dunham, "The Bicycle Era in American History" (PhD diss., Harvard University, 1956), 196–204; Dale A. Somers, "A City on Wheels: The Bicycle Era in New Orleans," *Louisiana History: The Journal of the Louisiana Historical Association* 8, no. 3 (Summer 1967): 223; Glen Norcliffe, *The Ride to Modernity: The Bicycle in Canada, 1869–1900* (Toronto: University of Toronto Press, 2001), 193–97; Records of the Harvard Bicycle Club, 1879–1889, Harvard University Archives. Many of the early clubs followed the guidelines established in Charles Eadward Pratt, *The American Bicycler: A Manual for the Observer, the Learner, and the Expert* (Cambridge: Riverside Press, 1879), 165–86.

39. "The LAW and Legal Rights," *Outing*, January 1886, 454; Phillip P. Mason, "The League of American Wheelmen and the Good Roads Movement: 1880–1905" (PhD diss., University of Michigan, 1957), 37; Dunham, "The Bicycle Era in American History," 196–97.

40. *New York Bicycle Directory* (New York: New Bicycle Directory Publishing Co., 1896); *Brooklyn Daily Eagle Almanac*, Vol. X (Brooklyn: Press of *Brooklyn Daily Eagle* Book and Job Department, 1895), 118–20; Encyclopedia of Chicago, "Bicycling," accessed September 19, 2009, http://www.encyclopedia.chicagohistory.org/pages/136 .html; Owen D. Gutfreund, *Twentieth-Century Sprawl: Highways and the Reshaping of the American Landscape* (New York: Oxford University Press, 2004), 62; Perry R. Duis and Glen E. Holt, "Chicago as It Was: City on Wheels," *Chicago*, June 1979, 190; "Gossip of the Cyclers," *New York Times*, September 26, 1897.

41. *Fifty Miles Around New York* (New York: The New York State Division of the League of American Wheelmen, 1896); "Don't Ask Them to Join," *LAW Bulletin and Good Roads*, July 3, 1896, 9; Riess, *City Games*, 57; Articles of Incorporation of Citizens Bicycle Club, New-York Historical Society, New York; Constitution and By-Laws of the Century Cycle Club, MS 383, Box 3 Folder 2, Howard S. Fisk Bicycle Club Collection, 1887, 1895–1905, The Historical Society of Washington, DC.

42. A. H. Godfrey, "Cycling Clubs and Their Spheres of Action," *Outing*, July 1897, 342–50.

43. Articles of Incorporation and By-Laws of the Citizens Bicycle Club of the City of New York, 1883, New-York Historical Society.

44. Minutes of Meetings of the Century Cycle Club, MS 383, Howard S. Fisk Bicycle Club Collection, 1887, 1895–1905, The Historical Society of Washington, DC.

45. *Illinois Cycling Club Life*, May 1895; *Dash*, August 31, 1895; *Illinois Cycling Club Life*, December 1896; *Illinois Cycling Club Life*, June 1899; Mayo, *The American Country Club*, 14–24.

46. "That's What's the Matter," *Times* (Oswego, NY), June 28, 1896, in Newspaper Clippings Related to Cycling and Cycling Clubs, New-York Historical Society, New York.

47. *Proceedings of the Fourth Annual Convention of the American Society of Municipal Improvements* (Milwaukee: Swain & Tate Co., 1897), 320.

48. E.H. Lacon Watson, "Bicycle Tours—and a Moral," *Westminster Review*, July–December 1894, 168.

49. *Eighth Annual Report of the Department of Public Safety* (Philadelphia: City of Philadelphia, 1896), 13.

50. For example, see *Dash*, the club paper of the Lake View Cycling Club in Chicago, and *Scorcher*, the club paper for the South Side Cycling Club, also in Chicago.

51. "Society's Cycling Club," *New York Times*, December 10, 1894; "The World Awheel," *Munsey's Magazine*, May 1896, 155.

52. Wade N. Praeger, "Fin de Cycle Seattle, the American Bicycle Craze of the 1890s" (master's thesis, Western Washington University, 1997), 35; Smith, *A Social History of the Bicycle*, 117.

53. Mona Domosh, *Invented Cities: The Creation of Landscape in Nineteenth-Century New York and Boston* (New Haven: Yale University Press, 1996), 156; David Hammack, *Power and Society: Greater New York at the Turn of the Century* (New York: Russell Sage Foundation, 1982), 72; Mayo, *The American Country Club*, 26, 47–49, 63–72, 98.

54. Riess, *City Games*, 8; Mayo, *The American Country Club*, 27; "The Power

of the Wheel," *New York Journal*, June 19, 1896, in Newspaper Clippings Related to Cycling and Cycling Clubs, New-York Historical Society, New York. Some clubs specifically barred women from joining ("Women Riders Barred," *Wheel Life*, March 17, 1898). For more on women's cycling clubs, see Lorenz J. Finison, *Boston's Cycling Craze, 1880–1900: A Story of Race, Sport, and Society* (Amherst: University of Massachusetts Press, 2014), 103–21.

55. Minutes of Meetings of the Century Cycle Club, MS 383, Folder 3, in Howard S. Fisk Bicycle Club Collection, 1887, 1895–1905, The Historical Society of Washington, DC; Riess, *City Games*, 57.

56. Bjelopera, *City of Clerks*, 93–100.

57. "Bicycling in Chinatown," *Morning World-Herald* (Omaha), August 3, 1895; "Chinese Wheelmen," *San Francisco Chronicle*, January 1, 1892; "Chinamen Will Take to the Wheel," *Chicago Daily Tribune*, August 16, 1895; "Gossip of the Cyclers," *New York Times*, September 19, 1897; "In the Cycling World," *New York Tribune*, May 30, 1897; "Of Interest to Wheelmen," *New York City Daily Mercury*, June 19, 1896, in Newspaper Clippings Related to Cycling and Cycling Clubs, New-York Historical Society, New York; "Fifteen 'Grinders' Left," *Brooklyn Daily Eagle*, December 11, 1897; Finison, *Boston's Cycling Craze*, 128–29; "Entry Blanks are Out," *Chicago Daily Tribune*, April 25, 1897; "Route of the Bicycle Parade," *Chicago Daily Tribune*, October 16, 1898.

58. "Chinamen Will Take to the Wheel," *Chicago Daily Tribune*, August 16, 1895; "Reform by the Bicycle. The Wheel A Splendid Factor in Developing Citizenship," *Los Angeles Times*, July 26, 1896; Kathy Peiss, *Cheap Amusements: Working-Women and Leisure in Turn-of-the-Century New York* (Philadelphia: Temple University Press, 1986), 31; Lizabeth Cohen, *Making a New Deal: Industrial Workers in Chicago, 1919–1939* (New York: Cambridge University Press, 1990), 119–20.

59. Susan G. Davis, *Parades and Power: Street Theatre in Nineteenth-Century Philadelphia* (Philadelphia: Temple University Press, Philadelphia, 1986), 3.

60. "The Field Day," *Los Angeles Times*, May 30, 1894.

61. *American Hebrew*, June 19, 1896, 169. See also *Jewish Criterion*.

62. Magazine editors argued that wearing bloomers was ugly but represented less of a taboo than did the scantily clad women on the beach; that women should cycle for exercise, albeit moderately and "gently"; that "women should ride the wheel, if they wish health, pleasure and happiness . . ." Advertisement, *American Jewess*, March 1896; "Editor's Desk," *American Jewess*, July 1895; "Cycling as an Exercise for Women," *American Jewess*, April 1897; "The Woman Who Talks," *American Jewess*, September 1896; "Why Women Should Ride the Wheel," *American Jewess*, June 1896.

63. "Bicicletas," *Nuevo Mundo* (Albuquerque), June 5, 1897; "Para los ciclistas," *Clarin del Norte* (El Paso), August 11, 1906; "La Bicicleta," *Empresa* (Las Cruces), January 23, 1897; "La Bicicleta y Su Teoria," *Dos Republicas* (Los Angeles), August 15, 1896; advertisement, *Cacara Jicara* (New York), November 13, 1897; Paul Boyer, *Urban Masses and Moral Order* (Cambridge: Harvard University Press, 1978), 123.

64. "Colored Wheelmen Barred," *New York Times*, September 10, 1892; "Watermelon for Colored Wheelmen," *Washington Post*, August 14, 1897; "Colored Cyclers to form a League," *Chicago Daily Tribune*, September 16, 1895; "Colored Wheelmen's Re-

ception," *New York Times*, February 19, 1897; "The Bicycle a Boon," *Idaho Statesman*, October 4, 1896; "Colored Crackjacks," *Los Angeles Times*, November 27, 1895; Andrew Ritchie, "The League of American Wheelmen, Major Taylor, and the 'Color Question' in the United States in the 1890s," *Sport in Society* 6, no. 2–3 (June/October 2003): 20–23; "Negro Cyclists Plead for Membership in the League of American Wheelmen," *New York Journal*, February 3, 1898; *American Wheelmen*, August 13, 1896, 17; Somers, "A City on Wheels," 225.

65. "Race on Conduit Road," *Washington Post*, October 11, 1896; "With the Subjects of King Bicycle," *Atlanta Constitution*, August 9, 1896; "Colored Wheelmen to Organize," *Chicago Daily Tribune*, March 19, 1894; "A LAW unto Themselves," *Los Angeles Times*, August 4, 1895; "Schade is at the Top," *Washington Post*, October 19, 1896; "Colored Wheelmen Parade," *Washington Post*, October 21, 1896.

66. "Utilitarian Side of Cycling," *Cycle Age and Trade Review*, September 22, 1898, 602. This was one of the only traffic surveys that differentiated "colored" riders from the rest of the cyclists. While some black Chicagoans cycled to work, their numbers paled in comparison to that of the white population.

67. "Negro Cyclists Plead for Membership in the League of American Wheelmen," *New York Journal*, February 3, 1898. A long way from New York, a group of black cyclists served in a experimental military unit designed to test the usefulness of the bicycle in military affairs. Alexandra V. Koelle, "Pedaling on the Periphery: The African American Twenty-Fifth Infantry Bicycle Corps and the Roads of American Expansion," *Western Historical Quarterly* 41 (Autumn 2010): 305, 326.

68. US Census Bureau, "New York—Race and Hispanic Origin for Selected Large Cities and Other Places: Earliest Census to 1990," accessed August 1, 2013, http://www.census.gov/population/www/documentation/twps0076/ NYtab.pdf.

69. "Where Wheel Men Abound," *New York Herald*, September 16, 1894.

70. "The Cycle Parade" *New York Tribune*, July 13, 1902; "Fourth of July Dull in the Park," *Philadelphia Inquirer*, June 29, 1900.

71. For example, see "Isaac B. Potter," *Baltimore Afro-American*, April 9, 1898; *Baltimore Afro-American*, July 9, 1898.

72. "Negro Cyclist Ran into Lady," *Columbus Daily Enquirer*, October 20, 1901; "More 'Scorcher' Victims: A Fast-Riding Negro Cyclist Ran down Two Children Yesterday Afternoon," *Kansas City Star*, April 15, 1899; "Run over by a Colored Bicyclist," *Sun* (Baltimore), June 22, 1897; "Reckless Negro Bicyclist: He is under Arrest for Running down Mrs. Robinson," *St. Louis Republic*, September, 4, 1896; "Dr. T. B. Kingsbury, Run over and Badly Hurt, last Night, by a Colored Bicyclist," *Semi-Weekly Messenger*, December 14, 1897; "The Bicycle a Boon," *Idaho Statesman*, October 4, 1896; "Kemble Illustrates the Piccaninny Club Awheel," *San Francisco Examiner*, August 8, 1897; "Afro-American Cyclists," *St. Louis Republic*, August 30, 1898. At least one bicycle manufacturer speculated that as southern blacks became cyclists, white southerners no longer found the activity appealing; see Bruce D. Epperson, *Bicycles in American Highway Planning: The Critical Years of Policy-Making, 1969–1991* (Jefferson, NC: McFarland & Company, 2014), 30. For more on the issue of bicycle racing and segregation, see Major Taylor, *The Fastest Bicycle Rider in the World* (Worcester, MA: Wormley Pub. Co., 1928).

73. "Emancipation Day at Springfield, Ill.," *Washington Post*, September 23, 1896; "The Negro's Day of Jubilee," *Washington Post*, September 15, 1896.

74. Clifford Geertz, *The Interpretation of Cultures, Selected Essays* (New York: Basic Books, 1973), 448. It should be noted that this quote derives from an observation Geertz made about Balinese cockfighting, a subject not remotely close temporally, geographically, or thematically to bicycle parades in the 1890s. Nonetheless, the logic applies.

75. Davis, *Parades and Power*, 155.

76. Owen Wister, "Artists and the Wheel," *The Critic*, December 1895, as quoted in Praeger, "Fin de Cycle Seattle, the American Bicycle Craze of the 1890s."

CHAPTER 3

1. For a case study of such a phenomenon, see Peter Baldwin, *Domesticating the Street: The Reform of Public Space in Hartford, 1850–1930* (Columbus: Ohio State University Press, 1999).

2. "The Bicycle and its Rights," *Philadelphia Times*, July 20, 1896, in Newspaper Clippings Related to Cycling and Cycling Clubs, May 26, 1896–February 11, 1897, and undated collection, New-York Historical Society, New York.

3. As just one example, in 1891, Washington, DC licensed 548 public vehicles (e.g., omnibuses), not including the rapidly expanding cars in the street railway system. *Annual Report of the Commissioners of the District of Columbia for the Year Ended June 30, 1891* (Washington, DC: Government Printing Office, 1891).

4. For more on the development of how cities came to reorganize traffic in the twentieth century, particularly around the automobile, see Peter D. Norton, *Fighting Traffic: The Dawn of the Motor Age in the American City* (Cambridge: MIT Press, 2008).

5. Eric H. Monkkonen, *America Becomes Urban: The Development of US Cities and Towns, 1780–1980* (Berkeley: University of California Press, 1988), 164–67. To understand how cities came to regulate automobiles, see Norton, *Fighting Traffic*. For a broader overview of the relative power municipalities held, and the ways in which they crafted and enforced regulations throughout the nineteenth century, see William J. Novak, *The People's Welfare: Law and Regulation in Nineteenth-Century America* (Chapel Hill: University of North Carolina Press, 1996); and Brian Balogh, *A Government Out of Sight: The Mystery of National Authority in Nineteenth-Century America* (Cambridge: Cambridge University Press, 2009).

6. For example, see *San Francisco Park and Recreation Commission Minutes, 1885*, 51–53, San Francisco Public Library.

7. For example, see the debate about a proposed ordinance to legalize cycling in the streets in "The Aldermen," *Brooklyn Daily Eagle*, April 27, 1880.

8. Norman L. Dunham, "The Bicycle Era in American History" (PhD diss., Harvard University, 1956), 272; Charles Eadward Pratt, *What & Why: Some Common Questions Answered* (Boston: Press of Rockwell and Churchill, 1884), 44–48.

9. Dunham, "The Bicycle Era in American History," 272; "Park Department Matters," *New York Times*, July 8, 1880.

10. Dunham, "The Bicycle Era in American History," 280–81; "The Bicyclists Defeated," *New York Times*, July 19, 1882; "Bicycles and Tricycles," *New York Times*, April 1, 1882; "A Test Bicycle Case," *New York Times*, July 15, 1881; "The Rights of the Bicycle," *New York Times*, July 26, 1881; "News for the Wheelman," *New York Times*, July 1, 1897.

11. Stephen Goddard, *Colonel Albert Pope and His American Dream Machines: The Life and Times of a Bicycle Tycoon Turned Automotive Pioneer* (Jefferson, N.C.: McFarland & Company, 2000), 73; Dunham, "The Bicycle Era in American History," 281.

12. "The Rights of the Bicycle," *New York Times*, July 26, 1881; "The Bicyclists Defeated," *New York Times*, July 19, 1882; "Bicycles and Tricycles," *New York Times*, April 1, 1882; "A Test Bicycle Case," *New York Times*, July 15, 1881.

13. "Wheel News," *Outing*, June 1883, 238; "Speeches Made at the Banquet of the League of American Wheelmen, Monday, May 28, 1883, At Metropolitan Hotel, New York City (Continued.)," *Outing*, August 1883, 373–74.

14. "New-York Daguerreotyped," *Putnam's Monthly*, April 1853, 364; "A New-York Hotel," *New York Times*, June 19, 1852.

15. "Speeches Made at the Banquet of the League of American Wheelmen, Monday, May 28, 1883, at Metropolitan Hotel, New York City," *Outing*, July 1883, 309; "Speeches Made at the Banquet of the League of American Wheelmen, Monday, May 28, 1883, At Metropolitan Hotel, New York City (Continued.)," 373–74; "Wheelmen on Parade," *New York Times*, May 29, 1883; "Parade of the Wheelmen," *Brooklyn Daily Eagle*, May 28, 1883.

16. "Speeches Made at the Banquet of the League of American Wheelmen, Monday, May 28, 1883, at Metropolitan Hotel, New York City," 309.

17. "Articles of incorporation and By-laws of the Citizens Bicycle Club of the City of New York: Organized June 1st, 1882: Incorporated, August 30th, 1883," New-York Historical Society, New York.

18. "Concessions to Bicycle Riders," *New York Times*, Jun 17, 1883; *Twenty-Fifth Annual Report of the Brooklyn Park Commissioners for the year 1885* (Brooklyn, 1886), 40–41. For more on the urban "bachelor subculture," see Howard P. Chudacoff, *The Age of the Bachelor: Creating an American Subculture* (Princeton: Princeton University Press, 1999).

19. "Rights for the Bicyclers," *Brooklyn Daily Eagle*, June 15, 1887; "Heard by the Governor," *New York Times*, June 15, 1887.

20. *New York Laws*, chapter 702 (1887); "Heard by the Governor," *New York Times*, June 15, 1887; "Editor's Open Window," *Outing*, August 1887, 484.

21. "The Talk of New York," *Brooklyn Daily Eagle*, July 10, 1887.

22. Pratt, *What & Why*, 40.

23. Bob Mionske, *Bicycling and the Law: Your Rights as a Cyclist* (Boulder: Velo Press, 2007), 8–11; W. E. Swift v. the City of Topeka, 43 Kan. 671; 23 P. 1075; 1890 Kan. LEXIS 163 (Kan. May 10, 1890).

24. "In and About Springfield," *Republican* (Springfield, MA), October 17, 1897; Karen McCally, "Bloomers & Bicycles: Health and Fitness in Victorian Rochester," *Rochester History* 69, no. 2 (Spring 2008): 12; "Wanted: A Bicycle Ordinance," *Detroit Free Press*, August 29, 1896.

25. City of Philadelphia, "Department of Public Safety," *Journal of the Common*

Council of the City of Philadelphia from April 6, 1896 to September 24, 1896, Vol. I (Philadelphia: Dunlap Printing Company, 1896).

26. Robert G. Steel, *Bicycle Routes in Michigan, Giving a Complete Description of the Roads of Michigan used by Wheelmen in Riding between Different Cities and Towns, with Maps* (League of American Wheelmen, Michigan Division, 1896); "Philadelphia Wheelmen Awake," *Cycle Age and Trade Review*, January 26, 1899; "To Secure Better Roads," *New York Times*, May 1, 1895; *Good Roads Book and the Rules of the Road Magazine*, 23; "Marlborough a Prisoner," *New York Times*, October 19, 1895. For examples of bicycle ordinances, see *Compiled Ordinances of the City of St. Paul, Minnesota. Corrected and Revised to January 1, 1906* (St. Paul: St. Paul Review Publishing Co., 1908); *Code of Ordinances of The City of New York* (New York: Banks Law Publishing Company, 1908); and *General Orders of the Board of Supervisors Providing Regulations for the Government of the City and County of San Francisco*, 362–3.

27. "A New Boulevard Resolution," *New York Mail and Express*, September 9, 1896, in Newspaper Clippings Related to Cycling and Cycling Clubs, New-York Historical Society, New York; "To Save Cyclists and Their Wheels," *New York Journal*, September 9, 1896, in Newspaper Clippings Related to Cycling and Cycling Clubs, New-York Historical Society, New York; "Boulevard Bicyclists' Terror," *New York Sun*, July 4, 1896; "The Bicycle Problem," *Commercial Appeal* (Memphis), September 25, 1896, in Newspaper Clippings Related to Cycling and Cycling Clubs, New-York Historical Society, New York. There was a long history of animosity between cyclists and other drivers. In probably the most dramatic example of road rage, one teamster, angered by the rising number of bicycles, shot five passerby cyclists. Robert A. Smith, *A Social History of the Bicycle, Its Early Life and Times in America* (New York: American Heritage Press, 1972), 186.

28. The poll reported 2,528 ballots for restriction of traffic and thirty-four ballots against. "Alderman and Bicycles," *New York Herald*, September 26, 1896, in Newspaper Clippings Related to Cycling and Cycling Clubs, New-York Historical Society, New York.

29. *Proceedings of the Board of Aldermen of the City of New York From October 6 to December 29, 1896* (New York: Martin B. Brown, 1897), 12–13; "Cycle News," *New York Evening Recorder*, October 2, 1896, in Newspaper Clippings Related to Cycling and Cycling Clubs, New-York Historical Society, New York.

30. *Proceedings of the Board of Aldermen of the City of New York From October 6 to December 29, 1896*, 3–4, 15, 35–36; "Cycle News," *New York Evening Recorder*, October 2, 1896; "Would Stripe the Boulevard," *New York Sun*, October 4, 1896; "Bicycles on the Boulevard," *New York Sun*, October 20, 1896.

31. Clay McShane, *Down the Asphalt Path: The Automobile and the American City* (New York: Columbia University Press, 1994), 50–51; Norton, *Fighting Traffic*, 50. In Seattle, for example, the Queen City Cycle Club helped draft its city's cycling ordinances. Wade N. Praeger, "Fin de Cycle Seattle, the American Bicycle Craze of the 1890s" (master's thesis, Western Washington University, 1997), 74–76.

32. "News for the Wheelmen," *New York Times*, June 11, 1897; "News for the Wheelmen," *New York Times*, July 14, 1897.

33. "Gossip of the Cyclers," *New York Times*, February 11, 1895; *General Ordi-*

nances of the City of New York under the Greater New York Charter (New York: Banks Law Publishing Co., 1902), 128–130.

34. *General Ordinances of the City of New York under the Greater New York Charter*, 128–130.

35. Raymond H. Clarybooks, *The Making of Golden Gate Park: The Early Years: 1865–1906* (San Francisco: California Living, 1980), 75–76; "Topeka, Kas., Bicyclists Get Even with the City Council," *Chicago Daily Tribune*, July 7, 1896.

36. For example, see "Not a Paradise for Wheelmen," *Wheel and Cycling Trade Review*, May 17, 1895, 34.

37. "New Rules of the Road," *New York Times*, July 28, 1897; "Wheelmen and Sidewalks," *New York Times*, June 18, 1897; *Code of Ordinances of the City of New York*. The principle of defining the bicycle as a vehicle became so commonplace in the United States that it was even exported to its distant territories. In the Philippines, for example, American officials declared that "Every bicycle shall be regarded as a vehicle and subject to all ordinances and regulations relating thereto. It shall carry a light when in use after dark, and a bell or whistle at all times, which shall be sounded when approaching any street crossing or intersection or any vehicle or person occupying the street." *Annual Reports of the War Department for the Fiscal Year ended June 30, 1901 Report of the Lieutenant-General Commanding the Army. In Five Parts. Part 5* (Washington, DC: Government Printing Office, 1901).

38. "Cycle News and Gossip," *Baltimore Herald*, July 28, 1896.

39. A. J. Geiger v. the President, Managers and Company of The Perkiomen & Reading Turnpike Road, 167 Pa. 582; 31 A. 918; 1895 Pa. LEXIS 949 (Pa. April 29, 1895). Similar challenges were made in cases involving sidewalk riding. For example, see Commonwealth, Appellant, v. James B. Forrest, No. 136, 170 Pa. 40; 32 A. 652; 1895 Pa. LEXIS 1360 (Pa. July 18, 1895).

40. *Proceedings of the Board of Aldermen of the City of New York From October 6 to December 29, 1896* (New York: Martin B. Brown, 1897), 45.

41. *General Ordinances of the City of New York under the Greater New York Charter*, 130.

42. As quoted in Clarybooks, *The Making of Golden Gate Park*, 75–76.

43. *Proceedings of the Board of Aldermen of the City of New York from April 7 to June 30, 1896* (New York: Martin B. Brown, 1897), 329; "Three Thousand New Bikes," *Pittsburgh Times*, June 18, 1896, in Newspaper Clippings Related to Cycling and Cycling Clubs, New-York Historical Society, New York; *Proceedings of the City Council of the City of Chicago for the Municipal Year 1897–1898* (Chicago: John F. Higgins, 1898), 612–14. In Ohio, a bicycle tax was levied throughout the entire state by the act of the state legislature. "Ohio's Bicycle Tax," *Cycle Age and Trade Review*, April 28, 1898. Other cities taxed bicycles in other ways, like when San Francisco levied a tax on "cycleries" or businesses that rented bikes for hire. *General Orders of the Board of Supervisors Providing Regulations for the Government of the City and County of San Francisco* (San Francisco: Phillips & Smith), 1898, 126. Few of the municipal logbooks containing records of bicycle taxes remain, but for one example, see "Dauphin County Bicycle Register, 1899–1902," Pennsylvania State Archives.

44. *Proceedings of the Board of Aldermen of the City of New York from April 7 to*

June 30, 1896, 410; "Bicycle Tax; Baby Riders," *New York Evening World,* June 10, 1896, in Newspaper Clippings Related to Cycling and Cycling Clubs, New-York Historical Society, New York; "Gossip of the Cyclers," *New York Times,* May 22, 1898; Jesse J. Gant and Nicholas J. Hoffman, *Wheel Fever: How Wisconsin Became a Great Bicycling State* (Madison: Wisconsin Historical Society Press, 2013), 84–85; *Proceedings of the Fourth Annual Convention of the American Society of Municipal Improvements* (Milwaukee: Swain & Tate Co., 1897), 214–15; *LAW Bulletin and Goad Roads Magazine,* February 5, 1897; "Build Bicycle Paths," *San Francisco Call,* August 4, 1897; "Tacoma's Exclusive Cycle Bridge," *Cycle Age and Trade Review,* May 12, 1898, 1122; Isaac B. Potter, "The Bicycle Outlook," *Century Magazine,* September 1896, 785–90.

45. *Annual Report of the Commissioners of the District of Columbia for the Year Ended June 30, 1898, Vol. 1* (Washington, DC: Government Printing Office, 1898), 8–9, 13–14; "Washington's Regulations," *Cycle Age and Trade Review,* December 16, 1897, 162; "Washington Liverymen Protests," *Cycle Age and Trade Review,* December 23, 1897, 240; "Fred Schade's protest," January 10, 1898, in Vertical Files-Recreation Sports-Bicycling Box 20, Washington, DC Historical Society, Washington, DC; Moore v. the District of Columbia, No. 777. 2 App. D.C. 537; 1898 U.S. App. LEXIS 3180 (D.C. May 3, 1898).

46. Dale A. Somers, "A City on Wheels: The Bicycle Era in New Orleans," *Louisiana History: The Journal of the Louisiana Historical Association* 8, no. 3 (Summer 1967): 228; *Proceedings of the City Council of the City of Chicago for the Municipal Year 1896–1897* (Chicago: John F. Higgins, 1896), 1591.

47. *Proceedings of the Board of Aldermen of the City of New York from January 7 to March 21, 1896* (New York: Martin B. Brown, 1897), 185, 201, 348–50, 444.

48. "Go Easy, Bicyclists!," *Harper's Weekly,* May 23, 1896, 507–8.

49. *City of Detroit, Journal of the Common Council from January 12, 1897 to January 11, 1898* (Detroit: City of Detroit, 1898), 510.

50. "Up-To-Date Wheelmen," *Boston Herald,* August 30, 1896, in Newspaper Clippings Related to Cycling and Cycling Clubs, New-York Historical Society, New York. See also "A Code of Signals," *Buffalo Enquirer,* June 5, 1896, in Newspaper Clippings Related to Cycling and Cycling Clubs, New-York Historical Society, New York.

51. "The Power of the Wheel," *New York Journal,* June 19, 1896, in Newspaper Clippings Related to Cycling and Cycling Clubs, New-York Historical Society, New York.

52. "The Bicycle," *Semi-Weekly Messenger,* (Wilmington, NC), December 17, 1897.

CHAPTER 4

1. "Unbounded Horseless Possibilities Opened Up," *Toronto Truth,* August 8, 1896, in Newspaper Clippings Related to Cycling and Cycling Clubs, May 26, 1896–February 11, 1897, and undated collection, New-York Historical Society, New York.

2. "Bicycle Problems and Benefits," *Century Magazine,* July 1895, 475.

3. US Department of Agriculture, *Report of the Commissioner of Agriculture, 1888* (Washington, DC: Government Printing Office, 1889), 47.

4. Micahel R. Fein, *Paving the Way: New York Road Building and the American State, 1880–1956* (Lawrence: University Press of Kansas, 2008), 27.

5. Phillip P. Mason, "The League of American Wheelmen and the Good Roads Movement: 1880–1905" (PhD diss., University of Michigan, 1957), 5, 23.

6. "Hub of all Wheeldom," *Washington Post*, September 6, 1896.

7. "The Pulpit and the Bicycle," *Arena*, August 1895, xix.

8. "The Future of the Bicycle," *New York Times*, June 26, 1881; "The Bicycle Fever," *Times* (Richmond), June 4, 1896.

9. League of American Wheelmen, New York Division, *Fifty Miles around Brooklyn: A Handbook of Cycling Roads and Routes with Maps and Illustrations* (New York: New York State Division of the League of American Wheelmen, 1896); C. F. Wadsworth, *Cyclists' Road Guide to Chicago and Vicinity: Including Maps of Milwaukee, Racine, Beloit, Evanston, Rockford, Geneva, Elgin, Aurora, and others* (Chicago: C. F. Wadsworth, 1895); *Chicago Cycler's Guide for 1896* (Chicago: Chicago Cycler's Guide, 1896), 17; Joseph Bliss, Bicycle Routes: MS. S, 1894–1903, Bancroft Library, University of California, Berkeley; Frank J. Schwartz cycling logbook, 1883–1888, New-York Historical Society, New York; Arthur P. S. Hyde Diaries, 1892–1896, New-York Historical Society, New York; Harry Adams Hersey papers, 1892–1979, Massachusetts Historical Society, Boston.

10. For a detailed breakdown of the most common pavement types across major cities, see *Paving and Municipal Engineering*, April, 1896, 235. For more history on paving materials and the growing importance of asphalt, see Clay McShane, *Down the Asphalt Path: The Automobile and the American City* (New York: Columbia University Press, 1994), 57–63; I. B. Holley, Jr., "Blacktop: How Asphalt Paving Came to the Urban United States," *Technology and Culture* 44, no. 4 (October 2003): 703–33.

11. Christopher W. Wells, *Car Country: An Environmental History* (Seattle: University of Washington Press, 2012), 14, 24; *Proceedings of the City Council of the City of Chicago for the Municipal Year 1894–1895* (Chicago: John F. Higgins, 1896), 2247–52; Jon C. Teaford, *The Unheralded Triumph: City Government in America, 1870–1900* (Baltimore: Johns Hopkins University Press, 1984), 6–26. For more on the legal and jurisdictional history of roadways in the nineteenth century, see William J. Novak, *The People's Welfare: Law and Regulation in Nineteenth-Century America* (Chapel Hill: The University of North Carolina Press, 1996), 121–31. For a different perspective on the issue of power and decision-making in municipal politics as a whole in this era, see David Hammack, *Power and Society: Greater New York at the Turn of the Century* (New York: Russell Sage Foundation, 1982). See also Kenneth Fox, *Better City Government: Innovation in American Urban Politics, 1850–1937* (Philadelphia: Temple University Press, 1977).

12. "Notes upon Road Progress," *Bearings*, February 19, 1891.

13. George B. Clementson, *The Road Rights and Liabilities of Wheelmen* (Chicago: Callaghan & Co., 1895); "Benefits of the League," *New York Times*, March 24, 1895; Mason, "The League of American Wheelmen and the Good Roads Movement," 64–65, 76, 103; "Benefits of the League."

14. Albert A. Pope, *Relation of Good Streets to the Prosperity of a City: An Address* (Boston, 1890); Stephen Goddard, *Colonel Albert Pope and His American Dream Machines: The Life and Times of a Bicycle Tycoon Turned Automotive Pioneer* (Jefferson, NC: McFarland & Company, 2000), 117–19; Albert A. Pope, *The Movement for Better*

Roads: An Address (Boston: Pope Manufacturing Co., 1892); Albert A. Pope, *Road Making as a Branch of Instruction in Colleges* (Boston, 1892); Stephen Hardy, *How Boston Played: Sport, Recreation, and Community, 1865–1915* (Boston: Northeastern University Press, 1982), 160.

15. "Good Roads," *Binghamton Leader*, June 16, 1896, in Newspaper Clippings Related to Cycling and Cycling Clubs, New-York Historical Society, New York; "The Wheelmen's Plank for Good Roads," *Chicago Tribune*, June 15, 1896; Michael Taylor, "The Bicycle Boom and the Bicycle Bloc: Cycling and Politics in the 1890s," *Indiana Magazine of History* 104 (September 2009): 213–40; "The World Awheel," *Munsey's Magazine*, May 1896, 156. As a report from a group of municipal engineers noted, ". . . the number of wheelmen has so increased that they represent quite a power at the polls, and without giving allegiance to any particular party they could easily be able in any local election, to elect to office those who would at least show them justice in establishing rules and regulations for the proper use of the streets and sidewalks." *Proceedings of the Fourth Annual Convention of the American Society of Municipal Improvements* (Milwaukee: Swain & Tate Co., 1897), 320.

16. George D. Bushnell, "When Chicago Was Wheel Crazy," in *The Chicago Sports Reader: 100 Years of Sports in the Windy City*, ed. Steven A. Riess and Gerald R. Gems (Urbana: University of Illinois Press, 2009), 86.

17. State of New Jersey, *Fourth Annual Report of the Commissioner of Public Roads for the Year Ending October 31st, 1897* (Trenton: MacCrellish & Quigley, 1898), 54.

18. "Of Interest to New York," *LAW Bulletin and Good Roads*, October 30, 1896, 567; *LAW Bulletin and Good Roads*, February 26, 1897, 211; Bushnell, "When Chicago Was Wheel Crazy," 88; Carter H. Harrison, *Stormy Years: The Autobiography of Carter H. Harrison, Five Times Mayor of Chicago* (Indianapolis: Bobbs-Merrill Company Publishers, 1935), 104–5; Edith Ogden Harrison, Writings and Outgoing Correspondence, "Bicycles and Billiards," n.d., Midwest MS Harrison Box 19, Folder 952, Newberry Library, Chicago; Encyclopedia of Chicago, "Bicycling," accessed September 19, 2009, http://www.encyclopedia.chicagohistory.org/pages/136.html. In St. Paul, Minnesota, too, as well as in many other cities, a candidate representing the "wheelmen's interests" ran on a probicycle platform for a seat in the state government. "Gossip of the Twin Cities," *Cycle Age and Trade Review*, May 12, 1898. For more on the "bicycle bloc" and the role of cyclists in politics, see Taylor, "The Bicycle Boom and the Bicycle Bloc."

19. *Chicago Wheelman*, March 29, 1899. Harrison was also a frequent guest of Chicago's Bicycle Clubs. For example, see *Illinois Cycling Club Life*, July 1899.

20. "News for the Wheelmen," *New York Times*, July 18, 1897; "The Modern Bicycle," *New York Times*, August 13, 1894; "Of Benefit to Wheelmen," *New York Times*, April 7, 1897.

21. Hank Chapot, "The Great Bicycle Protest of 1896," *Processed World* 2, no. 1 (2001): 64–68. Similarly, in Toronto cyclists alleged that the streetcar operators liked to water the tracks, making the pavement extra slippery for cyclists. Christopher Armstrong and H. V. Nelles, *The Revenge of the Methodist Bicycle Company: Sunday Streetcars and Municipal Reform in Toronto, 1888–1897* (Toronto: Peter Martin Associates Limited, 1977), 170.

22. "Night Parade of Brooklyn Cyclists," *New York Journal*, September 27, 1896, in

Newspaper Clippings Related to Cycling and Cycling Clubs, New-York Historical Society, New York; "Brooklyn to Have a Night Parade," *New York Journal*, September 26, 1896, in Newspaper Clippings Related to Cycling and Cycling Clubs, New-York Historical Society, New York; *Chicago Times Herald*, September 24, 1896, in Newspaper Clippings Related to Cycling and Cycling Clubs, New-York Historical Society, New York; "On the Wheel," *Standard Union* (Brooklyn), September 30, 1896, in Newspaper Clippings Related to Cycling and Cycling Clubs, New-York Historical Society, New York; *Municipal Engineering*, December 1896, 391. For more on urban parades, see Susan G. Davis, *Parades and Power: Street Theatre in Nineteenth-Century Philadelphia* (Philadelphia: Temple University Press, 1986); Mary Ryan, *Women in Public: Between Banners and Ballots, 1825–1880* (Baltimore: Johns Hopkins University Press, 1992); Mary Ryan, "The American Parade: Representation of the Nineteenth-Century Social Order," in *The New Cultural History*, ed. Lynn Hunt (Berkeley: University of California Press, 1989).

23. "Big Parade of the Wheelmen," *Evening Post* (San Francisco), July 8, 1896, in Newspaper Clippings Related to Cycling and Cycling Clubs, New-York Historical Society, New York; "Cyclers March the Streets in Mute Appeal for Good Pavements," *San Francisco Chronicle*, July 26, 1896; "An Incipient Riot on Market Street," *San Francisco Chronicle*, July 26, 1896.

24. "Cyclers March the Streets in Mute Appeal for Good Pavements," *San Francisco Chronicle*, July 26, 1896.

25. Frederic W. Speirs, *The Street Railway System of Philadelphia: Its History and Present Condition* (Baltimore: Johns Hopkins University Press, 1897), 63–66.

26. Bushnell, "When Chicago Was Wheel Crazy," 88; *Proceedings of the Fourth Annual Convention of the American Society of Municipal Improvements*, 214–15.

27. In general, the private firms that ran streetcar lines faced few restrictions, particularly in comparison to Europe where municipalities regulated public transit more heavily. See John P. McKay, "Comparative Perspective on Transit in Europe and the United States, 1850–1914," in *Technology and the Rise of the Networked City in Europe and America*, ed. Joel A. Tarr and Gabriel Dupuy (Philadelphia: Temple University Press, 1988), 6–7; Sylvester Baxter, "Public Control of Urban Transit," *The Cosmopolitan*, November 1894, 54–60; Paul Barrett, *The Automobile and Urban Transit: The Formation of Public Policy in Chicago, 1900–1930* (Philadelphia: Temple University Press, 1983); and Clay McShane and Joel A. Tarr, *The Horse in the City: Living Machines in the Nineteenth Century* (Baltimore: Johns Hopkins University Press, 2007).

28. "An Evening on the Boulevard," *Harper's Weekly*, August 28, 1897, 864. For more on the importance of boulevards in the shaping of an urban environment, see Allan B. Jacobs, Elizabeth Macdonald, and Yodan Rofe, *The Boulevard Book: History, Evolution, Design of Multiway Boulevards* (Cambridge: MIT Press, 2002).

29. "Good Roads of France Her Greatest Blessing," *Brooklyn Daily Eagle*, July 31, 1898; "The Pulpit and the Bicycle," *Arena*, August 1895, xx; "The Passing Hour," *Bicycling World*, January 25, 1895, 372; N. P. Lewis, "From Cobblestones to Asphalt to Brick," *Paving and Municipal Engineering*, April 1896, 232; Charles Mulford Robinson, "The Sociology of a Street Layout," in "Housing and Town Planning," special issue, *Annals of the American Academy of Political and Social Science* 51 (January 1914): 196.

30. For example, see the campaign in New York to improve the "abominable" conditions of New York's Eighth Avenue. "A Danger to Wheelmen," *New York Times*, May 7, 1895.

31. *Chicago Wheelman*, March 29, 1899.

32. "In the Cycling World," *New York Tribune*, September 27, 1896; "An Asphalt Strip for Cyclers," *New York Times*, June 11, 1896; *LAW Bulletin and Good Roads*, April 23, 1897, 437; *LAW Bulletin and Good Roads*, February 24, 1899; "Alderman and Bicycles," *New York Herald*, September 26, 1896, in Newspaper Clippings Related to Cycling and Cycling Clubs, New-York Historical Society, New York; "Brooklyn Riders Plan Asphalt Strips," *Cycle Age and Trade Review*, January 26, 1899; *Municipal Engineering*, October 1896, 245; "To Benefit Bicycle Riders," *New York Times*, October 24, 1895; "Streets for Wheels," *American Wheelmen*, June 20, 1896, in Newspaper Clippings Related to Cycling and Cycling Clubs, New-York Historical Society, New York.

33. Lewis, "From Cobblestones to Asphalt to Brick," 234–35.

34. "The Wheel, Present and Future," *Journal* (Milwaukee), September 23, 1896; *San Francisco Municipal Reports for the Fiscal Year 1896–1897* (San Francisco: Hinton Printing Company, 1897), 13; "For Brooklyn Cyclers," *New York Times*, June 30, 1895.

35. Teaford, *The Unheralded Triumph*, 227; George William Tillson, *Street Pavements and Paving Materials: A Manual of City Pavements* (New York: John Wiley & Sons, 1900), 186; *LAW Bulletin and Good Roads*, November 27, 1896, 694; Wells, *Car Country*, 24.

36. Fein, *Paving the Way*, 4–5, 18–20; Nathaniel Southgate Shaler, "The Betterment of our Highways," *Atlantic Monthly*, October 1892, 506.

37. Mason, "The League of American Wheelmen and the Good Roads Movement," 119–22; "Letter to the Editor from Senator William Richardson," *Good Roads*, January 1892, 45; "Good Roads," *New York Times*, March 20, 1898. For more on some of the early state legislation in terms of good roads, see Owen D. Gutfreund, *Twentieth-Century Sprawl: Highways and the Reshaping of the American Landscape* (New York: Oxford University Press, 2004), 9–11; "Good Roads Committee Report," *Cycle Age and Trade Review*, February 10, 1898, 562; and Fein, *Paving the Way*, 43.

38. *Good Roads*, April 1892, 208. A strikingly similar complaint (perhaps a reiteration of the original) was voiced at a farmers' convention in 1893: "We don't want any eastern bicycle fellers or one-hoss lawyers with patent leather boots, to tell us how to fix the roads that we use" (As quoted in, Wells, *Car Country*, 28).

39. Isaac B. Potter, *Gospel of Good Roads: Letter to an American Farmer* (New York: Evening Post Job Printing House, 1891); Fein, *Paving the Way*, 31.

40. Mason, "The League of American Wheelmen and the Good Roads Movement," 173–75; Gregory C. Lisa, "Bicyclists and Bureaucrats: The League of American Wheelmen and Public Choice Theory Applied," *Georgetown Law Journal* 84 (1995–1996): 387–395; Gutfreund, *Twentieth-Century Sprawl*, 11–16; Bruce E. Seely, *Building the American Highway System: Engineers as Policy Makers* (Philadelphia: Temple University Press, 1987), 11–23.

41. "Benefits of the League," *New York Times*, March 24, 1895; "The Modern Bicycle," *New York Times*, August 13, 1895; Isaac B. Potter, *Cycle Paths: A Practical Hand-Book, Containing the Best Available Information to Guide Members of the League of*

American Wheelmen and Others in Placing in Substantial Form their Protest Against Bad Roads by the Construction and Maintenance of those Temporary Blessings Known as Cycle Paths (League of American Wheelmen, 1898), 85; "How to take care of your Motor Car," *Outing*, 1905, 373.

42. For a contrasting view, see Wells, *Car Country*, 25–26.

43. *Municipal Engineering* regularly followed bicycle-related issues, ranging from asphalt projects to renewed guidelines for traffic law. For example, see *Municipal Engineering*, July 1896, 34; *Municipal Engineering*, October 1896, 245; *Municipal Engineering*, November 1896, 307; *Municipal Engineering*, December 1896, 376, 391–95.

44. Wells, *Car Country*, xxxi.

45. As Peter Norton argues, it was not until around 1930 that the meaning of the street truly became fixed. By then, it was understood as a motor thoroughfare. Peter Norton, *Fighting Traffic: The Dawn of the Motor Age in the American City* (Cambridge: MIT Press, 2008), 4–7.

CHAPTER 5

1. "Bicycle Problems and Benefits," *Century Magazine*, July 1895, 474–75.

2. Peter G. Furth, "Bicycling Infrastructure for Mass Cycling: A Transatlantic Comparison," in *City Cycling*, ed. John Pucher and Ralph Buehler, 105–39 (Cambridge: MIT Press, 2012).

3. For example, the proposal to erect a bicycle path on the Brooklyn Bridge emanated from the fact that an average of almost three bicycle accidents occurred daily on the bridge. "Bridge Bicycle Accidents," *Brooklyn Daily Eagle*, June 14, 1897.

4. For a detailed examination from an engineer on the preferred construction, location, and costs of paths, see Ira Osborn Baker, *A Treatise on Roads and Pavements* (New York: John Wiley & Sons, 1906), 624–32.

5. The early history of bicycle paths remains nebulous, but for sure, the Coney Island Cycle Path was an early and important large-scale path in a major city. Roughly around the same time, other cities considered similar proposals. As early as 1893 in San Francisco, for example, plans for an exclusive bicycle pathway "extending to the beach" and later billed as the first "bicycle path for the exclusive use of wheelmen" emerged but took several years to be completed. *San Francisco Municipal Reports for the Fiscal Year 1892–1893* (San Francisco: James H. Barry, 1893), 604–5; *San Francisco Municipal Reports for the Fiscal Year 1896–1897* (San Francisco: Hinton Printing Company, 1897), 168–69. There were a number of earlier paths, even dating back to the high-wheel era, but they tended to be short and located outside of heavily urban areas, and they sometimes catered to more than just bicycles.

6. "A Straight Run to the Sea," *New York Times*, August 26, 1894.

7. Ibid.; "For the Cycle Path Fund," *New York Times*, November 29, 1894; "Brooklyn's Big Bicycle Parade," *Harper's Weekly*, June 29, 1895, 604–7; "Gossip of the Cyclers," *New York Times*, May 28, 1899; "For Better Highways," *Brooklyn Daily Eagle*, April 2, 1895; Lorenz J. Finison, *Boston's Cycling Craze, 1880–1900: A Story of Race, Sport, and Society* (Amherst: University of Massachusetts Press, 2014), 177–79.

8. "Build Bicycle Paths," *San Francisco Call*, August 4, 1897; *Compiled Ordinances*

of the City of St. Paul, Minnesota. Corrected and Revised to January 1, 1906; "Bicycle Paths," *Pioneer Press* (St. Paul, MN), October 4, 1896, in Newspaper Clippings Related to Cycling and Cycling Clubs, New-York Historical Society, New York; The St. Paul Cycle Path Association, "Cycling Routes around the Twin Cities" (map), 1899. For more on the issue of taxation and the mix of private/public funding in the process of constructing bicycle paths, see James Longhurst, "The Sidepath Not Taken: Bicycles, Taxes and the Rhetoric of the Public Good in the 1890s," *Journal of Policy History* 25, no. 4 (2013): 557–86. One of the more interesting facets of the bicycle-path building in Minneapolis is that much of the growth came after the nationwide boom in cycling ended. Ross Petty, "Post Boom Bicycling in Minneapolis: Counting Transportation Use," in *Cycle History 20: Proceedings of the 20th International Cycle History Conference, Freehold, New Jersey (USA), July 30–August 1, 2009*, ed. Gary W. Sanderson (Cheltenham, UK: John Pinkerton Memorial Publishing Fund, 2010), 73–80.

9. *Baltimore News*, October 13, 1896, in Newspaper Clippings Related to Cycling and Cycling Clubs, New-York Historical Society, New York; James Barton, "From the Pacific to the Atlantic on a Bicycle," *State Journal* (Columbus, OH), June 7, 1896, in Newspaper Clippings Related to Cycling and Cycling Clubs, New-York Historical Society, New York; "Move for a Bicycle Path," *San Francisco Call*, August 18, 1895; Robert Bruce, "Bicycle Side-Path Building in 1900," *Outing*, May 1900, 182; Longhurst, "The Sidepath Not Taken"; Robert L. McCullough, "Cycling's 19th Century Path Finders" (paper presented at the 25th International Cycling History Conference, Baltimore, MD, August 7–9, 2014).

10. There was some interest in bicycle paths outside of the United States in the 1890s. In Europe, select cities laid roadways exclusively for cyclists. But as the case of Germany illustrates, large-scale construction of cycling paths was years away. Not until automobile sales skyrocketed in the 1920s did the need to segregate traffic receive support from the state. Even though in the last years of the 1920s cyclists in Germany numbered around twelve million while motorists amounted to less than one million, an ordinance to improve the circulation of motor vehicles ultimately required German cyclists to use cycling paths and stay off the roads when available. But in the 1890s, as Americans increasingly sought to isolate bicycle traffic from carriage traffic, most Germans were content to see their roads populated with an assortment of vehicles traveling at various speeds. In the few cases in which German cyclists clamored for separate roadways, it was often because the roads were poorly paved and designed for heavy vehicles. In general, though, European cities built and maintained roads that put American cities' roads to shame, which in some ways rendered separate bicycle paths less necessary and, for some good roads advocates, illuminated the futility of bicycle paths. Outside of Europe, Australians and New Zealanders laid paths in some of their urban districts, but as one observer noted, "the cycle path is first and last an American institution." Whether that was a source of pride or embarrassment depended on the rider. Volker Briese, "Bicycle Path Construction in Germany, 1897–1940," in *Cycle History 5: Proceedings of the 5th International Cycle History Conference, Cambridge, England, September 2–4, 1994*, ed. Rob van der Plas (San Francisco: Bicycle Books, 1995); "Side Paths," *LAW Bulletin and Good Roads*, July 10, 1895, 51; Bruce, "Bicycle Side-Path Building in 1900," 182.

11. "To Pedal Up in the Air," *Chicago Daily Tribune*, June 7, 1897; "Chicago's Elevated Cycleway," *LAW Bulletin and Good Roads*, May 26, 1899; *Buffalo Courier*, October 9, 1896, in Newspaper Clippings Related to Cycling and Cycling Clubs, New-York Historical Society, New York; *Review of Reviews*, June 1896, 648. London, Paris, and Berlin also considered, but never built, elevated cycling roads.

12. T. D. Denham, "California's Great Cycle-Way," *Pearson's Magazine*, September 1901, 305–7; "Unique Scheme for Wheelmen," *San Francisco Call*, January 23, 1897.

13. Denham, "California's Great Cycle-Way," 305–7; "Bicycle Path for Pasadena," *San Francisco Call*, January 31, 1898; "Cycle Way Formally Opened," *San Francisco Call*, January 2, 1900; "A Magnificent California Enterprise," *Los Angeles Times*, February 19, 1899.

14. "Los Angeles County: Cities and Suburban Places," *Los Angeles Times*, November 25, 1902; "Ask Permission to Remove Old Landmark," *Los Angeles Herald*, October 23, 1907.

15. Clay McShane, *Down the Asphalt Path: The Automobile and the American City* (New York: Columbia University Press, 1994), 62.

16. "Another Cycle Path," *New York Commercial Advertiser*, June 27, 1896; "Cycling Notes," *Evening World* (New York), June 16, 1896; "Summary of Events," *The Friend: A Religious and Literary Journal*, June 6, 1896, 308; "On the Wheel," *Standard Union* (Brooklyn), July 20, 1896, in Newspaper Clippings Related to Cycling and Cycling Clubs, New-York Historical Society, New York. The "return path" opened on June 27, 1896, just over one year after the original Coney Island Cycle Path opened.

17. "Cycling in the Park," *San Francisco Call*, July 13, 1896, in Newspaper Clippings Related to Cycling and Cycling Clubs, New-York Historical Society, New York; *Third Annual Report of the Board of Park Commissioners of the City of Cleveland 1895* (Cleveland, 1896); "No Cycle Path Needed," *New York Daily Tribune*, April 5 1897.

18. "Potter Says He Will Fight," *Brooklyn Daily Eagle*, May 7, 1896; "Bassett's Big Figures," *New York Evening World*, June 24, 1896; "News of the Wheelmen," *New York Sun*, June 17, 1896; "Cycling in the Park," *San Francisco Call*, July 13, 1896, in Newspaper Clippings Related to Cycling and Cycling Clubs, New-York Historical Society, New York.

19. "Potter Says He Will Fight," *Brooklyn Daily Eagle*, May 7, 1896; "Special Park Police," *Brooklyn Daily Eagle*, May 9, 1896.

20. "Cycling Clubs and their Spheres of Action," *Outing*, August 1897, 490; "Ocean Parkway Ordinance," *Brooklyn Daily Eagle*, May 15, 1896; "News of the Wheelmen," *New York Sun*, June 10, 1896.

21. "News of the Wheelmen," *New York Sun*, June 10, 1896. Even though Potter had championed cycle paths before, he did so reluctantly and only "as a valued auxiliary to the greater cause" of good roads. Isaac B. Potter, *Cycle Paths: A Practical Hand-Book* (Boston: League of American Wheelmen, 1898), 8.

22. "Cyclists' Mass Meeting," *New York Sun*, May 16, 1896.

23. "Bicycles and Street Rights," *Brooklyn Daily Eagle*, May 20, 1899.

24. "A Slap at Alex Schwalbach," *Brooklyn Daily Eagle*, May 14, 1896; "The Bicycle in its Relation to Good Roads," *Scientific American*, September 19, 1896.

25. "Lay of a New Jersey Wheelman," *LAW Bulletin and Good Roads*, August 14, 1896, 234.

26. "Cyclists' Mass Meeting," *New York Sun*, May 16, 1896; "Pushing the Pedals," *New York Evening Sun*, June 10, 1896; *Proceedings of the Board of Aldermen of the City of New York from October 6 to December 29, 1896* (New York: Martin B. Brown, 1897), 12; C. T. Raymond, "Roads and Side-Paths," *LAW Bulletin and Good Roads*, January 1, 1897.

27. *Thirty-Seventh Annual Report of the Department of Parks of the City of Brooklyn the Third of the County of Kings and the First to the Mayor of the Greater New York for the Year 1897* (Brooklyn, 1897), 168; *Thirty-Sixth Annual Report of the Department of Parks of the City of Brooklyn the Second of the County of Kings for the Year 1896* (Brooklyn, 1896), 11, 180–81; *Thirty-Fifth Annual Report of the Department of Parks of the City of Brooklyn for the Year 1895* (Brooklyn, 1895), 26, 107; "Routes to Coney Island," *New York Times*, April 28, 1895; "Information for Cyclists," *New York Evening Sun*, June 29, 1896; "Night Parade of Brooklyn Cyclists," *New York Journal*, September 27, 1896. Back in Golden Gate Park, San Francisco, where the ordinance requiring riders to use the paths in lieu of the main drives failed to become law, almost all of the riders used the bicycle-only paths by choice. "The Wheelmen," *San Francisco Call*, January 25, 1896.

28. Petty, "Post Boom Bicycling in Minneapolis," 73–80; Longhurst, "The Side-path Not Taken"; Blake McKelvey, *Rochester on the Genesee: The Growth of a City* (Syracuse: Syracuse University Press, 1993), 140–41; Bruce, "Bicycle Side-Path Building in 1900," 183; Charles Zueblin, *American Municipal Progress: Chapters in Municipal Sociology* (New York: MacMillan Company New York, 1902), 252.

29. David Hammack, *Power and Society: Greater New York at the Turn of the Century* (New York: Russell Sage Foundation, 1982), 304.

30. There were a few examples in which municipalities engaged in a public/private partnership to build and profit from bicycle paths. For example, see Wade N. Praeger, "Fin de Cycle Seattle, the American Bicycle Craze of the 1890s" (master's thesis, Western Washington University, 1997), 72–79.

31. "'Star' Cycle Path was Opened Gloriously," *Star* (St. Louis), November 15, 1896; A. B. Choate, "Bicycle Side-Path Trunk Lines," *Outing*, October 1900, 115–16.

32. Christine Boyer, *Dreaming the Rational City: The Myth of American City Planning* (Cambridge: MIT Press, 1983), xi. Nonetheless, as John Fairfield has argued, cities were, in certain ways, "planned," even in this preplanning era. Politicians and individuals consciously debated and implemented far-reaching policies affecting city building far into the future. But the contemporary debates revealed that "city building should remain an essentially individual process in which the average citizen" (which would certainly include cyclists) "had a crucial and largely private role to play." John D. Fairfield, *The Mysteries of the Great City: The Politics of Urban Design 1877–1937* (Columbus: Ohio State University Press, 1993), 3–7. See also Jon A. Peterson, *The Birth of City Planning in the United States, 1840–1917* (Baltimore: Johns Hopkins University Press, 2003).

33. Mona Domosh, *Invented Cities: The Creation of Landscape in Nineteenth-Century New York and Boston* (New Haven: Yale University Press, 1996), 3.

34. Kevin J. Krizek, "Cycling, Urban Form and Cities: What Do We Know and How Should We Respond?," in *Cycling and Sustainability*, ed. John Parkin, 119–22 (Bradford, UK: Emerald Group Publishing, 2012).

CHAPTER 6

1. US Census Bureau, *Twelfth Census of the United States: Statistics of Population* [1900], vol. 1, pt. 1 (Washington, DC, 1901), 430–36. For more on how contemporaries understood and "perceived" the problems of urban life, see Andrew Lees, *Cities Perceived: Urban Society in European and American Thought, 1820–1940* (New York: Columbia University Press, 1985). For more on the general waves of urban reform in Gilded Age cities, see Paul Boyer, *Urban Masses and Moral Order* (Cambridge: Harvard University Press, 1978), 123–91.

2. Jon C. Teaford, *The Unheralded Triumph: City Government in America, 1870–1900* (Baltimore: Johns Hopkins University Press, 1984), 150–55; M. Christine Boyer, *Dreaming the Rational City: The Myth of American City Planning* (Cambridge: MIT Press, 1983), 33–60; Bonz Szczygiel, "'City Beautiful' Revisited: An Analysis of Nineteenth-Century Civic Improvement Efforts," *Journal of Urban History* 29 (January 2003): 107–32.

3. Stanley K. Schultz, *Constructing Urban Culture: American Cities and City Planning, 1800–1920* (Philadelphia: Temple University Press, 1989), xvii.

4. The American Wheelman, "A New View of Sunday Cycling," in *Lyra Cyclus; or, the Bards and the Bicycle*, ed. Edmond Redmond (Rochester: 1897), 129–30.

5. Arthur Meier Schlesinger, *The Rise of the City, 1878–1898* (New York: The Macmillan Company, 1933), 128; Boyer, *Dreaming the Rational City*, 16–17; Charles W. Mann, *School Recreations and Amusements* (New York: American Book Company, 1896), 171. For more on Hall and his concern about children losing contact with nature, or, as Gail Bederman describes, being "over civilized," see Gail Bederman, *Manliness and Civilization: A Cultural History of Gender and Race in the United States, 1880–1917* (Chicago: University of Chicago Press, 1995), 77–120.

6. Steven A. Riess, *City Games: The Evolution of American Urban Society and the Rise of Sports* (Urbana: University of Illinois Press, 1989), 6–7. See also Peter Baldwin, *Domesticating the Street: The Reform of Public Space in Hartford, 1850–1930* (Columbus: Ohio State University Press, 1999), 5.

7. Mann, *School Recreations and Amusements*, 171–72.

8. Ebenezer Howard, *Garden Cities of Tomorrow* (London: Swan Sonnenschein & Co., 1902); Peter J. Schmidt, *Back to Nature: The Arcadian Myth in Urban America* (New York: Oxford University Press, 1969), xviii, 4; John Higham, "The Reorientation of American Culture in the 1890s," in *The Origins of Modern Consciousness*, ed. John Weiss (Detroit: Wayne State University Press, 1965), 26–45.

9. "Bicycle Problems and Benefits," *Century Magazine*, July 1895, 474–75; Joseph B. Bishop, "Social and Economic Influence of the Bicycle," *Forum*, August 1896, 685; "A Growing Fad," *LAW Bulletin and Good Roads*, October 16, 1896, 513–14; Sylvester Baxter, "Economic and Social Influences of the Bicycle," *Arena*, October 1892, 583; "The Gentle Art of Cycling," *MacMillan's Magazine*, January 1898, 204.

10. Jean Porter Rudd, "My Wheel and I," *Outing*, May 1895, 128.

11. Oftentimes guidebooks aimed at urban cyclists included information about local ferries and railroads. For example, see *Good Roads Book and the Rules of the Road Magazine*, 1898.

12. *New York City Army and Naval Journal*, June 20, 1896, in Newspaper Clippings Related to Cycling and Cycling Clubs, New-York Historical Society, New York; "The Long Island Railroad Broke a Record on Saturday," *Brooklyn Daily Eagle*, July 6, 1897; "Transporting Bicycles," *Brooklyn Daily Eagle*, January 16, 1898. The issue of carrying bicycles as baggage on railroads was controversial and oft debated in the period. Many states mandated that railroads carry bicycles as baggage, without extra charge.

13. Barbara Young Welke, *Recasting American Liberty: Gender, Race, Law, and the Railroad Revolution, 1865–1920* (Cambridge: Cambridge University Press, 2001), x–xi; "The Road and its Rewards," *Outing*, June 1900, 299; "The Gentle Art of Cycling," *MacMillian's Magazine*, January 1898, 204; "The Wheel in California," *Overland Monthly*, October 1893, 391; Winfred Ernest Garrison, *Wheeling through Europe* (St. Louis: Christian Publishing Company, 1900), 109–11, as quoted in "Bicycle Touring in the Late Nineteenth Century," in *Cycle History 12: Proceedings of the 12th International Cycling History Conference, San Remo, Italy, September 2001*, ed. Duncan R. Jamieson (San Francisco: Van der Plas, 2002); J. & E. R. Pennell, "Twenty Years of Cycling," *Fortnightly Review*, August 1, 1897, 190.

14. *Appletons' Dictionary of New York and its Vicinity* (New York: D. Appleton and Company, 1902), 88–89; "Signs of the Times," *LAW Bulletin and Good Roads*, July 31, 1896, 153.

15. For example, see Rand, McNally & Co., *Rand, McNally & Co's Handy Guide to the Country around New York for the Wheelman, Driver, and Excursionist* (New York: Rand, McNally & Co., Publishers, 1896).

16. "Brooklyn Wheelmen," *New York Recorder*, June 10, 1896, in Newspaper Clippings Related to Cycling and Cycling Clubs, New-York Historical Society, New York; Advertisement for Van Buren's-By-The-Sea in League of American Wheelmen, *Fifty Miles Around New York: A Book of Maps and Descriptions of the Best Roads, Streets, and Routes for Cyclists and Horsemen* (New York: New York State Division of the League of American Wheelmen, 1896).

17. "Unfrequented Bicycle Roads in the Vicinity of San Francisco," *San Francisco Call*, April 18, 1897; "Twas an Ideal Day for Cyclers," *Philadelphia Press*, August 31, 1896, in Newspaper Clippings Related to Cycling and Cycling Clubs, New-York Historical Society, New York.

18. "People in Chicago taking Bicycle Picnics," *Chicago Times Herald*, June 9, 1896, in Newspaper Clippings Related to Cycling and Cycling Clubs, New-York Historical Society, New York; "Picnics a La Bicycle," *Kansas City Star*, May 24, 1896.

19. J. R. Morgan, "The Ubiquitousness of the Bicycle," *New York City Metropolitan*, August 1896, in Newspaper Clippings Related to Cycling and Cycling Clubs, New-York Historical Society, New York; "Good Word for Bicycling," *New York Evening World*, June 19, 1896, in Newspaper Clippings Related to Cycling and Cycling Clubs, New-York Historical Society, New York; Arthur P. S. Hyde Diaries, 1892–1896, New-York Historical Society, New York; "The Pulpit and the Bicycle," *Arena*, August 1895, xvii-xx;

Advertisement for 3inOne in League of American Wheelmen, *Fifty Miles Around New York.*

20. Thomas Stevens, *Around the World on a Bicycle, Volume II: From Teheran to Yokohama* (New York: Charles Scribner's Sons, 1889); Peter Zheutlin, *Around the World on Two Wheels: Annie Londonderry's Extraordinary Ride* (New York: Citadel, 2007); F. C. Wildes, Copied Diary of a Bicycle Trip, July 7 to August 30, '99, Newberry Library, Chicago; H. A. Hersey, 1892 Diary, Massachusetts Historical Society, Boston; Joseph Bliss, Bicycle Routes: MS. S, 1894–1903, Bancroft Library, University of California, Berkeley; J. Parmly Paret, *The Woman's Book of Sports: A Practical Guide to Physical Development and Outdoor Recreation* (New York: D. Appleton and Company, 1901), 83–86; "News of the Wheelmen," *New York Times*, April 19, 1892; League of American Wheelmen, *Fifty Miles Around New York*; Pope Manufacturing Company, *Tourists' Manual and Book of Information of Value to all Bicyclers* (Boston: Pope Manufacturing Co., 1892); Luther Henry Porter, *Cycling for Health and Pleasure: An Indispensable Guide to the Successful Use of the Wheel* (New York: Dodd, Mead and Company, 1896), 58.

21. Gary Allan Tobin, "The Bicycle Boom of the 1890s: The Development of Private Transportation and the Birth of the Modern Tourist," *Journal of Popular Culture* 7, no.4 (Spring 1974): 845; Michael R. Fein, *Paving the Way: New York Road Building and the American State, 1880–1956* (Lawrence: University Press of Kansas, 2008), 28.

22. Eastman Kodak Company, *Bicycle Kodaks* (Rochester: Eastman Kodak Co., 1897), 1–2; Advertising Supplement, *Review of Reviews*, June 1896, 62; Kenneth I. Helphand, "The Bicycle Kodak," *Environmental Review* 4, no. 3 (1980): 24–33; Phillip G. Hubert, Jr., "The Bicycle: The Wheel of To-Day," *Scribner's Magazine*, June 1895, 702; William R. Taylor, *In Pursuit of Gotham: Culture and Commerce in New York* (New York: Oxford University Press, 1992), 30; Zachary Mooradian Furness, *One Less Car: Bicycling and the Politics of Automobility* (Philadelphia: Temple University Press, 2010), 41; Arthur P.S. Hyde Diaries, 1892–1896, 66, New-York Historical Society, New York.

23. League of American Wheelmen, *New York State Division, Tour Book: New York State Division, League of American Wheelmen* (Cortland, NY: Standard Press, 1895); "Cycling Parades," *New York Evening Journal*, October 19, 1896, in Newspaper Clippings Related to Cycling and Cycling Clubs, New-York Historical Society, New York.

24. Charles Eadward Pratt, *What & Why: Some Common Questions Answered* (Boston: Press of Rockwell and Churchill, 1884), 64; Higham, "The Reorientation of American Culture in the 1890s"; John Rickards Betts, "The Technological Revolution and the Rise of Sport, 1850–1900," *Mississippi Valley Historical Review* 40, no. 2 (September 1953): 232; Elliott J. Gorn, *The Manly Art: Bare-Knuckle Prize Fighting in America* (Ithaca: Cornell University Press, 1986), 179–80; C. Lombroso, "The Bicycle and Crime," *Pall Mall Magazine*, 1900, 31.

25. Gihon, "The Bicycle as a Sanitary Measure," in *Public Health Papers and Reports Vol. XXII*, ed. American Public Health Asssociation (Concord, NH: Republican Press Association, 1897), 47–48; "A Word for the Wheel," *New York City Home Journal*, July 1, 1896, in Newspaper Clippings Related to Cycling and Cycling Clubs, New-York Historical Society, New York; Theodore R. MacClure, "Bicycling: From Social, Business, and Healthful Standpoints," *Physician and Surgeon*, October 1898, 449–454; "Cycling and Health," *Bicycling World*, December 21, 1894. For a poem about scorching

cyclists that emphasized the dangerous ways that speeding cyclists contorted their bodies, see Newt Newkirk, "The Man with the Hump," *LAW Bulletin and Good Roads*, August, 1899, 56.

26. MacClure, "Bicycling: From Social, Business, and Healthful Standpoints," 114; "The Point of View," *Scribner's Magazine*, February 1896, 256; "Recommended by Dr. Hammond," *New York Times*, January 5, 1896; "The Bicycle Fever," *Times* (Richmond), June 4, 1896; Benjamin Ward Richardson, *Vita Medica: Chapters of Medical Life and Work* (London: Longmans, Green, and Co., 1897), 246.

27. "Recommended by Dr. Hammond," *New York Times*, January 5, 1896; Porter, *Cycling for Health and Pleasure*, 13–15.

28. "The Bicycle for Persons with Hernia," *New York Medical Journal*, April 29, 1899, 606.

29. Maria E. Ward, *The Common Sense of Bicycling: Bicycling for Ladies* (New York: Brentano's, 1896), 172; Frances E. Willard, *A Wheel Within a Wheel: How I Learned to Ride the Bicycle with Some Reflections by the Way* (Chicago: Woman's Temperance Publishing Association, 1895), 55–56; MacClure, "Bicycling: From Social, Business, and Healthful Standpoints," 115; J. West Roosevelt, "A Doctor's View of Bicycling," *Scribner's Magazine*, June 1895, 707–9; Benjamin Ward Richardson, "What to Avoid in Cycling," *North American Review*, August 1895, 179; Graeme M. Hammond, "The Bicycle in the Treatment of Nervous Diseases," *Journal of Nervous and Mental Disease*, 1892, 37–46.

30. Bederman, *Manliness and Civilization*, 84–88; T. J. Jackson Lears, *No Place of Grace: Antimodernism and the Transformation of American Culture, 1880–1920* (Chicago: University of Chicago Press, 1994), 47–58. For an analysis that focuses particularly on women and nervous diseases like neurasthenia, see Carroll Smith-Rosenberg, *Disorderly Conduct: Visions of Gender in Victorian America* (New York: Alfred A. Knopf, 1985), 197–216. For more on the relationship between urban nervousness, neurasthenia, and modernity, see Andreas Killen, *Berlin Electropolis: Shock, Nerves, and German Modernity* (Berkeley: University of California Press, 2006).

31. John H. Girdner, *Newyorkitis* (New York: Grafton Press, 1901), 25–39.

32. J. H. K., "Therapeutic Value of the Bicycle," *Modern Medicine and Bacteriological World*, April 1893, 100–102; "The Wheel and Disease," *American Wheelman*, July 16, 1896, 32; Lombroso, "The Bicycle and Crime," 316; Hammond, "The Bicycle in the Treatment of Nervous Diseases," 37–46.

33. Richard Harmond, "Progress and Flight: An Interpretation of the American Cycle Craze of the 1890s," *Journal of Social History* 5 (Winter 1971–1972): 246. One doctor went so far as to condemn bicycles for contributing to the "nervous condition" in a malady he termed, the "vibratory habit." "Echoes and News," *The Medical News*, May 2, 1896, 499; Gihon, "The Bicycle as a Sanitary Measure," 53. See also E. H. Lacon Watson, "Bicycle Tours—and a Moral," *Westminster Review*, July–December 1894, 169.

34. As the novelist Booth Tarkington wrote about streetcars, but which could have equally applied to bicycles: "In good weather the mule pulled the car a mile in a little less than twenty minutes, unless the stops were too long; but when the trolley-car came, doing its mile in five minutes and better, it would wait for nobody. Nor could its passengers have endured such a thing, because the faster they were carried the less time

they had to spare! In the days before deathly contrivances hustled them through their lives, and when they had no telephones—another ancient vacancy profoundly responsible for leisure—they had time for everything: time to think, to talk, time to read, time to wait for a lady!" Booth Tarkington, *The Magnificent Ambersons* (Garden City, NY: Doubleday, Page & Co., 1918), 11–12.

35. Leo Marx, *The Machine in the Garden: Technology and the Pastoral Ideal in America* (New York: Oxford University Press, 1967).

36. "Future Bicycling," *Bicycling World*, November 30, 1894, 16; Marguerite Merington, "Woman and the Bicycle," *Scribner's Magazine*, June 1895, 703; Lombroso, "The Bicycle and Crime," 314–16; W. J. McGee, "Fifty Years of American Science," *Atlantic Monthly*, September 1898, 311–312; Joseph J. Corn, *The Winged Gospel: America's Romance with Aviation* (Baltimore: Johns Hopkins University Press, 2001), 40–41.

37. For more on how advertisers tapped into the health consciousness of consumers, see T. J. Jackson Lears, "From Salvation to Self-Realization: Advertising and the Therapeutic Roots of the Consumer Culture, 1880–1930," in *The Culture of Consumption: Critical Essays in American History, 1880–1980*, ed. Richard Wightman Fox and T. J. Jackson Lears (New York: Pantheon Books, 1983).

38. "Monarch Bicycles Advertisement," *Cosmopolitan*, April 1901; "Columbia Ladies' Safety Advertisement," *Cosmopolitan*, November 1891.

39. Pope Manufacturing Company, *Columbia Bicycle Catalog for 1893*, 46–48. See also "How the Finest Bicycles Are Made," *Review of Reviews* (advertising supplement), 1894, 19–20.

40. Pond's Extract Co., *Cycling in the Country. Twenty-Five charming Trips Combining Both Long and Short Runs through the Beautiful Regions Adjacent to New York* (New York: Pond's Extract Co., 1897).

41. Schultz, *Constructing Urban Culture*, 112.

42. Ibid., 118; Christopher W. Wells, *Car Country: An Environmental History* (Seattle: University of Washington Press, 2012), 16.

43. Martin V. Melosi, *Effluent America: Cities, Industry, Energy, and the Environment* (Pittsburgh: University of Pittsburgh Press, 2001), 39, 58; Joel A. Tarr, *The Search for the Ultimate Sink: Urban Pollution in Historical Perspective* (Akron: The University of Akron Press, 1996), 323.

44. *Annual Report of the Commissioners of the District of Columbia for the Year Ended June 30, 1898, Vol. 1.* (Washington, DC: Government Printing Office, 1898), 461. Many street commissioners and engineers in other cities echoed these sentiments. For example, see N. P. Lewis, "From Cobblestones to Asphalt to Brick," *Paving and Municipal Engineering*, April 1896, 232.

45. Martin V. Melosi, *The Sanitary City: Environmental Services in Urban America from Colonial Times to the Present* (Pittsburgh: Pittsburgh University Press, 2008), 121; Daniel Eli Burnstein, *Next to Godliness: Confronting Dirt and Despair in Progressive Era New York City* (Urbana: University of Illinois Press, 2006), 32–55; George E. Waring, Jr., "The Cleaning of a Great City," *McClure's Magazine*, September 1897, 921; "News of the Bicyclists," *New York World*, June 20, 1896, in Newspaper Clippings Related to Cycling and Cycling Clubs, New-York Historical Society, New York; "Awheel

in the Tyrol," *New York Mail and Express*, September 30, 1896, in Newspaper Clippings Related to Cycling and Cycling Clubs, New-York Historical Society, New York.

46. "Cyclists at Dinner," *New York Times*, February 19, 1897; "Gossip of the Cyclers," *New York Times*, May 22, 1898.

47. Henry P. Morrison, "The Sidewalks of New York City," *Good Roads*, February 1904, 77; Fein, *Paving the Way*, 31; Baxter, "Economic and Social Influences of the Bicycle," 579–83; Baldwin, *Domesticating the Street*, 50–60.

48. Raymond W. Smilor, "Toward an Environmental Perspective: The Anti-Noise Campaign, 1893–1932," in *Pollution and Reform in American Cities, 1870–1930*, ed. Martin V. Melosi (Austin: University of Texas Press, 1980); Stephen Crane, *Maggie: A Girl of the Streets and Other Tales of New York* (New York: Penguin, 2000), 184; Baxter, "Economic and Social Influences of the Bicycle," 579–583; "Unbounded Horseless Possibilities Opened Up," *Toronto Truth*, August 8, 1896, in Newspaper Clippings Related to Cycling and Cycling Clubs, New-York Historical Society, New York; "How Fool Driving Affects the Popularity of the Automobile," *Outing*, February 1906, 664. It should be noted that bicycle paths catered exclusively to cyclists and took up valuable space within the city. That said, cyclists could, and often did, ride through the city on the streets with other traffic and did not require paths exclusively for their use.

49. Frederick Law Olmsted to R. P. Hammond, Jr., October 5th, 1886, in Board of Park Commissioners, *The Development of Golden Gate Park* (San Francisco: Bacon & Company, 1886), 22; Thomas Bender, *Toward an Urban Vision: Ideas and Institutions in Nineteenth Century America* (Baltimore: Johns Hopkins University Press, 1975); David Schuyler, *The New Urban Landscape: The Redefinition of City Form in Nineteenth-Century America* (Baltimore: Johns Hopkins University Press, 1986), 36; *First Report of the Park and Outdoor Art Association* (Louisville, 1897), 22; Gunther Barth, *City People: The Rise of Modern City Culture in Nineteenth-Century America* (Oxford: Oxford University Press, 1980), 37.

50. Schultz, *Constructing Urban Culture*, 155–56; Schmidt, *Back to Nature*, 70; Teaford, *The Unheralded Triumph*, 252.

51. "Concessions to Bicycle Riders," *New York Times*, June 17, 1883; *Twenty-Fifth Annual Report of the Brooklyn Park Commissioners: for the Year 1885* (Brooklyn: Printed for the Commissioners, 1886), 40–41; Jerome P. Bjelopera, *City of Clerks: Office and Sales Workers in Philadelphia, 1870–1920* (Urbana: University of Illinois Press, 2005), 100–101; *Third Annual Report of the Board of Park Commissioners of the City of Cleveland, 1895* (Cleveland, 1896), 27; *Thirty-Fifth Annual Report of the Department of Parks of the City of Brooklyn for the Year 1895* (New York, 1895), 129–130; *Thirty-Sixth Annual Report of the Department of Parks of the City of Brooklyn the Second of the County of Kings for the Year 1896* (Brooklyn, 1897), 208; "Twas an Ideal Day for Cyclers," *Philadelphia Press*, August 31, 1896, in Newspaper Clippings Related to Cycling and Cycling Clubs, New-York Historical Society, New York; *LAW Bulletin and Good Roads*, May 14, 1897; "Yields to the Wheel," *Chicago Tribune*, July 26, 1896; Bishop, "Social and Economic Influence of the Bicycle," 680–91.

52. Olmsted to Hammond, Jr., October 5, 1886, in Board of Park Commissioners, *The Development of Golden Gate Park*, 22; Schuyler, *The New Urban Landscape*, 6;

Roy Rosenzweig and Elizabeth Blackmar, *The Park and the People: A History of Central Park* (Ithaca: Cornell University Press, 1992), 251.

53. *Annual Report of the Executive Department of the City of Boston, For the Year 1896 Part II* (Boston: Municipal Printing Office, 1897), 46–47. It is unclear if Frederick Law Olmsted himself drafted the petition as his active involvement in the firm slowed in 1895.

54. Rosenzweig and Blackmar, *The Park and the People*, 244.

55. George D. Bushnell, "When Chicago Was Wheel Crazy," in *The Chicago Sports Reader: 100 Years of Sports in the Windy City*, ed. Steven A. Riess and Gerald R. Gems (Urbana: University of Illinois Press, 2009), 89.

56. Barth, *City People*, 39; *San Francisco Municipal Reports For the Fiscal Year 1889–90* (San Francisco: W. M. Hinton & Co. Printers, Published by Order of the Board of Supervisors, 1890); *Cycling Record Book, Season 1898, Siegel, Cooper and Company, Compliments of the Big Store* (Cleveland: Cooper and Company, 1898); Arnold, Schwinn & Co., *Fifty Years of Schwinn-Built Bicycles: The Story of the Bicycle and its Contributions to Our Way of Life* (Chicago: Arnold, Schwinn & Co., 1945), 47; Stephen Hardy, *How Boston Played: Sport, Recreation, and Community, 1865–1915* (Boston: Northeastern University Press, 1982), 147.

57. Baldwin, *Domesticating the Street*, 121–134.

58. "Cycle News," *New York Recorder*, July 2, 1896, in Newspaper Clippings Related to Cycling and Cycling Clubs, New-York Historical Society, New York; "News of Wheels and Wheelman," *Chicago Times Herald*, June 7, 1896, in Newspaper Clippings Related to Cycling and Cycling Clubs, New-York Historical Society, New York.

59. "The Return of the Horse," *The Bookman*, March–August 1901, 425; *News Enquirer* (Charleston), October 20, 1896, in Newspaper Clippings Related to Cycling and Cycling Clubs, New-York Historical Society, New York; "Safety of Wheelmen at Night," *New York Tribune*, September 8, 1896; City of Philadelphia, "Appendix," *Journal of the Common Council of the City of Philadelphia from April 6, 1896 to September 24, 1896, Vol. 1* (Philadelphia: Dunlap Printing Company, 1896), 23; Edith Ogden Harrison, Writings and Outgoing Correspondence, "Bicycles and Billiards," n.d, Midwest MS Harrision Box 19, Folder 952, Newberry Library, Chicago.

60. "Bicycle Riders Locked Up," *New York Times*, September 17, 1893; "Lights on Vehicles at Night," *New York Times*, November 5, 1899; Indiana University, "The World Awheel," accessed August 13, 2010, http://www.indiana.edu/~liblilly/awheel/awheel7.html.

61. *Proceedings of the City Council of the City of Chicago for the Municipal Year 1896–1897* (Chicago: Press of John F. Higgins, 1897), 690, 760.

62. William Chapman Sharpe, *New York Nocturne: The City After Dark in Literature, Painting, and Photography* (Princeton: Princeton University Press, 2008), 84; "Safety of Wheelmen at Night," *New York Tribune*, September 8, 1896; Pratt, *What & Why*, 17.

63. Peter C. Baldwin, "'Nocturnal Habits and Dark Wisdom': The American Response to Children in the Streets at Night, 1880–1930," *Journal of Social History* 35, no. 3 (Spring 2002): 596–97; "Wheelmen All Stirred up by—Is Bicycling Immoral?," *New*

York Journal, August 16, 1896, in Newspaper Clippings Related to Cycling and Cycling Clubs, New-York Historical Society, New York.

64. Baldwin, "Nocturnal Habits and Dark Wisdom," 594; Peter C. Baldwin, *In the Watches of the Night: Life in the Nocturnal City, 1820–1930* (Chicago: University of Chicago Press, 2012); Sharpe, *New York Nocturne*, 6; "An Evening on the Boulevard," *Harper's Weekly*, August 28, 1897. For an interesting example of how Broadway was used as a promenade, an avenue for theater, and a stage on which to assert status and class, see Mona Domosh, "Those 'Gorgeous Incongruities': Polite Politics and Public Space on the Streets of Nineteenth-Century New York City," *Annals of the Association of American Geographers* 88, no. 2 (June 1998): 209–26.

65. "Rights of Wheelmen are Recognized," *New York Herald*, October 7, 1896, in Newspaper Clippings Related to Cycling and Cycling Clubs, New-York Historical Society, New York; "Is Bicycling Immoral?," *New York Journal*, August 1, 1896, in Newspaper Clippings Related to Cycling and Cycling Clubs, New-York Historical Society, New York; "A Wise Injunction," *Rochester Herald*, June 21, 1896, in Newspaper Clippings Related to Cycling and Cycling Clubs, New-York Historical Society, New York.

66. MacClure, "Bicycling: From Social, Business, and Healthful Standpoints," 411; "Secret of the Bicycle," *Scribner's Magazine*, July 1896, 132; A. C. True, "The Solidarity of Town and Farm," *Arena*, March 1897, 546.

CHAPTER 7

1. Henri Lefebvre, *The Production of Space* (Cambridge, MA: Blackwell, 1991), 127.

2. David Harvey, *The Condition of Postmodernity: An Enquiry into the Origins of Cultural Change* (Oxford: Blackwell, 1989), 232. One early observer even noted that the power of the bicycle is that it "erases time and space." M. D. Bellencontre, *Hygiéne du Vélocipéde* (Paris: L. Richard, Libraire-éditeur, 1869), 38, as quoted in Christopher Thompson, *The Tour de France: A Cultural History* (Berkeley: University of California Press, 2006), 29.

3. Stephen Kern, *The Culture of Time and Space, 1880–1918* (Cambridge: Harvard University Press, 1983), 1–3, 110–13, 123.

4. Paul Adam, *La Morale des Sports* (Paris, 1907), 449–50, as quoted in Kern, *The Culture of Time and Space*, 111; "Bicycle-Riding," *Harper's Weekly*, January 12, 1895, 27; Sylvester Baxter, "Economic and Social Influences of the Bicycle," *The Arena*, October 1892, 578; "A Point of View," *Scribner's Magazine*, October 1894, 527. See also Robert Park, "The City: Suggestions for the Investigation of Human Behavior in the Urban Environment," in *Classic Essays on the Culture of Cities*, ed. Richard Sennett (Englewood Cliffs, NJ: Prentice-Hall, 1969), 125–27.

5. "Wheelmen as Soldiers," *Hoboken Observer*, July 2, 1896, in Newspaper Clippings Related to Cycling and Cycling Clubs, May 26, 1896–February 11, 1897, and undated collection, New-York Historical Society, New York. See also "The Wonderful Wheel," *New Orleans Picayune*, June 14, 1896.

6. "Bicycle Room in a Church," *LAW Bulletin and Good Roads*, May 21, 1897, 611; "The Bicycle and its Triumphs," *Atlanta Journal*, June 27, 1896, in Newspaper Clippings

Related to Cycling and Cycling Clubs, New-York Historical Society, New York; "The Pulpit and the Bicycle," *Arena*, August 1895.

7. "In Buffalo," *Printers' Ink*, September 6, 1899, 8; City of Minneapolis, *Annual Reports of the Various City Officers of the City of Minneapolis, Minnesota, for the Year 1897* (Minneapolis: Harrison & Smith Printers, 1898), 768; "The Bicycle Racks," *Evening News* (San Jose), August 7, 1896; "Councilman Miner Swings His Ax on the Bicycle Racks About the Town," *Evening News* (San Jose), November 20, 1899; *Appletons' Dictionary of New York and its Vicinity* (New York: D. Appleton and Company, 1902), 170.

8. Advertisement, *Printers' Ink*, September 6, 1899, 39; "Bicycle in Practical Use," *Denver Republican*, November 15, 1896, in Newspaper Clippings Related to Cycling and Cycling Clubs, New-York Historical Society, New York; Davis v. Petrinovich, 112 Ala. 654; 21 So. 344; 1896 Ala. LEXIS 383 (Ala., November 1896); Charles Eadward Pratt, *What & Why: Some Common Questions Answered* (Boston: Press of Rockwell and Churchill, 1884), 62–64; "Messenger Boys to Use Bicycles," *New York Times*, May 3, 1896. For more on the early bicycle telegraph messengers, see Gregory J. Downey, *Telegraph Messenger Boys: Labor, Technology, and Geography, 1850–1950* (New York: Routledge, 2002); and Ross D. Petty, "The Bicycle as a Communications Medium: A Comparison of Bicycle Use by the U.S. Postal Service and Western Union Telegraph Company," in *Cycle History 16: Proceedings of the 16th International Cycling History Conference, University of California, September 2005*, ed. Andrew Ritchie (San Francisco: Van der Plas, 2006).

9. "Police Patrol Awheel," *New York Times*, December 13, 1895; "Mounted Salvationists," *New York Times*, June 5, 1884.

10. Kenneth T. Jackson, *Crabgrass Frontier: The Suburbanization of the United States* (New York: Oxford University Press, 1985), 45–48, 111, 124; George Harris, "Supplementary Educational Agencies," *Educational Review*, February, 1902, 122; "The Velocipede Mania," *Scientific American*, December 23, 1868, 407; Phillip Hubert, Jr., "The Bicycle: The Wheel of To-Day," *Scribner's Magazine*, June 1895, 693, 697; Baxter, "Economic and Social Influences of the Bicycle"; "The Bicycle as a Social Factor," *Philadelphia Record*, September 16, 1896.

11. Marmaduke Humphrey, "A Cycle Show in Little," *Godey's Magazine*, April 1896, 367; "A Folding Bicycle," *Bicycling World*, September 27, 1895, 771; "Practical Bicycle Holder," *American Wheelman*, July 9, 1896, 19; Maria E. Ward, *The Common Sense of Bicycling: Bicycling for Ladies* (New York: Brentano's, 1896), 139; *Godey's Magazine*, April 1896, 370; "Where Wheel Men Abound," *New York Herald*, September 16, 1894; *A. G. Spalding & Bros. Makers of Credends Bicycles and Cycling Sundries Catalog*, 1890.

12. "Bicycle-Riding," *Harper's Weekly*, January 12, 1895, 27; Eric H. Monkkonen, *America Becomes Urban: The Development of U. S. Cities & Towns, 1780–1980* (Berkeley: University of California Press, 1988), 218; New York Court of Appeals, "In the Matter of the Application of the Buffalo Traction Company," *Records and Briefs* (New York, 1895), 177–83, 317–22, accessed June 1, 2013, http://books.google.com/books?id=cYZa3_TFsp0C&printsec=frontcover&source=gbs_ge_summary_r&cad=0#v

=onepage&q&f=false; "In and about Springfield," *Republican* (Springfield, MA), October 17, 1897.

13. *Proceedings of the Fourth Annual Convention of the American Society of Municipal Improvements* (Milwaukee: Swain & Tate Co., 1897), 318–20. A professor of civil engineering at the University of Illinois made similar remarks. Ira Osborn Baker, *A Treatise on Roads and Pavements* (New York: John Wiley & Sons, 1906), 624–32.

14. For example, see *City of Emporia v. Wagoner*, as referenced in *The Pacific Reporter, Volume 49* (St. Paul: West Publishing Co., 1897), 701.

15. Professors who cycled seemed to be so common that some schools even started their own faculty bicycle clubs. For example, members of Harvard University's Faculty of Arts and Science formed the U 5 Club (The Bicycle Department) in 1894. U 5 Club Records, Harvard University Archives.

16. "The City's Cycling Streets," *New York Times*, May 12, 1895; Andrew Fleming West, "The American College," in *Education in the United States: A Series of Monographs Prepared for the United States Exhibit at the Paris Exposition 1900*, ed. Nicholas Murray Butler (Albany: J. B. Lyon Company, 1900), 233; Gilbert B. Morrison, "School Architecture and Hygiene," in *Education in the United States*, ed. Butler, 449–50; "The Wheel in Institutions of Learning," *Chicago Inter-Ocean*, June 7, 1896; "The Wheel in our Institutions of Learning," *Chicago Inter-Ocean*, May 24, 1896; Jerome P. Bjelopera, *City of Clerks: Office and Sales Workers in Philadelphia, 1870–1920* (Urbana: University of Illinois Press, 2005); E. C. Smith v. W. B. Horton, No. 1882 92 Tex. 21; 46 S.W. 627; 1898 Tex. LEXIS 142 (Tex., March 26, 1898); "The Decline of the Bicycle," *New York Times*, September 13, 1900; Norman L. Dunham, "The Bicycle Era in American History" (PhD diss., Harvard University, 1956), 448; "Bicycles Brought Washington's First Traffic Problems," *Sunday Star*, August 9, 1942, in Vertical Files-Recreation, Sports-Bicycling, Box 20, Historical Society of Washington, DC; "Bicycle Stable," *Afro-American* (Baltimore), November 25, 1899; "Bicycle Lodge," *Bicycling World*, May 3, 1895, 1090; *Chicago Cycler's Guide* (Chicago: Chicago Cycler's Guide, 1896), 9; "Wheeling into Favor," *Kansas City Star*, September 17, 1896; Burdett A. Rich and Henry P. Farnham, eds., *The Lawyers Reports Annotated: Book LV* (Rochester: Lawyers' Co-operative Publishing Company, 1902), 308–9.

17. Budget Meakin, *Model Factories and Villages: Ideal Conditions of Labour and Housing* (London: T. Fisher Unwin Paternoster Square, 1905), 234; National Civic Federation, *Conference on Welfare Work, Held at the Waldorf Astoria, New York City, March 16, 1904* (New York: Press of A. H. Kellogg, 1904), 28, 94–98, 156; William Howe Tolman, "Industrial Betterment," in *Monographs on American Social Economics*, ed. Herbert B. Adams (New York: The Social Service Press, 1900), 41–42.

18. *Proceedings of the Fourth Annual Convention of the American Society of Municipal Improvements*, 319; "Buildings need Bicycle Facilities," *New York Press*, June 18, 1896, in Newspaper Clippings Related to Cycling and Cycling Clubs, New-York Historical Society, New York.

19. "Cyclist Run Down," *New York Evening World*, June 29, 1896, in Newspaper Clippings Related to Cycling and Cycling Clubs, New-York Historical Society, New York.

20. City of Minneapolis, *Annual Report of the City Engineer for the year ending Dec. 31, 1895* (Minneapolis: City of Minneapolis, 1896), 22–25; City of Minneapolis, *Annual Report of the City Engineer of the City of Minneapolis* (Minneapolis: City of Minneapolis, 1906), 16–17.

21. City of Minneapolis, *Annual Report of the City Engineer of the City of Minneapolis*, 16–17; City of Minneapolis, *Annual Report of the City Engineer for Year Ending Dec. 31, 1895*, 22–25. The estimates for warm weather cyclists in 1895 are based on data from the 1906 traffic count. In that year, the average number of bicycles per day was 423 percent higher in the August-October period than the November-December period, while the average number of vehicles per day (excluding automobiles) averaged 37 percent higher.

22. United States Census Office, "Table 88-Population at least 10 Years of Age Engaged in Gainful Occupation," *Abstract of the Twelfth Census of the United States, 1900* (Washington: Government Printing Office, 1902), 126; The League of American Bicyclists, accessed September 27, 2014, http://bikeleague.org/content/new-bike-commute-data-released; Ross D. Petty, "Bicycle History by the Numbers: Minneapolis 1895-1911," in *Cycle History 20: Proceedings of the 20th International Cycle History Conference, Freehold, New Jersey (USA), July 30–August 1, 2009*, ed. Gary W. Sanderson (Cheltenham, UK: John Pinkerton Memorial Publishing Fund, 2010), 73–80.

23. Petty, "Bicycle History by the Numbers," 73–80; Minneapolis City Engineers Office, "Map of Minneapolis" (paving map), 1897; City of Minneapolis, *Annual Report of the City Engineer for the Year Ending Dec. 31, 1895*, 22–25.

24. "Figures on Wheels," *Chicago Daily Tribune*, September 18, 1898; "Utilitarian Side of Cycling," *The Cycle Age and Trade Review*, September, 22, 1898, 602; John Pucher and Ralph Buehler, "At the Frontiers of Cycling: Policy Innovations in the Netherlands, Denmark, and Germany," accessed April 4, 2013, http://policy.rutgers.edu/faculty/pucher/Frontiers.pdf.

25. "In and About Springfield," *Republican* (Springfield, MA), October 17, 1897; "Appendix No. 16," *Journal of the Common Council of the City of Philadelphia, from April 6, 1896 to September 24, 1896, Vol. I* (Philadelphia: Dunlap Printing Company, 1896), 20–24; The League of American Bicyclists, "American Community Survey—All Cities Data Compiled by the League of American Bicyclists," accessed July 8, 2013, http://www.bikeleague.org/content/bicycle-commuting-data. Some of the riders in the Philadelphia count may have been recorded more than once. Nevertheless, at just one of the checkpoints (the corner of Broad and Arch Streets), on just one day, city officials counted 8,521 cyclists.

26. *St. Louis Courier-Journal*, July 11, 1897, as quoted in Joe Ward, "Bicycle Commuting in the Late 19th Century," accessed May 5, 2013, http://www.louisvillebicycleclub.org/Default.aspx?pageId=917133.

27. "Bicyclists and the Railroads," *San Francisco Call*, June 1, 1897.

28. Robert C. Post, *Urban Mass Transit: The Life Story of a Technology* (Greenwood Press, Westport, CT, 2007), 58; Charles W. Cheape, *Moving the Masses: Urban Public Transit in New York, Boston, and Philadelphia, 1880–1912* (Cambridge: Harvard University Press, 1980), 7; Theodore Hershberg et al., "The 'Journey-to-Work': An Empirical Investigation of Work, Residence and Transportation, Philadelphia, 1850 and 1880," in

Philadelphia: Work, Space, Family and Group Experience in the Nineteenth Century; Essays toward an Interdisciplinary History of the City, ed. Theodore Hershberg, 151–53 (New York: Oxford University Press, 1980). Although Hershberg focused on the period ending in 1880, he included data points until 1920 and noted that "the use of public transportation for commuting to work on a regular basis by most workers did not become the primary purpose of the system until after . . . 1910."

29. Monkkonen, *America Becomes Urban*, 160–61; Christopher Armstrong and H. V. Nelles, *The Revenge of the Methodist Bicycle Company: Sunday Streetcars and Municipal Reform in Toronto, 1888–1897* (Toronto: Peter Martin Associates Limited, 1977), 169–71; Hershberg, "The 'Journey-to-Work,'"143–51; Jon C. Teaford, *The Unheralded Triumph: City Government in America, 1870–1900* (Baltimore: Johns Hopkins University Press, 1984), 239; Sylvester Baxter, "Public Control of Urban Transit," *Cosmopolitan*, November 1894, 58; Post, *Urban Mass Transit*, 53; Barbara Young Welke, *Recasting American Liberty: Gender, Race, Law, and the Railroad Revolution, 1865–1920* (Cambridge: Cambridge University Press, 2001), 17, 99; New York Court of Appeals, "In the Matter of the Application of the Buffalo Traction Company," 177–83.

30. Interstate Commerce Commission, *Twelfth Annual Convention of Railroad Commissioners. May 1900* (Washington, DC: Government Printing Office, 1900); "The Street Car's Rival: Bicycle Has Certainly Hurt the Railway Business," *Emporia Gazette*, February 7, 1898; "Street Railways Lose Money," *Cycle Age and Trade Review*, January 8, 1898, 333; *Street Railway Journal*, July 1897, 419; Calvin G. Godrich, *A History of the Minneapolis Street Railway Company: Covering 35 Years—1873–1908* (Minneapolis: Brooks Press, 1909), 16.

31. "The New York State Street Railway Association," *Street Railway Journal*, October 1897, 633; Interstate Commerce Commission, *Twelfth Annual Convention of Railroad Commissioners*, 36; "Transportation of Bicycles," *Street Railway Journal*, July 1897, 425; *Street Railway Journal*, August 1897, 500; *Street Railway Journal*, June 1897, 370; *Street Railway Journal*, February 1897, 123; Post, *Urban Mass Transit*, 58.

32. For example, in Philadelphia in 1880, the average journey to work was still within a one-mile radius. Although this distance continually expanded throughout the next few decades, in absolute terms, commuting distances remained relatively short. Hershberg, "The 'Journey to Work,'" 143–51.

33. Sam Bass Warner, *Streetcar Suburbs: the Process of Growth in Boston, 1870–1900* (Cambridge: Harvard University Press, 1962); Jackson, *Crabgrass Frontier*; Dolores Hayden, *Building Suburbia: Green Fields and Urban Growth, 1820–2000* (New York: Vintage Books, 2003).

34. "The Practical Bicycle," *Philadelphia Record*, June 22, 1896, in Newspaper Clippings Related to Cycling and Cycling Clubs, New-York Historical Society, New York.

CHAPTER 8

1. Surprisingly, there are few in-depth studies of women and bicycles. Most books about bicycles allude to the issue but do not explore it fully, and many books about gender and the nineteenth-century city ignore women cyclists altogether. One such study, Sharon E. Wood's *The Freedom of the Streets: Work, Citizenship, and Sexuality in a*

Gilded Age City (Chapel Hill: University of North Carolina Press, 2005), even uses a picture of a woman cyclist on its cover (arguably to convey the "freedom of the streets") but does not devote any of its pages to the issue of female cyclists. Of course, certain issues, like women's cycling dress, have received more attention than others. Most of the book-length scholarly works that do focus on women's cycling issues have not been published. For example, see Sheila Hanlon, "The Lady Cyclist: A Gender Analysis of Women's Cycling Culture in 1890s London" (PhD diss., York University, 2009); Sarah Overbaugh Hallenbeck, "Writing the Bicycle: Women, Rhetoric, and Technology in Late Nineteenth-Century America" (PhD diss., University of North Carolina at Chapel Hill, 2009); and Marie Brock, "The Bicycle as Vehicle to Women's Emancipation as Reflected in Popular Culture, 1888–1900," (master's thesis, University of Houston-Clear Lake, 2004).

2. Maurice Thompson, "What We Gain in the Bicycle," *Chautauquan*, August 1897, 549; Frances E. Willard, *A Wheel Within a Wheel: How I Learned to Ride the Bicycle with Some Reflections by the Way* (Chicago: Woman's Temperance Publishing Association, 1895), 13–14. Considering that around one-quarter of the entire cycling population was female, likely more than one million women became cyclists in the 1890s. At roughly the same time as Americans, women cyclists in foreign cities also adopted the wheel in record numbers. How the bicycle altered women's lives and changed notions of gender varied across the globe, but for one perspective that in many ways parallels the experience of women riders in the United States, see C. Simpson, "Respectable Identities: New Zealand Nineteenth-Century 'New Women'—On Bicycles!," *International Journal of the History of Sport* 18, no. 2 (2001): 54–77. For more on women and tricycling, see Lorenz J. Finison, *Boston's Cycling Craze, 1880–1900: A Story of Race, Sport, and Society* (Amherst: University of Massachusetts Press, 2014), 43–52.

3. Patricia Marks, *Bicycles, Bangs, and Bloomers: The New Woman in the Popular Press* (Lexington: University Press of Kentucky, 1990), 186; Luther Henry Porter, *Cycling for Health and Pleasure: An Indispensable Guide to the Successful Use of the Wheel* (New York: Dodd, Mead and Company, 1896), 21; Mary L. Bisland, "Woman's Cycle," *Godey's Magazine*, April 1896, 386. For an introductory overview of understanding technology through a gendered lens, see Judy Wajcman, "Feminist Theories of Technology," *Cambridge Journal of Economics* 34 (2010): 143–52. Some of the concerns facing female cyclists, including their inability to operate bicycles, reappeared when women began to drive automobiles; see Virginia Scharff, *Taking the Wheel: Women and the Coming of the Motor Age* (Albuquerque: University of New Mexico Press, 1991), 30–33.

4. C. C. Cooper, "The Result of Bicycle Riding Among Women and Girls," *St. Louis Clinique: A Monthly Journal of Clinical Medicine and Surgery*, November 1891, 576–78; "It has Two Sides" *St. Louis Clinique*, November 1898, 609–10; "Women, Girls, and Bicycles," *New York Times*, May 21, 1893; Katherine Murtha, "Cycling in the 1890s: An Orgasmic Experience?," *Canadian Woman Studies* 21, no. 3 (Winter/Spring 2002): 119–21; Sarah Hallenbeck, "Riding Out of Bounds: Women Bicyclists' Embodied Medical Authority," *Rhetoric Review* 29, no. 4 (2010): 327–45.

5. Albert L. Gihon, "The Bicycle as a Sanitary Measure," in *Public Health Papers and Reports, Vol. XXII*, ed. American Public Health Association (Concord, NH; Republican Press Association, 1897), 53–54; *LAW Bulletin and Good Roads*, February 10, 1899.

6. Mary P. Ryan, *Women in Public: Between Banners and Ballots, 1825–1880* (Baltimore: Johns Hopkins University Press, 1990); Wood, *The Freedom of the Streets*, 7; Mona Domosh, "Those 'Gorgeous Incongruities': Polite Politics and Public Space on the Streets of Nineteenth-Century New York City," *Annals of the Association of American Geographers* 88, no 2 (June 1998): 209–26; Phillip Gordon Mackintosh, "A Bourgeois Geography of Domestic Bicycling: Using Public Space Responsibly in Toronto and Niagara-on-the-Lake, 1890–1900," *Journal of Historical Sociology* 20, no.1–2 (March–June 2007): 126–57; Hanlon, "The Lady Cyclist," 100; Maureen E. Montgomery, *Displaying Women: Spectacles of Leisure in Edith Wharton's New York* (New York: Routledge, 1998), 99; "Evadne's Column," *Bicycling World*, June 21, 1895, 149; Barbara Young Welke, *Recasting American Liberty: Gender, Race, Law, and the Railroad Revolution, 1865–1920* (Cambridge: Cambridge University Press, 2001), 57. For historical studies on women and public space, see Wood, *The Freedom of the Streets*; Sarah Deutsch, *Women and the City: Gender, Space, and Power in Boston, 1870–1940* (New York: Oxford University Press, 2000).

7. Deutsch, *Women and the City*, 284; "The World Awheel," *Munsey's Magazine*, May 1896, 157.

8. Kathy Peiss, *Cheap Amusements: Working-Women and Leisure in Turn-of-the-Century New York* (Philadelphia: Temple University Press, 1986), 7; Carroll Smith-Rosenberg, *Disorderly Conduct: Visions of Gender in Victorian America* (New York: Alfred A. Knopf, 1985), 173; Clay McShane and Joel A. Tarr, *The Horse in the City: Living Machines in the Nineteenth Century* (Baltimore: Johns Hopkins University Press, 2007), 79; Gunther Barth, *City People: The Rise of Modern City Culture in Nineteenth-Century America* (Oxford: Oxford University Press, 1980), 121–146; Robert M. Fogelson, *Downtown: Its Rise and Fall, 1880–1950* (New Haven: Yale University Press, 2001), 14–15; John F. Kasson, *Rudeness & Civility: Manners in Nineteenth-Century Urban America* (New York: Hill and Wang, 1990), 215; William Leach, *Land of Desire: Merchants, Power, and the Rise of a New American Culture* (New York: Pantheon Books, 1993); Maureen A. Flanagan, *Seeing with Their Hearts: Chicago Women and the Visions of the Good City, 1871–1933* (Princeton: Princeton University Press, 2002); Deutsch, *Women and the City*; Alison Isenberg, *Downtown America: A History of the Place and People who Made It* (Chicago: University of Chicago Press, 2004), 16–31.

9. Mona Domosh, "The 'Women of New York': A Fashionable Moral Geography," *Environment and Planning D: Society and Space* 19 (2001): 578; Marguerite Merington, "Woman and the Bicycle," *Scribner's Magazine*, June 1895, 703; *Bicycling World*, May 10, 1895, 1101; "The Pulpit and the Bicycle," *Arena*, August 1895, xvii–xx. For an interesting article on how female cyclists used bicycle maps to increase their mobility, see Christina E. Dando, "Riding the Wheel: Selling American Women Mobility and Geographic Knowledge," *ACME: An International E-Journal for Critical Geographies* 6, no.2 (2007): 174–210.

10. "Woman Awheel," *Cleveland Critic*, July 4, 1896, in Newspaper Clippings Related to Cycling and Cycling Clubs, New-York Historical Society, New York; "The Woman and the Wheel," *Baltimore American*, June 14, 1896, in Newspaper Clippings Related to Cycling and Cycling Clubs, New-York Historical Society, New York; "Wheel Gossip," *Cleveland Leader*, September 21, 1896, in Newspaper Clippings Related to Cycling and Cycling Clubs, New-York Historical Society, New York.

11. "Cora Urquhart Potter's Views," *New York Times*, January 5, 1896. In one women's club in New England, members were promised that when cycling their "whole moral nature would take a turn for the better, while the revolutions of the wheel were bringing us health and improved complexions . . ." "Report of Discussion Committee of the New England Women's Club, May 30, 1896," Records of the New England Women's Club, Schlesinger Library, Radcliffe College, Boston. For more anecdotes about how cycling helped to improve a woman's health, see Porter, *Cycling for Health and Pleasure*, 15–20.

12. Sarah Hallenbeck, "User Agency, Technical Communication, and the 19th-Century Woman Bicyclist," *Technical Communication Quarterly* 21, no. 4 (2012): 290–306. For more on how bicycles developed into gender-specific machines, see Nicholas Oddy, "Bicycles," in *The Gendered Object*, ed. Pat Kirkham (Manchester: Manchester University Press, 1996), 60–69; Hanlon, "The Lady Cyclist," 39–91. For more on masculinity in this era, see Mark C. Carnes and Clyde Griffen, eds., *Meanings for Manhood: Constructions of Masculinity in Victorian America* (Chicago: University of Chicago Press, 1990); Gail Bederman, *Manliness and Civilization: A Cultural History of Gender and Race in the United States, 1880–1917* (Chicago: University of Chicago Press, 1995); Steven A. Riess, *City Games: The Evolution of American Urban Society and the Rise of Sports* (Urbana: University of Illinois Press, 1989), 56.

13. Ellen Gruber Garvey, "Reframing the Bicycle: Advertising-Supported Magazines and Scorching Women," *American Quarterly* 47, no. 1 (March 1996): 66–101; Ad for Andrus' Bicycle Skirt Guard, *American Wheelmen*, July 2, 1896, 23; Hallenbeck, "User Agency," 290–306.

14. Maria E. Ward, *The Common Sense of Bicycling: Bicycling for Ladies* (New York: Brentano's, 1896), 12–13, 99; Hallenbeck, "User Agency," 290–306.

15. Maud C. Cooke, *Social Etiquette* (Boston: Geo. M Smith & Co., 1896), 344–46; "A Wise Injunction," *Rochester Herald*, June 21, 1896, in Newspaper Clippings Related to Cycling and Cycling Clubs, New-York Historical Society, New York. For more on the subject of etiquette and etiquette books in nineteenth-century America, see John F. Kasson, *Rudeness & Civility*.

16. *Cycling Record Book, Season 1898* (Cleveland: Siegel, Cooper and Company, 1898), 39.

17. "Evadne's Column," *Bicycling World*, July 19, 1895, 394; *American Wheelmen*, May 28, 1896; *Wheelwoman*, June 1896; *Picayune* (New Orleans), August 9, 1891, as quoted in Somers, "A City on Wheels: The Bicycle Era in New Orleans," *Louisiana History: The Journal of the Louisiana Historical Association* 8, no. 3 (Summer 1967): 235; *The Modern Bicycle and its Accessories* (New York: The Commercial Advertiser Association, 1896), 90; "Social Graces," *Good Housekeeping*, March 1898, 95.

18. "Grand Parade of Cyclers," *New York Times*, June 21, 1891. It is noteworthy that women occupied a central place within the parade at all. As Mary Ryan has shown, women were often relegated to symbolic representations, and it was not until the final decades of the nineteenth century that women served as actual participants in parades. Mary Ryan, *Women in Public*, 31, 42; Mary Ryan, "The American Parade: Representation of the Nineteenth-Century Social Order," in *The New Cultural History*, ed. Lynn Hunt (Berkeley: University of California Press, 1989), 147–149.

19. Papers of Kirk Munroe, Library of Congress; Whistle Code Philadelphia Bicycle Club 1880, Marion S. Carson Collection, Library of Congress; "Articles of incorporation and by-laws of the Citizens Bicycle Club of the City of New York," New-York Historical Society, New York; Arthur P. S. Hyde Diaries, 1892–1896, New-York Historical Society, New York.

20. Mary Ryan, "The American Parade," 138; "Grand Parade of Cyclers," *New York Times*, June 21, 1891; "Cyclists' Street Parade," *New York Times*, July 13, 1902; Maria Ward, *Bicycling for Ladies*, 115; Jennifer Hargreaves, *Sporting Females: Critical Issues in the History and Sociology of Women's Sports* (London: Routledge, 1994). For a view on the limitations of the bicycle's effect, particularly related to women and the bicycle, see Anita Rush, "The Bicycle Boom of the Gay Nineties: A Reassessment," *Material History Bulletin* 18 (Fall 1983): 1–12. Another parade five years later in Brooklyn aroused similar debates. Citing the "outré figures" that dominated an earlier parade in New York, the organizers gave specific instructions mandating that the cycling paraders maintain their modesty. Even still, the subsequent news commentary about the wheel-women who participated focused most heavily on how they looked and what they wore. "Wheels Ruled the Road," *New York Tribune*, June 18, 1896.

21. Bederman, *Manliness and Civilization*, 11–15.

22. Patricia Campbell Warner, *When the Girls Came Out to Play: The Birth of American Sportswear* (Amherst: University of Massachusetts Press, 2006), 5; Sarah A. Gordon, "'Any Desired Length': Negotiating Gender through Sports Clothing, 1870–1925," in *Beauty and Business: Commerce, Gender, and Culture in Modern America*, ed. Phillip Scranton (New York: Routledge, 2001).

23. "A Wise Injunction," *Rochester Herald*, June 21, 1896, in Newspaper Clippings Related to Cycling and Cycling Clubs, New-York Historical Society, New York; Peter Zheutlin, *Around the World on Two Wheels: Annie Londonderry's Extraordinary Ride* (New York: Turnaround, 2007); Warner, *When the Girls Came Out to Play*, 6–7, 61–83. For more on professional women cyclists, see Clare S. Simpson, "Capitalising on Curiosity: Women's Professional Cycle Racing in the Late-Nineteenth Century," in *Cycling and Society*, ed. Dave Horton et al. (Burlington, VT: Ashgate Publishing Co, 2007).

24. *Wheel and Cycle Trade Review*, May 15, 1896. Additionally, 660 of the female riders were described as being in "bicycle costume," but not bloomers. In an unrelated count in 1898 Chicago, observers noted that most women wore bicycle clothes and that "as to bifurcated skirts and liberated legs, the era of woman's emancipation is evidently at hand." "Figures on Wheels," *Chicago Daily Tribune*, September 18, 1898.

25. "Hub of all Wheeldom," *Washington Post*, September 6, 1896; "Bloomers versus Skirts," *The Cherry and Black*, April 1896; "Gossip of the Cyclers," *New York Times*, May 22, 1898; "Object to Women Bicyclists," *New York Times*, June 15, 1895; "Not a Boy at all," *New York Times*, November 5, 1893; City of Detroit, *Journal of the Common Council from January 12, 1897 to January 11, 1898* (Detroit: City of Detroit, 1898), 81; "The Passing Hour," *Bicycling World*, April 26, 1895, 1017; Karen McCally, "Bloomers & Bicycles: Health and Fitness in Victorian Rochester," *Rochester History*, vol. 69, no.2 (Spring 2008): 1–23; "Y.M.C.A. vs. Bloomers," *Bicycling World*, October 18, 1895; Patricia A. Cunningham, *Reforming Women's Fashion, 1850–1920: Politics, Health, and Art* (Kent: Kent State University Press, 2003), 60–61; Warner, *When the Girls Came*

Out to Play, 105–27; Christine Neejer, "Cycling and Women's Rights in the Suffrage Press," (master's thesis, University of Louisville, 2011), 62–65; Sally Helvenston Gray and Mihaela C. Peteu, "'Invention, the Angel of the Nineteenth Century': Patents for Women's Cycling Attire in the 1890s," *Dress* 32 (2005): 27–42. For an interesting back-and-forth between a New York and a North Carolinian perspective on women's use of bicycles and bloomers in the south vis-à-vis the north, see "Southern Women and the Bicycle," *Daily Charlotte Observer*, June 9, 1895. For some examples of various cycling costumes, including bloomers, see Nancy Bradfield, *Costume in Detail: 1730–1930* (New York: Costume & Fashion Press, 1997), 228–91.

26. Gordon, "Any Desired Length," 26–27, 36; "Cyclists and their Clothes," *Boston Herald*, June 28, 1896, in Newspaper Clippings Related to Cycling and Cycling Clubs, New-York Historical Society, New York; "The Point of View," *Scribner's Magazine*, June 1896, 783; "The Era of the Bicycle," *San Francisco Bulletin*, June 26, 1896, in Newspaper Clippings Related to Cycling and Cycling Clubs, New-York Historical Society, New York; Neejer, "Cycling and Women's Rights in the Suffrage Press"; Warner, *When the Girls Came Out to Play*, 117.

27. Rosenberg, *Disorderly Conduct*, 176, 245–46; Peiss, *Cheap Amusements*, 7; Mary L. Bisland, "Woman's Cycle," *Godey's Magazine*, April 1896, 385. See also Deutsch, *Women and the City*, 87; "The Women of To-morrow," *Bicycling World*, January 11, 1895, 303.

28. Peiss, *Cheap Amusements*, 6, 163; Charles W. Mann, *School Recreations and Amusements* (New York: American Book Company, 1896), 172; Garvey, "Reframing the Bicycle," 66–101; Jerome P. Bjelopera, *City of Clerks: Office and Sales Workers in Philadelphia, 1870–1920* (Urbana: University of Illinois Press, 2005), 94–95. For more on the world of urban leisure and amusement, see David Nasaw, *Going Out: The Rise and Fall of Public Amusements* (New York: Basic Books, 1993).

29. "Woman Awheel," *Cleveland Critic*, July 4, 1896, in Newspaper Clippings Related to Cycling and Cycling Clubs, New-York Historical Society, New York; Clare S. Simpson, "Managing Public Impressions: Strategies of Nineteenth-Century Female Cyclists," *Sporting Traditions, Journal of the Australian Society for Sports History* 19, no. 2 (May 2003): 10; "Wheels Whirled in Fine Array," *New York Herald*, June 28, 1896, in Newspaper Clippings Related to Cycling and Cycling Clubs, New-York Historical Society, New York; James D. Norris, *Advertising and the Transformation of American Society, 1865–1920* (New York: Greenwood Press, 1990), 79; Carla Willard, "Conspicuous Whiteness: The New Woman, the Old Negro, and the Vanishing Past of Early Brand Advertising," in *Turning the Century: Essays in Media and Cultural Studies*, ed. Carol A. Stable (Boulder: Westview Press, 2000), 193–98; Nancy G. Rosoff, "'A Glow of Pleasurable Excitement': Images of the New Athletic Woman in American Popular Culture, 1880–1920," in *Sport, Rhetoric, and Gender: Historical Perspectives and Media Representations*, ed. Linda K. Fuller (New York: Palgrave Macmillan, 2006). For an overview of how advertisements and popular magazines portrayed women on bicycles and, more generally, women operating machines, see Julie Wosk, *Women and the Machine: Representations from the Spinning Wheel to the Electronic Age* (Baltimore: Johns Hopkins University Press, 2001).

30. Harvey Green, *The Light of the Home: An Intimate View of the Lives of Women*

in Victorian America (New York: Pantheon Books, 1983), 144–63; Marguerite Mering-ton, "Woman and the Bicycle," *Scribner's Magazine*, June 1895. See also "Utilitarian Side of Cycling," *Cycle Age and Trade Review*, September 22, 1898, 602. This traffic count and similar ones reveal that men cycled for purposes of commuting at a much higher rate than did women.

31. Anonymous Diaries, 1899–1946, Schlesinger Library, Radcliffe College, Boston.

32. Cooke, *Social Etiquette*, 343–45; "Fair Boston Cyclists," *Boston Post*, June 7, 1896, in Newspaper Clippings Related to Cycling and Cycling Clubs, New-York His-torical Society, New York; "Doings of Cyclists," *Morning Ado*, September 23, 1896, in Newspaper Clippings Related to Cycling and Cycling Clubs, New-York Historical Society, New York; Montgomery, *Displaying Women*, 12 (emphasis in original).

33. Montgomery, *Displaying Women*, 5–9; "Fashion, Fact, And Fancy," *Godey's Magazine*, April 1896, 449; Thorstein Veblen, *The Theory of the Leisure Class: An Economic Study of Institutions* (New York: Macmillan Company, 1899).

34. Deutsch, *Women and the City*, 12, 23, 78–79.

35. "Object to Women Bicyclists," *New York Times*, June 15, 1895.

36. Flanagan, *Seeing with Their Hearts*, 60.

37. Autumn Stanley, *Raising More Hell and Fewer Dahlias: The Public Life of Charlotte Smith, 1840–1917* (Bethlehem, PA: Lehigh University Press, 2009), 11–12; "Women Face Devery Before Saloon Crowd," *New York Times*, October 27, 1903; Au-tumn Stanley, "The Champion of Women Inventors," *American Heritage*, 8, no.1 (Sum-mer 1992); "Wicked Bachelor Politicians," *New York Times*, September 6, 1897.

38. "Cyclists and Crusaders," *Munsey's Magazine*, November 1896, 255; "Women to Protest," *New York Commercial Advertiser*, July 2, 1896; "Is the Bicycle an Aid to Im-morality?," *New York Journal*, July 19, 1896; "Against the Wheel!," *New York Tribune*, August 21, 1896.

39. "A Charlotte Ruse," *LAW Bulletin and Good Roads*, July 17, 1896, 78; "Look out, Pretty Bicyclist, You are Watched!," *New York Journal*, September 27, 1896, in Newspaper Clippings Related to Cycling and Cycling Clubs, New-York Historical Society, New York.

40. "Anti-Cycling Mass Meetings," *Brooklyn Daily Eagle*, August 20, 1896. For evidence about how men typically resisted the idea of "New Women," see Bederman, *Manliness and Civilization*, 13.

41. "Not the Devil's Advance Agent," *New York Press*, July 3, 1896, in Newspaper Clippings Related to Cycling and Cycling Clubs, New-York Historical Society, New York.

42. "Woman and the Wheel," *LAW Bulletin and Good Roads*, July 17, 1896, 81–83.

43. "Anti-Cycling Mass Meetings," *Brooklyn Daily Eagle*, August 20, 1896; "In De-fence of Miss Charlotte Smith's Accusation of Bicycle Immorality," *New York Journal*, August 23, 1896, in Newspaper Clippings Related to Cycling and Cycling Clubs, New-York Historical Society, New York; Montgomery, *Displaying Women*.

44. "Wheelmen All Stirred up by–Is bicycling Immoral?," *New York Journal*, Au-gust 16, 1896, in Newspaper Clippings Related to Cycling and Cycling Clubs, New-York Historical Society, New York; Walter Germain, *The Complete Bachelor: Manners for Men* (New York: D. Appleton and Company, 1896), 145; "Is Bicycling Immoral?," *New*

York Journal, August 1, 1896, in Newspaper Clippings Related to Cycling and Cycling Clubs, New-York Historical Society, New York; "Where Wheel Men Abound," *New York Herald*, September 16, 1894.

45. "Anti-Cycling Mass Meetings," *Brooklyn Daily Eagle*, August 20, 1896; "It would, Indeed, be Easter Day for the World if Bicycle Could Be Banished for the Streets," *Wheeling Register*, April 18, 1897; "This City Didn't Try It: Crusade Against Bicycling by Women Collapses in New York," *Philadelphia Inquirer*, January 8, 1897.

46. Ambrose Bierce, *The Devil's Dictionary* (Plain Label Books, 1929), 292–93.

47. Mary L. Bisland, "Woman's Cycle," *Godey's Magazine*, April 1896, 385–87.

48. For example, see Joseph Bliss, Bicycle Routes: MS. S, 1894–1903, Bancroft Library, University of California, Berkeley; Arthur P. S. Hyde Diaries, 1892–1896, New-York Historical Society, New York.

49. Willard, *A Wheel Within a Wheel*, 12, 38–39, 73. For a more in-depth reading of the text and its implications on urban cyclists, see "'Wheel Within a Wheel': Frances Willard and the Feminisation of the Bicycle," in *Cycle History 9: Proceedings, 9th International Cycling History Conference*, ed. Glen Norcliffe and Rob van der Plas (Ottawa: Van Der Plas Publications, 1999). See also Phillip Gordon Mackintosh and Glen Norcliffe, "Men, Women and the Bicycle: Gender and Social Geography of Cycling in the Late Nineteenth-Century," in *Cycling and Society*.

50. "Champion of her Sex" *New York World*, February 2, 1896; "Shall Women Ride the Bicycle?," Elizabeth Cady Stanton, Speeches and Writings, 5–6, Library of Congress; Lisa S. Strange and Robert S. Brown, "The Bicycle, Women's Rights, and Elizabeth Cady Stanton," *Women's Studies* 31 (2002): 609–26; Neejer, "Cycling and Women's Rights in the Suffrage Press."

51. "It would, Indeed, be Easter Day for the World if Bicycle Could Be Banished for the Streets," *Wheeling Register*, April 18, 1897. See also "Fair Boston Cyclists," *Boston Post*, June 7, 1896, in Newspaper Clippings Related to Cycling and Cycling Clubs, New-York Historical Society, New York; *Argonaut*, February 18, 1895, 2; Henry Adams, *The Education of Henry Adams: An Autobiography* (Boston: Houghton Mifflin, 2000), 330.

52. Willard, *A Wheel Within a Wheel*, 73.

CHAPTER 9

1. Joseph B. Bishop, "Social and Economic Influence of the Bicycle," *Forum*, August, 1896, 681.

2. Richard Harmond, "Progress and Flight: An Interpretation of the American Cycle Craze of the 1890's," *Journal of Social History* 5 (Winter, 1971–1972): 251; Norman L. Dunham, "The Bicycle Era in American History" (PhD diss., Harvard University, 1956), 484; David V. Herlihy, *Bicycle: The History* (New Haven: Yale University Press, 2004), 297; Arnold, Schwinn & Co., *Fifty Years of Schwinn-Built Bicycles: The Story of the Bicycle and its Contributions to Our Way of Life* (Chicago: Arnold, Schwinn & Co., 1945), 29. Although there were some contemporary reports in bicycle trade magazines about the effects of the short-lived Spanish-American War on bicycle sales, any claims about the relationship between the "splendid little war" and the dramatic slowdown in bicycle use are unsubstantiated.

3. Ross Petty, "Post Boom Bicycling in Minneapolis: Counting Transportation Use," in *Cycle History 20: Proceedings of the 20th International Cycle History Conference, Freehold, New Jersey (USA), July 30–August 1, 2009*, ed. Gary W. Sanderson (Cheltenham, UK: John Pinkerton Memorial Publishing Fund, 2010), 77. It should be noted that bicycle paths in Minneapolis, as in some other major cities, came relatively late within the bicycle era. Many of the paths built in and around major cities surfaced only in the final few years of the 1890s and some even in the first couple of years of the twentieth century, well after the bicycle's peak in popularity. Relatively few of the paths, with the notable exception of the Coney Island Cycle Path, predated 1896.

4. Glen Norcliffe, "Popeism and Fordism: Examining the Roosts of Mass Production," *Regional Studies* 31, no.3 (1997): 273–76; Bruce Epperson, "'It Cannot be that they Have Made no Profit': The Great Bicycle Trust, 1899–1903," in *Cycle History 16: Proceedings of the 16th International Cycling History Conference, University of California, September 2005*, ed. Andrew Ritchie (San Francisco: Van Der Plas, 2006), 98; Thomas Cameron Burr, "Markets as Producers and Consumers: The French and U.S. National Bicycle Markets, 1875–1910" (PhD diss., University of California, Davis, 2005), 300; Bruce Epperson, "Failed Colossus: Strategic Error at the Pope Manufacturing Company, 1878–1900," *Technology and Culture* 41, no.2 (April 2000): 300–320; "The Survival Fittest," *Cycle Age and Trade Review*, November 1, 1900, 1; Robert H. Merriam, "Bicycles and Tricycles," in US Census Bureau, *Census of Manufacturers: 1905* (Washington, DC, 1907), 287–97. For more on the slowing bicycle sales, the slumping bicycle industry, and the formation of the American Bicycle Trust, see Bruce D. Epperson, *Peddling Bicycles to America: The Rise of an Industry* (Jefferson, NC: McFarland & Company, 2010), 148–88.

5. "Downfall of the Bicycle," *The World To-Day*, October 1902, 1887–88; J. Earl Clauson, "Rediscovering the Bicycle," *Outing*, 1912, 673.

6. "A Few Straight Questions," *Cycle Age and Trade Review*, February 21, 1901, 415.

7. Ibid.; "To Promote New Century Prosperity," *Cycle Age and Trade Review*, January 3, 1901, 229.

8. Bruce Epperson, "How Many Bikes?" in *Cycle History 11: Proceedings of the 11th International Cycling History Conference, Osaka, Japan, 23–25 August 2000*, ed. Andrew Ritchie and Rob van der Plas (San Francisco: Van der Plas; Poole: Chris Lloyd, 2001), with a minor revision provided to the author; *Highway Statistics: Summary to 1945, Public Roads Administration, Federal Works Agency* (Washington, DC: United States Government Printing Office, 1947), 16–27. See also Karl Hodges, "Did the Emergence of the Automobile End the Bicycle Boom?," in *Proceedings of the 4th International Cycle History Conference, Boston, Massachusetts, USA., October 13–15, 1993*, ed. Lallement Memorial Committee (San Francisco: Bicycle Books, 1994), 39–42. Admittedly the number of registered motor vehicles does not account for the total number of automobiles in use, since some states did not yet mandate automobile registration. It should also be noted that multiple people could ride in a car, whereas tandem bicycles were fairly uncommon. Finally, even as domestic bicycle production plunged after 1899, the percentage of these bicycles exported out of the country rose, meaning a significant decline in domestic consumption of bicycles.

9. City of Minneapolis, *Annual Report of the City Engineer for the year ending*

Dec. 31, 1895 (Minneapolis: City of Minneapolis, 1896), 22–25; City of Minneapolis, *Annual Report of the City Engineer of the City of Minneapolis* (Minneapolis: City of Minneapolis, 1906), 16–17; Petty, "Post Boom Bicycling in Minneapolis"; Eric H. Monkkonen, *America Becomes Urban: The Development of US Cities & Towns, 1780–1980* (Berkeley : University of California Press, 1988), 174–75; H. P. Burchell, "The Automobile as a Means of Country Travel," *Outing*, August 1905, 537.

10. James J. Flink, *America Adopts the Automobile, 1895–1910* (Cambridge: MIT Press, 1970), 217. One Chicago wheelwoman even wrote that the motorcar "killed" the bicycle. "Bicycles and Billiards," n.d., Edith Ogden Harrison, Writings and Outgoing Correspondence, MS Harrison, Box 19, Folder 952, Newberry Library, Chicago. Gijs Mom notes that some of the early hostility that automobile enthusiasts faced "reminded motorists of what had happened ten to twenty years before" in terms of the bicycle. They subsequently organized themselves and tried to overcome, to an even greater degree than cyclists had been able to, the challenges of integrating automobiles into American society and onto its roads. Gijs Mom, *The Electric Vehicle: Technology and Expectations in the Automobile Age* (Baltimore: Johns Hopkins University Press, 2004), 47.

11. Arnold, Schwinn & Co., *Fifty Years of Schwinn-Built Bicycles*, 22; "Fairly Howling," *Motor World*, October 11, 1900, as quoted in Flink, *America Adopts the Automobile*, 35; Flink, *America Adopts the Automobile*, 7.

12. Robert C. Post, *Urban Mass Transit: The Life Story of a Technology* (Westport, CT: Greenwood Press, 2007), 65; Mark S. Foster, "The Automobile and the City," in *The Automobile and American Culture*, ed. David Lanier Lewis and Laurence Goldstein (Ann Arbor: University of Michigan Press, 1983), 25; Perry R. Duis and Glen E. Holt, "Chicago as It Was: City on Wheels," *Chicago*, June 1979, 192. See also Henry R. Sutphen, "Touring in Automobiles," *Outing*, May 1901, 197–202; and Clay McShane, *Down the Asphalt Path: The Automobile and the American City* (New York: Columbia University Press, 1994), 148. The language that contemporary proponents of the automobile used was also eerily similar to the ways in which bicycle advocates promoted the bicycle as a health-inducing, class-leveling machine. For example, an early champion of the automobile might have written these same words, only a few years earlier, with regard to the bicycle: "The roads are open to everyone; the fields offer everyone in intoxication of clean air and wide horizons, the magic of changing scenes that dispel sadness and boredom, the genial and invigorating breezes that give the short-winded city-dwellers back their health. The wide world is for everyone." As quoted in Mom, *The Electric Vehicle*, 37.

13. Flink, *America Adopts the Automobile*, 35; Daniel H. Burnham and Edward H. Bennett, *Plan of Chicago* (Chicago: The Commercial Club, 1908); Paul Barrett, *The Automobile and Urban Transit: The Formation of Public Policy in Chicago, 1900–1930* (Philadelphia: Temple University Press, 1983), 73–80; McShane, *Down the Asphalt Path*, 206–9. The *Plan of Chicago* actually makes only one reference to the bicycle, citing that "The rapidly increasing use of the automobile promises to carry on the good work begun by the bicycle in the days of its popularity in promoting good roads and reviving the roadside inn as a place of rest and refreshment."

14. *Interstate Commerce Commission. Twelfth Annual Convention of Railroad*

Commissioners. May 1900 (Washington, DC: Government Printing Office, 1900); "The Street Car's Rival: Bicycle Has Certainly Hurt the Railway Business," *Emporia Gazette,* February 7, 1898; "Street Railways Lose Money," *Cycle Age and Trade Review,* January 8, 1898, 333; Paul Rubenson, "Missing Link: The Case for Bicycle Transportation in the United States in the Early 20th Century," in *Cycle History 16: Proceedings of the 16th International Cycling History Conference, University of California, September 2005,* ed. Andrew Ritchie (San Francisco: Van der Plas Publications, 2006), 72–84. For an example of an argument that presumes that the electric streetcar replaced the bicycle, see Frank J. Berto, "The Electric Streetcar and the End of the First American Bicycle Boom," in *Cycle History 17: Proceedings of the 17th International Cycling History Conference,* ed. Andrew Ritchie (San Francisco: Van der Plas Publications, 2008), 91–100. For an excellent analysis of bicycle, automobile, and streetcar use in Minneapolis after the bicycle boom, see Petty, "Post Boom Bicycling in Minneapolis," 73–80.

15. "Is the Use of the Bicycle Decreasing?," *Philadelphia Inquirer,* December 1, 1898. For comments from those who, at the time, saw the crash as an inevitable result of an overdone fad, see "Passing of the Bicycle," *Baltimore American,* March 29, 1903; J. Parmly Paret, *The Woman's Book of Sports: A Practical Guide to Physical Development and Outdoor Recreation* (New York: D. Appleton and Company, 1901), 76; and "Downfall of the Bicycle," *World To-Day,* October 1902, 1888.

16. "The Return of the Horse," *Bookman,* July 1901, 426.

17. "Modern Tendencies," *Autumn Leaves,* November 1905, 509–510.

18. "The Decline of the Bicycle," *New York Times,* September 3, 1900; Burr, "Markets as Producers and Consumers," 287–88, 324; Luis A. Vivanco, *Reconsidering the Bicycle: An Anthropological Perspective on a New (Old) Thing* (New York: Routledge, 2013), 26.

19. There were some anecdotal reports indicating that certain riders no longer valued the health-inducing benefits of exercise as much as they had. For one example, Isaac Potter, a former president of the LAW, speaking at Carnegie Hall in 1907, remarked, "I don't ride a bicycle any longer myself, because I pay less regard to my health than I used to." Isaac B. Potter, "The Wheel and Wheels as Factors," *Good Roads,* April 1907, 112.

20. Fanny B. Workman, "Bicycle Riding in Germany," *Outing,* November 1892, 110–11; Stijn Knuts and Pascal Delheye, "Cycling in the City? Belgian Cyclists Conquering Urban Spaces, 1860–1900," *International Journal of the History of Sport* (2012): 13; Theo Stevens, "The Elitist Character of Early Dutch Cycling," in *Cycle History 12: Proceedings of the 12th International Cycling History Conference, San Remo, Italy, September 2001,* ed. Rob Van der Plas and Andrew Ritchie (San Francisco: Van der Plas, 2002), 126–28; "Far and Wide," *Bicycling World,* February 8, 1895, 495; "General Notes," *Anglo-Japanese Gazette,* September 1902, 46; *LAW Bulletin and Good Roads,* June 4, 1897, 671; Christopher Armstrong and H. V. Nelles, *The Revenge of the Methodist Bicycle Company: Sunday Streetcars and Municipal Reform in Toronto, 1888–1897* (Toronto: Peter Martin Associates Limited, 1977), 170; "Far and Wide," *Bicycling World,* January 4, 1895, 243; "Far and Wide," *Bicycling World,* January 18, 1895, 333; New Zealand House of Representatives, *Parliamentary Debates: Third Session of the Thirteenth Parliament, July 7, 1898* (New Zealand, 1898), 289–303; *Cycle Age and Trade Review,* November 25, 1897; *American Wheelman,* July 23, 1896, 43. There were even a few cy-

clists, including a handful of women, reported riding around Seoul, Korea. "Bicycle Experiences in Korea," in *The Korean Repository* (Seoul: Trilingual Press, 1896), 320–22.

21. David Rubinstein, "Cycling in the 1890s," *Victorian Studies* 21, no.1 (Autumn 1977): 47–51. For more on the history of the bicycle in England, see John Woodforde, *The Story of the Bicycle* (New York: Universe Books, 1971).

22. For a detailed comparison of the French and United States bicycle markets, see Burr, "Markets as Producers and Consumers." In 1896, 329,818 bicycles were registered in France, a country with about half the population of the United States, which by 1896 could count millions of bicycles. *Consular Reports: Commerce, Manufactures, etc.*, vol.55, nos. 203, 205, 206, and 207 (Washington, DC: Government Printing Office, 1897), 465–466.

23. For example, see Arsène Alexandre, "All Paris A-Wheel," *Scribner's Magazine*, August 1895, 195–201; "Cycling in England and France," *American Wheelman*, July 2, 1896, 33; "Paris Swells on Wheels," *New York Times*, September 25, 1893; James B. Townsend, "The Social Side of Bicycling," *Scribner's Magazine*, June 1895, 705–8.

24. Trine Agervig Carstensen and Anne-Katrin Ebert, "Cycling Cultures in Northern Europe: From 'Golden Age' to 'Renaissance,'" in *Cycling and Sustainability*, ed. John Parkin (Bradford, UK: Emerald Group Publishing, 2012), 24; Department of Commerce and Labor Bureau of Manufactures, *Monthly Consular and Trade Reports, September, 1907* (Washington, DC: Government Printing Office, 1907), 56; Ministry of Transport, Public Works and Water Management, *The Dutch Bicycle Master Plan: Description and Evaluation in an Historical Context* (March 1999), 14–16; Serena Beeley, *A History of Bicycles* (Secaucus, NJ: Wellfleet Books, 1992), 100; Anne-Katrin Ebert, "Cycling towards the Nation: The Use of the Bicycle in Germany and the Netherlands, 1880–1940," *European Review of History* 11, no. 3 (Autumn 2004): 349. For more on how the Netherlands became a nation of cyclists, see Sue-Yen Tjong Tjin Tai, Frank Veraart, and Mila Davids, "How the Netherlands became a Bicycle Nation: Users, Firms and Intermediaries, 1860–1940," *Business History* (September 2014), accessed September 8, 2014, http://www.tandfonline.com/doi/abs/10.1080/00076791.2014.928695 #.VA4F6WRdWRM.

25. Christopher Thompson, *The Tour de France: A Cultural History* (Berkeley: University of California Press, 2006), 15; Burr, "Markets as Producers and Consumers," 219; Ebert, "Cycling towards the Nation," 349; John C. Lehr and John H. Selwood, "The Two-Wheeled Workhorse: The Bicycle as Personal and Commercial Transport in Winnipeg," *Urban History Review* 28, no. 1 (October 1999): 8; Glen Norcliffe, *The Ride to Modernity: The Bicycle in Canada, 1869–1900* (Toronto: University of Toronto Press, 2001); "Bicycles in China," *World To-Day*, June 1903, 725. For more on the history of cycling in Shanghai, see Fang Zhou, "The Wheels that Transformed the City: The Historical Development of Public Transportation Systems in Shanghai, 1843–1937" (PhD diss., Georgia Institute of Technology, 2010).

26. Ebert, "Cycling towards the Nation," 348; Peter Jordan, *In the City of Bikes: The Story of the Amsterdam Cyclist* (New York: Harper, 2013), 99.

27. Paul Rubenson, "Patents, Profits & Perceptions: The Single-Tube Tire and the Failure of the American Bicycle, 1897–1933," in *Cycle History 15: Proceedings of the*

15th International Cycle History Conference, ed. Rob van der Plas (San Francisco: Van der Plas Publications, 2005), 87–97.

28. Anne-Katrin Ebert, "When Cycling gets Political: Building Cycling paths in Germany and the Netherlands, 1910–40," *The Journal of Transport History* 33, no. 1 (June 2012) 115–37; Ruth Oldenziel and Adri Albert de la Bruhèze, "Contested Spaces: Bicycle Lanes in Urban Europe, 1900–1955," *Transfers* 1, no. 2 (Summer 2011): 29–49; Carstensen and Ebert, "Cycling Cultures in Northern Europe," 30–36.

29. Ministry of Transport, *The Dutch Bicycle Master Plan*, 14–23; Ebert, "Cycling towards the Nation," 362; Fietsberaad, *The Bicycle Capitals of the World: Amsterdam and Copenhagen* (Utrecht: Fietsberaad, 2010). In the early years of the automobile, some advocates recognized the advantages of registering cars, licensing drivers, and paying taxes/fees. A 1905 article in *Horseless Age* described it as a "blessing in disguise" since licenses "restricted reckless drivers and lessened public opposition," while registration fees would be put to good use "for road construction and maintenance." Flink, *America Adopts the Automobile*, 173.

30. "Passing of the Bicycle," *Baltimore American*, March 29, 1903.

EPILOGUE

1. "No MetroCard Needed," *New York Times*, May 25, 2014; "Police Use High-Tech Lures to Reel in Bike Thieves," *New York Times*, May 28, 2014; "A Success, but Wobbly from the Start," *New York Times*, March 27, 2014; "A Girl Gets Mothers to Start Biking Again," *New York Times*, May 28, 2014; Brunner, "'Still Your Ride' Print Campaign," accessed August 5, 2014, http://www.brunnerworks.com/work/huffy/print-still-your -ride.aspx; "Bicyclist Killed by a Bus Rose Above Usual Anonymity of Deliverymen in the City," *New York Times*, January 25, 2014; "Round and Round They Go," *New York Times*, April 13, 2014; "Gadgets to Boost Bike Safety," *New York Times*, March 10, 2014; "Equipping the Ride of Your Life," *New York Times*, March 11, 2014; "Seeing the Light, and Finding Their Balance," *New York Times*, April 13, 2014; "A Free Ride for Hotel Guests on Branded Bikes," *New York Times*, March 30, 2014; "Wine on Wheels," *New York Times*, February 28, 2014; "On View: In the Bike Lane," *New York Times*, June 29, 2014; "After Ticket and Arrest, Alec Baldwin Gives New York a Piece of His Mind," *New York Times*, May 14, 2014; "Marlborough a Prisoner," *New York Times*, October 19, 1895.

2. For two recent books that examine the role of cycling in various parts of the twentieth century, see Bruce D. Epperson, *Bicycles in American Highway Planning: The Critical Years of Policy-Making, 1969–1991* (Jefferson, NC: McFarland & Company, 2014); and James Longhurst, *Bike Battles: A History of Sharing the American Road* (Seattle: University of Washington Press, 2015).

3. Ted Buehler and Susan Handy, "Fifty Years of Bicycle Policy in Davis, CA," accessed January 10, 2011, http://www.des.ucdavis.edu/faculty/handy/Davis_bike _history.pdf; Epperson, *Bicycles in American Highway Planning*, 96–112.

4. The City of New York, *PlaNYC: A Greener, Greater New York*, 87–88, 151, http:// www.nyc.gov/html/planyc/downloads/pdf/publications/full_report_2007.pdf.

5. NYC Bike Share, "System Data," accessed September 19, 2013, http://citibikenyc
.com/system-data; "De Blasio Deal Could Give Bike Sharing a New Imprint," *New York
Times*, July 28, 2014.

6. Jeff Mapes, *Pedaling Revolution: How Cyclists are Changing American Cities*
(Corvallis: Oregon State University Press, 2009), 191; League of American Bicyclists,
accessed September 27, 2014, http://bikeleague.org/sites/default/files/ACS_report
_70largest_final.pdf.

7. "The Future of Cycling," *New York Times*, February 7, 1897; J. Matthew Roney,
"Bicycles Pedaling into the Spotlight," Earth Policy Institute, accessed January 12, 2011,
http://www.earth-policy.org/index.php?/indicators/C48/.

INDEX

Page numbers in italics refer to figures and tables.

HISTORICAL STUDIES OF URBAN AMERICA

Edited by Lilia Fernández, Timothy J. Gilfoyle, Becky M. Nicolaides,
and Amanda I. Seligman
James R. Grossman, editor emeritus

Series titles, continued from front matter